# THE DELPHI MURDERS

## THE QUEST TO FIND 'THE MAN ON THE BRIDGE'

BY THE HOST OF *TRUE CRIME GARAGE*

# NIC EDWARDS

## WITH BRIAN WHITNEY

### WILDBLUE
PRESS

WildBluePress.com

*The Delphi Murders published by:*

*WILDBLUE PRESS*
*P.O. Box 102440*
*Denver, Colorado 80250*

*WILDBLUE PRESS is registered at the U.S. Patent and Trademark Offices.*

*ISBN 978-1-960332-15-8 Hardcover*
*ISBN 978-1-960332-14-1 Trade Paperback*
*ISBN 978-1-960332-16-5 eBook*

# THE DELPHI
# MURDERS

*"Parents should continually remind their children of 'stranger danger' and supervise them closely. They should also hug them frequently."*
—Carroll County Sheriff Tobe Leazenby (Retired)

# FOREWORD

Portions of this book were written in real time before the arrest of Richard Allen. This murder investigation was nearly six years active before charges were filed.

Here in these pages, you will find the timeline, the facts, and one man's thoughts, observations, and obsessions with an American murder investigation.

This tragedy was never far from my heart.

# INTRODUCTION

It arrives in my mailbox every Wednesday.

My mailbox has seen better days. It sits at the end of my driveway, black and uninviting, dented and dinged from my neighbors' friends constantly backing into it with their vans and pickup trucks. Six days a week it beckons me to walk out and retrieve whatever might be inside. Once I close my mailbox, I turn and make my return to my garage, shuffling through letters and advertisements as my flip-flops clop along the driveway.

Every week, right on time, I receive a copy of the *Carroll County Comet.* It's a little newspaper typically about ten to twelve pages long, maybe a little less during summer months when the local schools are out of session and high school and middle school sports are on break. It's delivered to me from a neighboring state, Indiana. I live in Ohio and like to pretend that a tan, sweaty man wearing a funny hat makes the two-hundred-fifty-mile trek weekly via horseback just to get me my Carroll County newspaper. I was born, raised, and still reside in central Ohio and I ain't going anywhere. So why would I care to receive this newspaper from a county two hundred fifty miles away, a place from which I know no one and I have never been?

A few years back, on an unseasonably warm Monday in February, a white male wearing a blue jacket walked a public nature trail and abducted two teenage girls in broad daylight. He took their lives, stole the innocence away from Carroll County, and then fled. In about one hour's time, a soulless, gutless subhuman brought tragedy and heartache to countless good, hardworking family-oriented people of Carroll County and beyond. We have been looking for him ever since.

The killer, the suspect, the man on the bridge, Bridge Guy—he has many monikers. Names we apply to the individual responsible for this great tragedy because we didn't know his identity. We knew he left behind his image, his voice, and the words, "Guys, down the hill."

All of this was captured via the most common of modern-day technological devices, a smartphone with a camera. These two brave little girls filmed the man on the bridge as he approached them on that unseasonably warm afternoon.

Justice for the girls. That's why I get the *Carroll County Comet* each week. Because my pea-sized brain seems to believe that if I look hard enough and long enough, I will find him. I have been searching for him everywhere for years, including on the pages of the *Comet*. Six days a week, I clop and flip-flop my way out to that old beat-up black harbinger of news so I can find him.

Each week there is a tribute posted in the *Comet* to keep the focus on justice for the girls, featuring pictures of Libby and Abby. But they are not the only victims. Unfortunately, tragedy befell four other little girls in Carroll County. Next door to Delphi, Indiana, the tiny rural community where Libby and Abby were living, is a town called Flora. In Flora, on November 21, 2016, four girls were killed in a house fire later deemed to be arson. Just like the Delphi double murders, no one has been arrested and charged in a case now called the Flora fire. The four little girls' names are Keyana Davis, Keyara Phillips, Kerrielle McDonald, and Kionnie Welch. They were sisters and much confusion surrounds their case.

My hat really goes off to those at the *Carroll County Comet,* not only for informing me that sweet Vidalia onions are only $1.29 a pound at Wallmann's Quality Foods but for being there for these six girls. The *Comet* has reported on these cases since the beginning and continues to be there today.

The *Comet* lists the Indiana State Police's arson hotline and the Abby and Libby tip line along with a reminder that there is a reward for information. "Justice for the Girls" sadly reminds me of another phrase from another horrific case. In this case, which we now commonly refer to as the Delphi double murders, or simply Delphi, we often hear or read the words "seeking information."

In early 2017, shortly after Abby and Libby were killed, billboards went up saying "seeking information." A short and simple way of asking all of us, "Have you seen this man?" or "Do you know this man?" The billboard consisted of a picture of the man on the bridge and photos of both Abby and Libby.

Law enforcement officials were hopeful that either someone would recognize the man as someone they knew or see the man somewhere and report him. Very quickly it became a nationwide hunt for the Indiana killer. Approximately six thousand digital billboards in forty-six different states were also seeking information.

Billboard campaigns in unsolved crimes are not uncommon. I have personally viewed several throughout my years. These were, but are not limited to, the Amy Mihaljevic case, the Raymond Timbrook cold case homicide, and Delphi. Two of these were at one time located within a mile of my home. They are a grim daily reminder of a terrible loss and that the person, or persons, responsible is still out there.

I wish they had chosen something less dry and more alarming for the billboards than "Do you know this man?" or "Have you seen this man?" The question, statement, or whatever one would like to call it should be haunting. That billboard should disturb and disrupt all our lives until the day we answer the question because even after we know the identity of the man on the bridge, we will still be seeking information. After all, information is not justice and what we are seeking is justice for the girls.

One campaign that was just as infamous as the one in the Delphi case was the "Who killed these girls?" billboards. In that case, police didn't have a picture of the suspect, so the victims took center stage. The victims were thirteen-year-old Amy Ayers, seventeen-year-old Eliza Thomas, seventeen-year-old Jennifer Harbison, and Jennifer's fifteen-year-old sister Sarah. The billboard featured pictures of each girl and those jarring words. Who killed these girls?

That billboard stems from one of the more horrifying cases in Texas. A case commonly known as the Yogurt Shop Murders.

The Yogurt Shop Murders are an unsolved quadruple homicide that took place at an I Can't Believe It's Yogurt! shop in Austin, Texas, on Friday, December 6, 1991. Jennifer and Eliza were employees, while Sarah and her friend Amy were in the shop to get a ride home with Jennifer after it closed. A couple, who left the shop just before eleven p.m., when Jennifer locked the front door to prevent more customers from entering, reported seeing two men sitting at a table inside the store. These men have never been identified and the case sits today just about as cold as can be.

Who killed these girls? Such a stunning set of words. But words should and do have real meaning. It's a haunting question that makes a statement at the same time. It is meant to haunt us all until we know the answer. Because someone knows who killed the girls in Austin. And someone knows who killed the girls in Delphi.

*Who Killed These Girls* is also the title of a great work of true crime by Beverly Lowery. Beverly wrote this book about twenty-five years after the horrific murders. Anyone who would wish to know more about that case should read it. One observation she makes is so profound yet so simply human. In her experience researching and writing her fine book, she was quick to notice how everyone from the cops to the family simply referred to these crimes as "the yogurt shop," replacing the details and victims' names with simply the location of where it happened. This is much less about saving time and more about sparing one another heartache and grim reminder of the crime.

As she points out, this is much like what we all do with 9/11. We've replaced the details and victims' names with the date of that tragic event. This holds true with Columbine, Newtown, and more recently Parkland.

A great detective told me once, "Nic, you don't want to dance in the blood for too long. And certainly not any longer than you must." That detective is my father, and he is right. We say things like "Yogurt Shop," "9/11," and "Parkland" so we all don't have to dance in the blood, and certainly not any longer than we must. In this case, in many of the conversations I have found myself in over the last five years, we simply say "Delphi" and it is understood exactly what we are talking about.

I reference Lowery's book *Who Killed These Girls* because of more than just one similarity to the murders of Libby and Abby. Sadly, it goes beyond just the billboard campaigns. Both cases share some unusual and frightening similarities—multiple female child victims in public locations where no one would have imagined such horror could take place. Both are cases that we were told from the onset by those on the front lines would be solved relatively quickly. But with the yogurt shop case, here we sit years later, still pondering that still very jarring, stunning, and haunting question. Who killed these girls?

You will notice a reoccurring theme throughout the pages of this book. First, I will be referencing other cases that span outside the perimeters of Carroll County, Indiana. These cases are both solved and still unsolved cases. Secondly, I also reference many other true-crime books.

I'm a true-crime podcaster, for those who may not know. Each week, I and my co-host tell another real-life true-crime story. We feature both solved and still unsolved cases. Most weeks I recommend a true-crime book to the audience.

This is my first true-crime book as an author and as I venture through these uncharted waters, I find myself following the lead of those I so admire and the true-crime stories of theirs that I have read. However, I am sure you've already noticed that I didn't follow Beverly Lowery's lead when choosing a title for this book. *Seeking Information* just didn't seem to convey the necessary thoughts and emotions that an unsolved double homicide should invoke. When referencing the composite sketch of the suspect in this case, journalist Barbara MacDonald told one of the Delphi victim's family members when talking about the first sketch, "That is the face of evil."

She is right. The face of evil. We've all been looking for that face for years, hoping to bring some justice for these two teenage girls.

Diane Erskin, Abby Williams' grandmother, said the following: "You study that face, and you look at the sketch. You try to think about how old they are. You try to make some connection. The first lesson we learn in science is for every action there is an equal and opposite reaction. That's in our makeup. As human beings, we are trying to justify and rationalize. This happened, so what is the cause? What is the action that caused it? Well, that doesn't work with evil. It just doesn't. There is no justification. There is no rationalization for this act. I don't know what the motivation is. If there even was a motivation. I don't know because it's evil. It's deceiving. It comes to kill, steal, and destroy."[1]

---

1. *Down the Hill: The Delphi Murders.* "Chapter 7: Madness" (HLN. March 11, 2020). https://podcasts.apple.com/us/podcast/down-the-hill-the-delphi-murders/id1494167201

# FRIENDS TIL THE END

When I was a kid, I used to think I loved a good mystery. But as the years have gone on, I realized that I don't love mysteries at all.

I hate them.

Mysteries, especially ones that involve a loss of life, invade my thoughts during the day and haunt my dreams at night. I can't let them go.

I got into true crime at an uncomfortably young age. My father, a police detective, often came home from work to see the books I was reading laying on the kitchen table with titles like *Berserk! Terrifying True Stories of Notorious Mass Murders and the Deranged Killers who Committed Them, Kids who Kill,* and *The Encyclopedia of Serial Killers.*

These were books that mostly focused on the gruesome and salacious details of multiple crimes. While each book was a real page turner, the material was far from what I desired. I wanted to know more about real police procedures, investigative strategies, and the psychology of such killers. While these books were interesting in their own regard, I certainly was in need of refining my book-hunting skills.

My father would sigh and say to me, "Nic, I don't get why anyone would want to read this stuff, let alone you. You're just a young kid, this stuff is going to rot your mind. It's kind of disturbing, to be honest."

But he didn't understand. It wasn't so much the blood and guts that got me into true crime; it was the mystery that hooked me. The unsolved aspect, the whodunit of the whole thing. Trying to find the killer who still walked free amongst us, or who did until he was finally caught and forced to pay for his crimes.

I started off with obsessions that were a tad more innocuous. In second grade, I became fascinated with dinosaurs, which quickly lead me to the Loch Ness Monster and Bigfoot, then the yeti and UFOs. I quickly locked in on the cryptozoology stuff, the study of animals or beings whose existence is unsubstantiated. Could these mythical beings be real? I felt like I was trying to solve a riddle.

I was born and raised in Columbus. I love this city; it feels like I and Columbus have grown at the same pace. I love the diversity of Columbus. Not just the diversity of the people that make up this great city, but the entertainment and restaurants offered here. There is a certain undefined artiness to Columbus. It's a "college town" but a big college town, which makes us unique.

Very near the heart of downtown Columbus is The Ohio State University. A school with one of the largest enrollments in the country. It's the land of higher learning, the pinnacle of health and medical advancements, and one cannot forget about Buckeye Nation. This is collegiate sports at the highest level. Columbus lives, breathes, and bleeds scarlet and grey, especially during the fall.

The other incredibly great thing about Columbus is the accessibility to be where you want to be. In about fifteen minutes or so you can be smack dab in the middle of the hustle and bustle of downtown or you could be in the burbs, which are all surrounded by small rural communities. There is something here for everyone—or at least enough for me.

I didn't have to look far as a kid to find a mystery to focus on. I became obsessed with Bessie, also known as the Lake Erie Monster.

The first recorded sighting of Bessie occurred in 1817, near Toledo. Two French settlers came across what they described as a huge monster on the beach, writhing in what they took to be its death throes. The settlers described it as around thirty feet in length and shaped like a large sturgeon, except it had arms. They quickly fled the scene. When they returned later, the creature had disappeared, presumably carried off by the waves after its death.

More sightings have occurred intermittently since then. One of the most famous happened in 1892 when a ship's crew saw a large area of water ahead of them churning and foaming. As they approached, they saw a huge sea serpent that appeared to be thrashing about in the water, as if wrestling an unseen foe. There were a few unsubstantiated sightings of the alleged monster in 1969, as well as in the 1980s. In 1993, a local marina owner offered a reward of five thousand dollars "for anyone who captures South Bay Bessie alive" but there have been no sightings as of late.

Sometimes when I was little, I would tag along with my mom to school where she was an elementary school principal. I spent hours at the library immersing myself in a series of books called *Amazing Mysteries of the World*. One afternoon while perusing these books, I came across a photo of the Loch Ness Monster. This was incredible to me; to my young mind, it was proof that the unbelievable could be true. When the photo was eventually debunked and shown to be a fake, I was crushed.

To feed my habit, I began watching the original run of *Unsolved Mysteries* and quickly became hooked. I lay on my stomach in the living room with my elbows digging into the carpet, completely mesmerized by that TV show.

One evening there was an episode about Ogopogo, a supposed monster who lives in the lakes of British Columbia. I couldn't stop thinking of it. I recorded the show and watched it repeatedly so I could pick up pieces of info I might have missed. The episode was burned into my brain.

Looking back, *Unsolved Mysteries* really wasn't that great of a TV show, but at the time, I lived for it. While I came for cryptozoology, *Unsolved Mysteries* also covered true crime. One episode featured a segment titled "Friends 'til the End." This episode was the kickstart of a lifelong fascination with true crime and following those real-life unsolved mysteries. "Friends 'til the End" was about two high school seniors living in Bryant, Arkansas. In my young mind, at least, they seemed like cool, popular kids. I wanted to be like them. They even had their own cars. They were best friends who were always together.

In the early morning hours of August 23, 1987, a seventy-five-car cargo train was headed to Little Rock, Arkansas. As the train approached the small town of Bryant, the engineer noticed what he thought might be something in its path. This obviously would be of great concern to the engineer. However, it is not uncommon for trains to have an encounter with an animal. Most of the time the animal has already expired. It is so common that many trains, especially old-school ones, have a device commonly called a cowcatcher or a pilot mounted to the front of the locomotive. In this case, however, the object on the tracks was not a cow or the even more common dog carcass. As the train drew closer, he saw what appeared to be two bodies lying on the tracks.

He laid on the horn and desperately tried to brake, but it was no use. Within about three seconds, he hit the boys. The train didn't stop for another half mile; when the bodies were found, they were mangled beyond belief.

The bodies were identified as sixteen-year-old Don Henry and seventeen-year-old Kevin Ives, seniors at Bryant High School. It seemed bizarre they would lay on the tracks while a huge freight train was racing towards them. It didn't just seem bizarre, it was bizarre.

The two friends were, in theory, out in the woods night hunting, using a method of "spotlighting" game. They often hunted near the spot on the tracks where their bodies were found.

Three hours later, they were hit by the train.

The state medical examiner, Dr. Fahmy Malak, concluded they had passed out on the tracks because of smoking a lot of marijuana. In fact, he claimed they smoked twenty joints and ruled the deaths an accident.

This made no sense at all. Who smokes twenty joints? Even if you did smoke that much, it would probably just give you a bad case of the munchies, not make you pass out on the train tracks.

Eventually, a new prosecutor was brought in and the case was reopened. He found evidence that suggested one boy was unconscious and the other died when the train ran over them. The deaths were officially ruled "probable homicides." Many believe the boys were murdered and were laid on the tracks as some sort of attempt at a cover-up, possibly related to drug trafficking.

In 1995, the investigation into Kevin and Don's murders was officially closed, the case still unsolved.

At ten years old, I was still into cryptozoology, but I was becoming more jaded. As a supposed plesiosaur, the Loch Ness Monster would have to come up for air regularly, but we only capture a photo of this enormous being every ten years. And why hadn't anyone ever found any bones of beings such as Nessie? It didn't make sense. This all started to seem silly.

One day I was talking to a buddy about my involvement with mysteries and he asked me what I thought about JFK.

I was confused and asked, "What do you mean?"

He said, "Well, what do you think about how he was killed?"

I wasn't sure what he was getting at. "Everyone knows that Lee Harvey Oswald shot him."

He looked at me like he was disappointed. "No, man. That's not what everyone knows, that's just what you've been told," and he broke down some of the more well-known alternate theories about Kennedy's death, such as his being killed by the CIA, KGB, or even mobsters.

I was blown away. Right at that moment, I knew there were way more important things to focus on than the Loch Ness Monster.

I was too young to realize there were other theories out there about what happened. When you are a kid, it's all about what your teachers and parents tell you; you never think there could be any other options. I began to study everything I could about other theories about what happened to JFK.

In 1996, I became fascinated by *Paradise Lost,* the HBO documentary about the West Memphis Three, teenagers charged with the murder of three young children. Supposedly, they killed the children as part of a satanic ritual. The three defendants were initially convicted, but after new evidence came to light, they later were released and their sentences were changed to time served.

In the documentary, I was introduced to Mara Leveritt, who ultimately went on to write *Devil's Knot,* which I consider to be the ultimate book about the case. I fell in love with her writing.

One day I was at the local library trolling through the small true-crime collection, which is always hidden in the back like you're supposed to feel deep shame for even looking at it. They should just have a sign that says BOOKS FOR CREEPY PEOPLE next to the section.

Every true-crime fan of a certain age knows this feeling, looking through the stacks of books just hoping to see something new, searching for some random true-crime book you've never read. True-crime books are odd. Some of them are awful and exploitative, while others are well-written and researched. A true aficionado takes their time when looking for a new true-crime book to read.

I noticed a book, published in 1999, called *The Boys on the Tracks: Death, Denial, and a Mother's Crusade to Bring*

*Her Son's Killers to Justice* by Mara Leveritt. I recognized her name right away. I picked it up and flipped it over to read the back cover and realized it was a book about that Friends til the End story that fascinated me so much. I had no idea the book even existed. It was one of the best true-crime books I have ever read.

I love it when things I am fascinated with return to me.

Then I started diving into the darker stuff, things with more of an edge, books with titles like *The Riverside Killer, Die for Me,* and *The Dracula Syndrome,* which is about cannibals.

One day my father saw me reading *The Dracula Syndrome* and he said to me, "Nic, I am not going to ask why you are reading that, I want to know why anyone would read that."

I didn't have an answer.

Books about unsolved cases fascinate me. As gruesome and tragic as these stories are, it can be rewarding if months or years later law enforcement solves the case, and a monster is brought to justice.

I've always believed in the boogeyman—but not some creepy monster under my bed. To me, he is the weird guy who lives down the street or the guy at the bus station who doesn't talk to anyone.

In 1989, the boogeyman was right around the corner from me.

Usually, when I got home from school, I went outside to play sports, but if it was raining, I would come home and plop myself in front of the TV. One day the weather was bad, so I was chilling out and watching the tube and I heard, "Coming up at five, ten-year-old Amy Mihaljevic from Bay Village went missing on Friday."

Right then, life got real for me. Something terrible had happened to this little girl that was out of her control, who lived in a place I had been, someplace close to me. This was not some make-believe case that happened far away. I felt a deep sense of unease, bordering on terror.

Bay Village, Ohio, is about two hours north of Columbus. On October 27, 1989, ten-year-old Amy Mihaljevic was kidnapped from the Bay Square Shopping Center parking lot. Weeks prior to this, Amy was contacted by telephone by a man who arranged to meet her after school on October 27 with a ruse of buying a gift for her mother, who had recently been promoted at work. Witnesses at the Bay Square Shopping Center saw Amy speaking with a white male, estimated to be in his thirties. Amy was last seen walking through the parking lot with him but there was no information about the vehicle they may have gotten into. After that, there was no sign of her; it was like she vanished.

On February 8, 1990, Amy's body was found by a jogger in a field, close to the road, in a rural area known as Ruggles Township. The crime scene indicated that Amy's body was most likely dumped there shortly after her abduction. Amy's cause of death was determined to be a combination of stab wounds to the neck and a blow to her head. The boots Amy was wearing, a denim backpack she was carrying, and turquoise earrings in the shape of horse heads were all missing and have never been found.

I spent a lot of time worrying about her. It kept me up at night. When I heard the news her body was found, it was like a train hit me. A little girl, one that lived close by me, was murdered and left on the side of the road. I wanted her to be found, but not this way. It affected me deeply in a way I can't explain and, in some way, just like many of the cases I have covered, it still does to this day.

That case almost scared me off true crime. But it didn't, or you wouldn't be reading this book right now.

As I left childhood and moved into adulthood, I got a job in property management after a stint as a bartender for a couple of years. I loved working for this company, I felt like I found a home. I am the kind of guy who, if I am not treated well or respected, I don't stick around very long, and this job I worked for thirteen years. The company became big but had started to downsize as it was in the process of relocating to New York City.

I was still fascinated with Ohio cold cases, one of which was the disappearance of ten-year-old Beverly Potts. She went missing from Halloran Park, which is on the west side of Cleveland, after attending an annual talent show. Despite being one of the largest police investigations in Cleveland history, nothing has ever been discovered as far as the little girl's fate is concerned. Up until that time, parents were, for the most part, fairly chill about where their kids were, but afterwards, kids were often warned about talking to strangers or they too would end up like Beverly Potts. Several suspects emerged over the years, but none can be definitively linked to the case.

Books about Ohio cold cases were rapidly becoming my favorite. I had always wanted to author a book about true crime, so I decided to start working on *Unsolved in Ohio*, a working title for a book I never finished. Yet. While working on the book, I did a deep dive into numerous unsolved cases. I spent a lot of time talking to detectives, driving to crime scenes, and reading old newspaper articles.

One of the cases I couldn't get enough of was known as the Bricca family murders, a crime still unsolved more than fifty years later.

On September 25, 1966, Gerald "Gerry" Bricca was seen taking out the trash at his family home on Greenway Avenue on Cincinnati's West Side. No one ever saw him alive again. Two days later, neighbors noticed newspapers had been piling up outside the home and thought it seemed suspicious.

Detectives were notified and responded to the house where they found Gerry, his twenty-three-year-old wife Linda, and the couple's four-year-old daughter Debbie dead. Gerry and Linda were found in their bedroom. Both had been stabbed multiple times in the chest, neck, and face, and both had been bound at some point in time. Gerry still had a sock stuffed in his mouth. Debbie, who was found in her bedroom, had also been killed with a knife.

The case was fascinating for so many reasons. It was still unsolved and at the time of the murders, there was a serial killer on the loose. The serial killer was known back then as the Cincinnati Strangler. The series of murders attributed to this killer caused a panic among the city's population. An arrest was made in the Strangler case after their Briccas were killed. Police, and the city for that matter, were trying to figure out if the cases were connected. Twenty-nine-year-old Posteal Laskey Jr. was tied to and later convicted of killing one of the Strangler victims. After he was apprehended, the Cincinnati Strangler killings stopped. Police believed they had caught the Strangler and they may have been right, but the Strangler case and the Bricca murders were not believed to be connected.

Some would later speculate that the Briccas may have been murdered by the Zodiac Killer because of the time period and because the bodies were "stacked" like they were in at least one of the Zodiac cases. This was an incredibly loose way to try connecting the Zodiac murders in California to the Bricca case in Ohio but an interesting thought nonetheless.

No one has ever been arrested or charged, but one man, who was supposedly having an affair with Linda, refused to cooperate with investigators and later killed himself.

In 2015, I was laid off from my property management job, but I was given around five months before my job ended. While I was disappointed, I was excited to work more on my book. I really ramped up my research. But at some point, you must stop collecting information and start writing. I loved the collecting-info part but the writing aspect of it? Not so much. That part was a lot more difficult. I knew how to find the information, collect it, and take notes, but getting it all out in a way that really told a captivating story was something I wasn't going to be able to teach myself overnight. But I knew I was a hard worker and if I put in the time and effort, I could find a way to tell these real-life unsolved cases. Especially the ones that they had never heard of before.

# THE GARAGE

The Captain is my brother.

There, I said it.

We have mentioned we were brothers before publicly, but never made a big deal of it. We occasionally saw people fighting online about the nature of our relationship, and we got a kick out of it, so we decided to let it remain a mystery.

We always have had that type of brotherly relationship where we fight one day and are best friends the next. He is a very talented dude, a legit musician who can play any instrument one can think of, and we played in a lot of rock and metal bands together when we were young.

He moved away to Indiana, so we spent a lot of time talking on the phone. He knew I liked true crime so sometimes he would indulge me, and we would just talk about one of these cases for hours. As it turns out, he ended up being laid off too, and decided to come home to Ohio. His last day of work was within a week or so of mine.

We were both listening to podcasts then, way back when you had to go to the internet and download the episodes individually. We loved talk radio, but podcasts were even better because they were focused on one subject.

In 2015, it was still the wild west for podcasts, everyone knew what they were, but they weren't as popular or polished as they are now. As he was moving back to Columbus, I suggested we do a podcast together for fun. It was a project that sounded like a challenge but maybe one that we would enjoy. We had no idea about what we would talk about, but it was an excuse to hang out and do something new after being laid off. I used to work around sixty hours a week, so I had a lot of time to kill now.

He told me, "I am down with doing a podcast. But we should pick something to talk about as opposed to just shooting the shit."

I said, "Agreed. What are you thinking?"

We talked it over and he had a few ideas, most of which centered around sports. I knew we needed something we could talk about for a long time, and something we had knowledge of above and beyond the average person, so I suggested true crime.

After giving it some thought, he said, "I don't know. You really think we can pull that off?"

"I've been working on this book, and I have a lot of info other people don't have. I have enough for several episodes."

He was noncommittal but he called back another time and said, "Okay, dude, I was thinking about your idea, and I like it What are we going to call it?"

"I know it sounds stupid but what about *True Crime Garage*?"

"That's one of the dumbest names I have ever heard."

"Hear me out. I listen to true-crime podcasts. Some are good and some are not. One thing I think is messed up is none of them have the words *true crime* in the title of the show. If we had a concrete company, we would call it something with concrete in the title, right?"

He replied, "Okay, what's up with the garage part then?"

"We're going to record it in my garage," I answered.

He was like, "Oh… right."

Or at least that is the version I am going to spill out this time around. This part of the story has been told many times and in several different ways. In some ways, it's a bit of a mystery how the name came about. Most likely I came up with the *true crime* part, which was easy. He probably came up with the *garage* part. So, if you like the name, we will share the credit. If you hate the name …well, then, I'll take the blame.

We would have been stunned if even a hundred people listened to us. Looking back now, I think putting "true crime" in the title of the show had a lot to do with it succeeding.

Around this time, I had become interested in the case of Tony Muncy. This kid reminded me of myself when I was his age. He was fifteen years old, a local kid from Ohio. I came across his case while looking around in the Columbus Library. I had a hard time not breaking down right there and then when I first read about what happened to him.

The worst thing in the entire world—and if you don't agree with me, there is something wrong with you—is the murder of a child. It makes people lose faith in God, it destroys lives, families, and even communities.

I live in Ohio, and I had never even heard of him before. Why? This case was sitting here unsolved and unknown, almost like it never even happened, like he never even existed. No one was talking about it; it wasn't even something you could find on the internet, let alone the news. It was unbelievably tragic, but other than this kid's family, it might as well have never happened for all the attention it received.

That could have been me. What happened to Tony could have happened to any of us. Although he was a kid I never knew, my heart was breaking for him and for me all at the same time.

I went from almost breaking down in public to being angry. Then I went from angry to determined. I was going to tell people about Tony. I was going to tell people it happened.

Tony disappeared in October 1983 after asking his dad for money so he could ride the bus to see his girlfriend from school. He was never seen alive again. His body was found in trash bags by the side of the road in a rural area. His limbs had been cut off. An autopsy revealed that Tony had been stabbed multiple times in the neck and upper back.

As much as I wanted to, I never felt like I could do his story justice, so I didn't want to cover it on the show. I felt it could be thought of as disrespectful unless I really did a great job with it, and I didn't have the confidence I could do that.

We had no sponsors for *True Crime Garage* and a very small audience, although it was larger than we were aware of. As odd as it sounds, we had no way to track the number of listeners we had. We thought we might have a few hundred people at the most. We weren't trying to get big, and we didn't think we were going to make any money.

One day, the Captain came to me with an idea. "Why don't we record a good, interesting story, put a lot of time into it and cover it well, then put it on iTunes and sell it for $1.99, just to see what would happen?"

We both know how hard it is to make a buck, so we decided if we did this, it had to be excellent. If not, we shouldn't charge anyone for it.

We decided it was time to tell Tony's story. We recorded and released it. I thought it came out great. Suddenly Tony had a footprint on the internet and people started caring. Tony's brother reached out with an email to thank us.

A month later, we got a big check from Apple because of the episode that people were so nice and gracious to buy. That was the first time we realized our hobby could make us money. More importantly, it showed us how much people cared about these victims.

In 2021, I was out picking up pizza; I like to go to my favorite place, order the pizza first, have a beer at the bar, then come home with the pies.

While carrying the pizzas to my car, I got a text from the Captain that said, THEY JUST SOLVED TONY'S CASE.

I thought I was the only one that cared. Little did I know, this entire time, the sheriff's department never gave up, they never stopped trying to find his killer. I must give major kudos to the Delaware County Sheriff's Office, who actively worked this cold case for years. They care. If you kill someone in Delaware County, they won't give up and they will hunt you down.

State and federal crime labs were able to determine several blood types based on evidence from the scene where Tony's body was found but technology and databases of that era were not able to provide much beyond that. The case went cold until it was reopened in 2010 in the hope that technological advances might be able to shed new light on the investigation. In June 2018, law enforcement learned about a cold case solved by the Snohomish County Sheriff's Office in Washington state.

There was DNA evidence in both cases. Investigators in Washington identified Daniel Anderson as the suspect in their case through a public DNA/genealogical database and shared the information with the detectives in Delaware, who sent a sample of their suspect's DNA to the lab. The results predicted with a high level of confidence that the suspect was one of three brothers, two of who were quickly eliminated.

The Ohio Bureau of Criminal Investigation confirmed that DNA found at the scene where Tony's body was found belonged to Anderson, who would have been thirty years old at the time of the crime and had a violent criminal history involving teenage boys. In early 2020, detectives identified Anderson as Tony's murderer. Anderson died sometime in 2013, and the cause of death has not been made public.

Through this experience, I was shown other people care about these cases as much as I do. It almost felt like I finally put out my book.

We were intrigued by the success of the show and the fact we made some money from it. We decided to do it again. The next time we did a show and charged $1.99 for it, we covered the Bricca family murder case. It went to number one on iTunes and stayed there for three days. We beat out Katie Perry.

That was the deciding factor to quit my job and do this full time just two years after I started.

I am going to do this as long as possible. I feel very blessed to do what I do, and I will continue to work hard at doing it the best I can.

In March 2017, we released a four-part series titled, "Boys on the Tracks."

*True Crime Garage* has always relied so heavily on word-of-mouth advertising. Our listeners are amazing. Not only do they tune in each week, but they tell their friends and family to tune in as well and pass along what cases and stories we are covering. This has helped our little show grow into something that neither I nor the Captain would have ever imagined. I hear from listeners time and time again, "Boys on the Tracks was the first time I listened to your show, so-and-so told me I had to check it out."

I have always found that the universe is a beautifully strange place and just a weird and wild concept in general. But I am reminded time and time again that if you take a strong interest in something, somehow these things return, they come back to find you just like you found them. While I didn't live those cases and wasn't affected by them personally, they have become a part of me. It's only fitting those cases helped our show find success.

# Down the Hill

It wasn't big news in Ohio the first day the girls were missing. Kids go missing all the time.

That changed when the bodies were found at noon on Tuesday.

There was very little desk time at my job. I spent my day running around, making sure things got done on time and the right way, meeting with clients and things of that nature. But the first thing I would do every morning was get on the computer and mess around for a few minutes before I started my day for real. I started by checking my email. Does my boss need anything? Does the team need anything? And of course, I might surf the net for a few minutes too. One morning I saw a news update: MISSING GIRLS FOUND MURDERED.

That is the kind of headline that grabbed me. When I hear a double homicide took place outdoors in a public area, I knew a lot of things had to happen.

I needed to know all the details. I began reading the article but there was nothing. I had to find a better article. I was supposed to be starting my workday but instead was looking for a better news story. I found some, but none of them had any more information.

Initially, all we knew was two girls had been missing overnight. Searchers called off the search around midnight.

While the weather was unseasonably warm, it was rough terrain, almost impossible to search at night.

I figured the perp would be caught quickly. Stranger-on-stranger crimes are rare. Typically, someone is killed by someone they know, often in their inner circle. One person pisses off the other and things get unbelievably ugly. These cases are usually solved quickly, often within the first forty-eight hours. An arrest is made or the police have a firm grasp on who their main suspect should be.

Usually, the younger the victim is, the closer the perp is to the victim. It makes sense—the younger we are, the smaller our social circle. With the girls being as young as they were, I figured the case would be solved soon.

When I got to work the next day, it was becoming national news. The public was told there was a picture of a person the police would like to interview. The photo was released to the public on February 22. Law enforcement said they were putting the photo out so the man could reach out and talk to the police.

It's interesting how detectives word things. I immediately realized this was the number one suspect. They were saying they talked to other people on the trails, but this was bait, hoping the suspect would come to them. They gave up that tactic soon because "Bridge Guy" didn't come forward. No one came in or called the station saying, "That's me in the picture." He never came into the station, he never called. He obviously didn't want to talk to them at all, not even a little bit.

Soon, they realized not only was it not going to work but that they confused the public as well.

A few days later, they said he was a suspect.

Now I was even more intrigued. Rarely would a case go unsolved for days when a photo is involved. It wasn't a great photo: it was pixelated, the man was probably seventy-five feet away, and it was taken on a cell phone back when they didn't have great cameras or photo capabilities. But we had a suspect, they had a photo, and the case had gone national.

I was happy. This was a case where they had evidence and they had leads. Now the pressure was on the suspect. It was only a matter of time. They were going to catch this bastard, or maybe before they caught him, he would kill himself.

As someone who reviews a lot of cases and crimes, I am drawn to the odder ones. This checked all the boxes—a double homicide, young victims, in a public area in an area I had never heard of. I not only had never heard of Delphi, but I had also never even heard of Carroll County. I had no idea where it was.

I was fully invested.

The man in the photo clearly wasn't the age of the girls. Was this some random killer out on the trails stalking women or little girls? Was this a real-life monster? If it was a stranger-on-stranger crime, it would be more difficult to solve.

When sexual predators are on the hunt, for them, it's like going to the grocery store and getting what they need for the week. Will anything do or are they looking for something more specific? They often go to areas where they know their type of desired victim would go. But these girls were in the middle of nowhere. Did he know they were going to be there or was this a crime of opportunity?

To make it more interesting, in this case, there were two victims, which is rare and complicates things for this type of predator. What if one of them got away?

The days went on. We still didn't know who this guy was, and it became apparent the police weren't sure what was going on. But now his photo was out, this was a good start to the investigation. Another good sign for the investigation was that the Indiana State Police were making the right moves. They put the suspect's picture out there and were crowdsourcing. Empower your citizens. They want to catch this guy just as much if not more than the police. Because until this killer is caught, no one's children are safe. If my initial suspicions were right, no one had connected this person to the crime...yet. That would soon change. It had to.

I am a light sleeper; I have dog ears. I can be asleep and hear something outside or three rooms away and it will wake me up, and once I am awake, I have a hard time going back to sleep.

One night, some phantom sound woke me up in the middle of the night. I went into the guest room and tried to sleep in there so I wouldn't bother my wife. I often read to be lulled to sleep. While I am a physical book guy, I read iPads at night.

It was 3:30 in the morning and the only light in the house was coming from my iPad. To my surprise, I saw law enforcement release an audio clip of the killer. I was confused. How the hell did they have an audio clip? There was a rumor a trail cam might have taken the photo, but now an audio clip?

I clicked on the link. As I heard a voice say, "Down the hill," every hair on my body stood up and a chill ran down my spine.

That's the killer. I just heard the killer's voice. The guy that went into the woods one day and killed two children. I saw the picture of evil and now I was hearing the voice of evil.

It scared the shit of me. As intrigued as I was, I had to shut it off.

In fact, I couldn't shut it off fast enough. It shook me. I lay there in the dark wishing I could go back three minutes and not have clicked on that thing. I will never forget that voice. I didn't get a wink of sleep that night.

That's when this thing got its hooks in me for real. The next morning, I couldn't think of anything but the case. But there was no new information. I wanted another taste but there was nothing.

This is what I knew at the time.

At about 1:40 in the afternoon of February 13, 2017, thirteen-year-old Abby Williams and fourteen-year-old Libby German were dropped off by Libby's older sister Kelsi at a trailhead on County Road 300 North. They were let off near the scenic Monon High Bridge, an abandoned railroad bridge that goes over Deer Creek in Carroll County, Indiana.

The prior evening, they had a sleepover at Libby's house. There weren't enough snow days that year in 2017 so the girls had February 13 off from school to make up for it. They had plenty of sleepovers together in the past, where they would stay up late watching TV and just hang out and talk, as teenage girls often do.

So on Monday, February 13, they slept in late. Derrick German is Libby's father, but she was raised by her grandparents, Mike and Becky Patty. Derrick had been in and out of her life; he was in her life at this point but wasn't playing the traditional father role. He was doing odd jobs for Becky's real estate business at the time, such as driving to a location and taking photos. That morning, Derrick cooked the girls breakfast, then left to take photos for Becky.

Libby called Becky around one o'clock. She and Abby were going to do some filing work for Becky that day to get money to go shopping. She asked if they could go to the Monon High Bridge, a place where she had gone numerous times before. It was almost a rite of passage for kids in the area. The bridge is very high and a little dangerous. Going there was something you did with your friends if you lived in Delphi. "What, you've never walked the Monon High Bridge? Let's go!" Abby had never done it; this was to be her first time with her best friend.

Becky told the girls if they could get a ride there with someone she knew and trusted, they could go.

Libby began bugging her older sister Kelsi for a ride. Eventually, Kelsi caved and said she would drive them to the bridge on the way to her boyfriend's. Soon they were on their way to the trails, roughly ten minutes away.

Kelsi's boyfriend called her at 1:38 p.m. She was on the phone with him when she dropped the girls off, so it was at least 1:38 when she did so, probably closer to 1:40.

Libby called Derrick before they left. He told her once he was done with the photos, he could pick them up. He would arrive between 3 and 3:30 and told Libby he would call or text when he got close.

They were dropped off by Kelsi across from a farm at an unofficial parking area. If you've hiked much at all, you know the vibe. The trees are cleared out and there is a little bit of gravel on the ground where cars can park. Everyone drops people off or picks them up there, and usually there are a few cars in the drive.

Kelsi said, "I love you," to Libby as the girls got out of the car and watched the girls walk to the trail.

The girls had to walk for a bit before they got to the bridge. As far as we know, there was no real agenda other than Abby walking across. They were probably lollygagging a bit, having a good time, talking girl stuff.

Libby posted a photo to Snapchat at 2:07. This photo is now well known, showing Abby crossing the Monon High Bridge. At 3:11, Derrick called Libby's cell phone as planned, but Libby didn't answer. At 3:13, he made another call. It too went to voicemail after ringing several times.

Minutes later, the calls from Derrick to Libby's phone started going directly to voicemail without ringing. This is often an indication that something has changed with the phone. Most likely the phone was now OFF or the battery had died.

By the time Derrick's second call to Libby went to voicemail, he had arrived at the pick-up location and parked his vehicle at the same general location where Libby and

Abby were originally dropped off. He exited his vehicle and walked the trail, looking for the girls. After a short distance, he came to an intersecting path. He saw, as he has described, an older man with a plaid or flannel shirt on (Flannel Shirt Guy). He asked this man if he had seen two girls, to which the man responded, "No but I saw a couple on the bridge." It turned out he was a worker who oversees the trail system.

The trails are numbered; the intersecting trails are the 501 Trail and the 505 Trail. From where Derrick parked, he walked a few moments on a short trail, then came to the 501, which is long and well-travelled. The 501 Trail, aka the Monon High Bridge Trail, goes all the way to the Freedom Bridge, which is a beautiful pedestrian bridge that extends over Highway 25, better known as the Hoosier Heartland Highway.

Since Flannel Shirt Guy was walking the 501 Trail, Derrick took the 505, assuming the girls must be that way instead. Derrick couldn't find them, so he doubled back.

Now it's 3:30. He called Becky and said he can't contact them or find them. He asked her to call the girls, saying maybe they will answer for her instead, which insinuated Becky was thought of as more of the person in charge in this situation.

Becky tried to call multiple times but there was no answer. While Derrick thought they might just be acting like defiant teenagers, I am guessing Becky was thinking Libby's phone was probably dead. At this point, no one was thinking something awful happened; either the phone is dead or they are being a bit irresponsible. What else could have happened to them?

Derrick walked all the way to the Freedom Bridge, then came back again. Other family members were now becoming involved. Derrick's sister Tara arrived at the trails to look for the girls. Becky called her husband Mike and told him what was going on. She then called Kelsi, who said all seemed fine when she dropped them off. Kelsi headed back to the trails herself to try to help.

So now, Derrick, Tara, Kelsi, and Becky were there looking for the girls. At some point, Cody, Libby's uncle, also came to help look. The group split up, most began driving down nearby roads while Kelsi and Cody walked the bridge looking for them. Kelsi and Cody then began walking on private land and knocked on a few doors asking if anyone had seen anything. No one had, or no one answered; it was still during the day and many people were still working.

Becky called AT&T, Libby's phone provider, to see if they could help in tracking the phone. Libby had only had her cell phone since Christmas and was still on her parents' phone plan.

The Snapchat photo of Abby was taken at 2:07 p.m. so we know they were alive and well then. Yet not even a full ninety minutes later, Derrick was there looking for them to no avail. Between 3:30 and four p.m., her family continued to attempt to get in touch with Libby, some leaving voicemails and some texting.

Mike Patty, Libby's grandfather, arrived on the scene, around five p.m. There is a private property owned by the Mears family near the trailhead parking area. Mike went to this home as he knows the Mears family. They hadn't seen anything. While there, he called a friend of his who is a police officer. Then Mike went back to the trails around 5:20. At 5:30, Libby's family called the police, notifying them that the girls had been missing since approximately 3:15 when they failed to arrive at the trailhead.

The police arrived shortly afterwards. A huge search was soon underway but was called off once it got too dark. Many of the family members and friends of the two girls continued to search into the night.

In a news release, Carroll County Sheriff Tobe Leazenby said there was no reason to suspect foul play or assume the girls were in immediate danger. It had just been a few hours after all. Anything could have happened.

Although some think otherwise, it made sense to call off the search. This area would be difficult to search at night; in fact, parts of it would be dangerous. There is some rough terrain out there and steep hills and the Monon High Bridge itself is dangerous any time of day.

Many small towns have places like this—an abandoned railroad bridge people go to for a quick nature walk, a place to have a picnic, or a place to hang out and get high. It's a seventy- to seventy-five-foot drop if you were to fall off that bridge. Anyone who has walked an abandoned railroad bridge (and I am one of them) knows that sometimes there are missing boards and even if not, there is usually a distance between them where you could easily lose your footing and twist an ankle.

I've seen pictures of this area in all seasons. Even with all the leaves off the trees, this is an area that is heavily wooded. This would make it tough to see things from any distance at all.

One thing that concerned many people, in the beginning, was the proximity to Indiana Highway 25, which could make it easy for abductors to snatch someone up and quickly get out of town. It's the same reason why banks near the freeway have a high probability of being held up and robbed.

But then you also have the possibility that the two girls were just not where they should be. That evening, there were likely several discussions that the two might be off partying with someone or hiding out at a friend's house. It certainly wouldn't be the first time a teenager did such a thing.

The next morning, February 14, 2017, the search effort picked up where they left off the night before. On the news, they asked anyone available to please come out and help search the area for the two girls.

But then the unthinkable happened and all hope was gone.

Just after noon, one of the search teams found two bodies about half a mile away from the Monon High Bridge.

We have never been told details by law enforcement, but we can deduce the following.

They were brought down a hill and then across a long private driveway. This is not the suburbs, so when I say *driveway*, it's not what most are picturing. This driveway looks like a long gravel and dirt road; you can't see any houses or other roads from this location. As soon as they go across this driveway, they would have to go down another hill, this one steeper than the last. This would put them right on the edge of Deer Creek. This could be another location where it's possible that the perpetrator—later known as Bridge Guy—says to the girls, "Down the hill." The bodies were found on the other side of this creek, about fifty feet from the north bank.

Police have still not publicly stated how the girls were murdered. Nor have they disclosed if the girls were clothed or if their clothing was wet with creek water. Law enforcement secured a large area of this bank of the creek with crime-scene tape as well as some of the areas on the east side of the bridge. We do not know if the girls were ordered to cross the creek at the shallow point or if they tried to run or if, in fact, they may have been killed, then carried across the creek to conceal the bodies further. But we do know that they were found across the creek. I'm going to guess, basing this simply off what the police did when they roped off a large area on the north bank, that they were probably killed on the side of the creek in which they were found. There was a lot of speculation that they were found in the creek. We can piece together from the words of law enforcement over time to know that is not true. Later we were told that the girls were killed where they were found. We don't know for certain at this time if they were found clothed, if they were naked or partially so, if their clothing was found or if it was never recovered at all. From later statements, we can surmise that some clothing had been removed.

On February 15, autopsies were conducted on the bodies.

That afternoon, Indiana State Police and the Carroll County Sheriff's Department held a press conference and confirmed they found Libby and Abby, and that the girls were murdered. Again, they did not state how they were killed. ISP also released a photo of a man they reported was seen on the trail around the time the girls disappeared. The image shows a white male with his hands in his pockets, wearing jeans and a navy-blue jacket, and possibly a hat.

The hat is still something people argue about but a lot of the news reports that came out around this time describe him wearing a hat. The image is helpful and hurtful to the investigation at the same time. We will get into the how and why of that later. It's so pixilated that there is a lot of room for interpretation as to what the guy looks like—which, if you're trying to catch a murderer, is kind of a big deal.

The police don't call the man a suspect but say they would like to talk to him. We've seen this tactic in other cases. By saying it in this manner, not calling him a *suspect* and just saying, "We would like to talk to him." There are times when a person will come forward and try to explain why they were in that area at that time, maybe try to get ahead of things, so to speak.

At this time, law enforcement did not say where the photo came from or where they obtained the photo. I thought it may have been captured by some type of trail camera but soon we learned it was taken by Libby with her phone.

On February 22, there was another news conference where police revealed that one of the victims, Libby, recorded video, and audio of the suspect on her cell phone. This is the audio recording released to the public which consisted of a man's voice saying, "Down the hill."

Here is the press conference in its entirety. Doug Carter is the superintendent of the Indiana State Police.

Words tends to escape during these periods of time. I've only had a couple other situations in my lifetime. I'll admit and stand before you and say that. Why Libby, why Abby? Why Delphi? Why Carrol County? Why the region, why the state, why even in the nation? I say that because this is a classic—a clear example that evil lives amongst us. To the family, the community, the region, the state. As the leader of the Indiana State Police, I say I am so very sorry.

Resources. It's unlikely that any of you will ever see nor will we ever see or experience again the level of resources that are attached to this investigation. To the media, my gosh, all I can say is, I give you my sincere thanks. See, this isn't like TV; there's a perception that that this can be solved very quickly—anything that we do can be solved very quickly—but this is a testament that that it can't, and we need you. We've needed you since last week. We need you today, we need you tomorrow, and likely, we'll need the media across this nation. From a simple guy, like me to you, I say, thank you. To the people dressed funny, like me, and those who represent the law enforcement profession, please understand we're human beings. Just like you. Anywhere in the nation with people standing behind me and I would suggest to you, that every time something like this happens, a little piece of us dies as well. But I also want you to understand how committed we are as a collective one. As a collective one. And we will continue.

This has been briefed all the way up to the director of the FBI, Director Comey, and Greg Masssa is going to talk a little bit. I had the opportunity to speak to my boss, Governor Holcomb, a couple different times about the situation and every time I do, I see this look that comes over his face—just like yours and this community's—and that's, that's the unfortunate experience of experiencing evil. We're not stopping.

The poster in front of you. Someone knows who this individual is. Someone knows who this individual is. Is it a family member? Is it a neighbor? Is it an acquaintance? Is it an associate? Or maybe that one guy who lives over at that one place that's just kind of not right? Maybe it's just jeans, maybe it's his jacket or sweatshirt, maybe it's a shirttail, maybe it's just posture, maybe it's the right hand in his pocket—you see even with technology, we need human intelligence. In other words, we need you. I'm not suggesting that science, that everything that we can do is science has been done. Because we are just getting started.

Abby and Libby deserve us, they deserve every single one of us. And not just the people standing up here on the stage that have given so much of their lives, to not just this but, but to this profession. Each and every one of you—each and every person—listening watching or seeing this in some form, we need you. Libby needs you; Abby needs you. Please do not rationalize tips away, rationalize what you think 'that might not be important' away by thinking, 'he it would never do that to another human being.' Or think, 'What I know doesn't matter.' Let folks, like the people that are standing behind me with such incredible passion and commitment and dedication to this profession, make that determination. Tips were anonymous; some might not walk to talk about it because «I don't wanna get involved,» because they know the individual and maybe a family member, probably has family—no one will ever know. No one will ever know; let the FBI answer that. No one on the planet better than—at helping us facilitate this—

than the FBI and they're just as entrenched in this as anybody. No one will know.

As poor as this picture is, somebody knows. And if you're watching, we'll find you. Who's next? I hate to ask you that question. I'd give my life to not have to but I know you've asked yourself that very question. We must recognize that you see we're all the same, we're all human beings, we must keep our resolve for Libby and Abby, for this community and frankly, to ensure that good trumps evil and it will—you're going to hear more in just a minute about what we know. Do not discount the voice that you will hear. We will stay committed with resolve very, very rarely exhibited with human behavior until this conclusion. Please be patient, become our partners, and communicate with us as often as you can. And now, from a very humble servant, the most blessed guy on this planet to represent the profession that I represent; to Abby and Libby, it's my hope and my prayer and experience in God's promise, eternal peace.[2]

Greg Massa, an FBI Special Agent, also spoke.

Good morning. As the assistant Special Agent in Charge, my role is to supervise and lead the FBI's criminal investigations across the state of Indiana. Nine days ago, we had an agent that was participating in the search for the missing victims and, from that moment until this morning, we have stood shoulder to shoulder with our law enforcement partners here. The FBI plays an important support role in this investigation—at this joint investigation. I'm very humbled by the response, that the resources that are

2. Frank Young. Delphi Press Conference 02.22.17/RTV6. February 23, 2017. https://www.youtube.com/watch?v=P1uSKrtYdDw

under my direction have brought and hopefully the contributions that we are making.

On any given day, we have twenty FBI agents that are here, providing investigative help; whether that's running down leads, conducting interviews, I'm helping with lead tracking system, providing intelligence analysis support, providing technical assistance every night. I update our FBI headquarters to our deputy assistant director and, as the superintendent mentioned, this has been briefed the FBI director on two occasions. So whatever resource that the FBI has available, whether it's here in the state of Indiana or nationally, we have brought those resources and we will continue to do so. We were committed to working around the clock as we have been over the last nine days and will continue to do so until this case is solved.

To the members of the community, when I met with our Behavioral Analysis Unit, and their expertise and in their experience, it is oftentimes, even unwitting, that that a member of the community may have information that is germane to this investigation. And I'd like, I'd like the community to, to go back nine days and go back to the afternoon of February 13—Monday, February 13—and just think if you had an interaction with an individual who inexplicably cancelled an appointment that you had had together or individual called into work sick and cancelled out an important appointment or a social engagement, and at the time gave what would have been a plausible explanation—my cell phone broke or I had a flat tire on my car—but in retrospect, that excuse no longer holds water. That, that may be important.

Likely, they still have behavioral indicators that this individual may have exhibited since the afternoon of (he says May 13 but should have said either February 13 or Monday the 13th.) Did this individual travel unexpectedly? Did they change their appearance? Did they shave their beard? Cut their hair? Change the color of their hair? The superintendent mentioned the clothes at this individual is wearing in the photo. Did they did they change the way they dress? Did their behavior change? If their sleep pattern is different now? Did they start abusing drugs or alcohol, where whereas they would not have? Have they been anxious, nervous, irritable? Have they followed this case and what the media is putting out with a with a sense that is not normal? Have they had ongoing discussions regarding their whereabouts on that afternoon, or thereafter?

Please, if you have that information call that into the tip line after this press conference. The FBI will be putting out a series of these indicators on our on our social media so it'll be available not only to the to the citizens of this community but across the state of Indiana and then nationally as well. We will also be utilizing digital billboards and in any way we can spread this this message, we will.

I'll just finalize my remarks, just to say that to my law enforcement partners behind me, to the community at large. Nine days ago, the FBI stood shoulder to shoulder with you we're not going anywhere, we will be here until this case is solved and I am confident this case will be solved. Thank you.[3]

It was hard not to speculate on how much more information law enforcement had and what else was recovered from Libby's phone, but the questions didn't stop there. The killer's voice sounds muffled—is that because the phone was concealed in her pocket? And how did they obtain this info from her phone? Was her phone in fact

---

3. Frank Young. Delphi Press Conference 02.22.17/RTV6. February 23, 2017. https://www.youtube.com/watch?v=P1uSKrtYdDw

found? At the time, I thought it was possible they pulled this image and audio from the Cloud. Later, we would learn that the phone was, in fact, recovered.

This is very interesting to ponder. Was the perp unaware she had a phone? Did he know about the phone but didn't see Libby using it to capture his image and voice? Did he know about the phone and was tech savvy enough to know that if he took it with him, the phone could lead the authorities directly to him?

This monster went to a trail system and killed two children out in the open. The risk he put himself in to do this is incredible. Sadly, a lot of sickos fantasize about doing something like this, but the situation would have to be just right for it to occur, something that would probably never happen, thankfully.

But this guy was driven to do this, so much so that he put himself at risk. Were the victims targeted? Did this person wake up that morning wanting to kill Libby or Abby? Did he really want to kill one of them and the other one was just collateral damage? These were young girls, why would anyone want to kill them if it wasn't just a lust murder, or lustmord?

According to Wikipedia, lust murder, also called sexual homicide, is a homicide that occurs in tandem with either an overt sexual assault or sexual symbolic behavior,[4] and according to the Urban Dictionary, *lustmord* is a state of ecstasy wherein one or more individuals torture and sexually violate a victim to the point of death.[5]

According to the FBI's National Center for the Analysis of Violent Crime, sexual homicide involves a sexual element as the basis for the sequence of acts leading to death. The performance and meaning of this sexual element varies with

---

4. "Lust murder." Wikipedia. 03 March 2023. https://en.wikipedia.org/wiki/Lust_murder

5. Urban Dictionary. "Urban Dictionary: Lustmord." https://www.urbandictionary.com/define.php?term=lustmord

the offender. The act may range from actual rape involving penetration (either before or after death) to a symbolic sexual assault, such as the insertion of foreign objects into the victim's bodily orifices.[6] There are almost always sexual aspects to these types of murders, especially when we know this is a grown man and these are children. Was this psycho a threat to the community? Would he kill again?

This was a mystery wrapped in a riddle trapped in an enigma.

In late February 2017, our show was starting to do well. We weren't making a lot of money, but we were selling ad space. We began getting emails from fans asking us to cover Delphi.

We talked about Delphi a few times a week on *True Crime Garage*, but we didn't have enough info to do a show. I also didn't want to affect the investigation in any way. I wanted this person caught. I didn't want to muddy the waters even more by passing along the wrong information.

When it came to *True Crime Garage*, it was hard to know what to cover, and it still is. We thought at one point about covering the Piketown murders, where eight family members were killed in the middle of the night in Pike County, Ohio. The case terrified residents in the surrounding rural community and prompted one of the most extensive criminal investigations in state history. Eventually, Jake Wagner and three of his family members were arrested and convicted of the crime.

The Captain didn't want to cover it because he knew some of the people involved peripherally; it was too close. Would it be disrespectful to the victims or families? Would people even come after us if we were doing a show on something local?

---

6. Douglas, John E., Ann W. Burgess, Allen G. Burgess, and Robert K. Ressler. *Crime Classification Manual: A Standard System for Investigating and Classifying Violent Crime.* (John Wiley & Sons, 2013.)

I couldn't give Delphi up. Every time I started to walk away, some new info would come in and the hooks would be back into me. We kept putting it off, we thought they were going to catch Bridge Guy. But people kept emailing and asking us to help, some people even said we owed it to the girls.

In May 2017, I quit my day job. I was going to do nothing but work on *True Crime Garage* for a year, even if I went broke.

One day, I said to the Captain, "You know that Delphi case I can't stop talking about?"

He said, "Yup."

I said, "Give me a week or two and I will have enough info to cover it on the show."

He looked confused. "But there is no info, how will we fill up a whole show?"

"It will be a challenge but we are doing this full time now; we will figure it out."

And we did. We did over two hours of coverage on Delphi; it was the first case we covered with me working on *True Crime Garage* full time.

People liked it. We got lots of praise for covering it long form.

Shortly after that, we were at CrimeCon, standing at our little booth, shaking hands and getting to know people. I had a big smile on my face; it was a big ego boost for me. Standing in the line of people waiting to talk to us, I saw a woman who looked very sad. When it was her turn to meet with us, she introduced herself to me as Libby's grandmother, Becky Patty. She said, "I just want to thank you for covering the case. It means a lot to all of us. I listened to 'Part One,' but I couldn't listen to the rest."

I almost collapsed, my mind was going a thousand miles a minute, knowing at some point she had to turn off the show because she lived it.

Her granddaughter was murdered in broad daylight by a monster. And she was still kind enough to try to make me feel good about myself for caring.

# LIBBY AND ABBY

Libby and Abby are known to most as nothing but victims. They were much more than that.

They were only victims for one moment of their lives.

At only thirteen and fourteen years old, they were still very innocent, just coming of age, not even old enough to be upsetting their moms and dads most of the time. They had things they loved to do, things they hated to do, people whom they loved. These were best friends, super tight, the type of friends when you see one and not the other you asked, "Hey, Abby, where's Libby?" and vice versa.

Libby and Abby—they almost sounded like twins, and they acted like it. We all should be lucky enough to have friends we are that close to in our lives.

Abby was an eighth grader at Delphi Community Middle School. She played saxophone in the school band and was on the volleyball team. She liked to read and loved to camp and swim. Being outdoors was her thing, and she enjoyed going with her family on camping trips to Michigan. She adored her cat Bongo and was very artistic. Many of her creations were on the walls of her mother's home.

Libby was into softball, volleyball, and swimming. She was also an enthusiastic band member and a great student. She was preparing for the Academic Bowl in her High Ability class.

She and her good friend Abby were looking forward to hanging out throughout high school.

Delphi is a town in Indiana with a population of roughly three thousand people[7] in Carroll County, Indiana. Delphi has kind of a mix between a rural and suburban feel. Many retirees live in Delphi and residents tend to lean conservative. Most own their homes. The public schools in Delphi are above average. It's been mentioned that for a town the size of Delphi, there sure are a lot of bars.

Delphi is the kind of town filled with hard-working blue-collar residents who are looking to raise their families or settle down in a quiet community. The kids grow up going through the schools together and usually end knowing up each other for the rest of their lives. It's easy to stay in touch in Delphi. The community certainly is not too big for anyone, and no one person is ever too big for the community. People grow up knowing their future wives and husbands for most of their childhood. It's a place of family and faith.

The Hoosier Heartland project is a four-lane highway constructed in the 1930s that connects Lafayette to Fort Wayne. The Freedom Bridge cuts across the highway and connects with the historic Monon Trail.

The Monon High Bridge was built in 1891. At sixty-three feet high, the bridge is one of the highest in Indiana. It carried trains high above Deer Creek until 1987. There are a lot of small areas on the bridge where you could move off to the side if a train was coming, although you wouldn't be too comfortable. The areas are just big enough that someone could stand there while the train passed.

The abandoned railroad bridge has since become a popular attraction for people who live in the area, despite its disrepair and exclusion from the official Delphi Historic Trail System. The bridge has been used as a backdrop for photo shoots like senior pictures, wedding photos, or to

---

7. "Delphi, Indiana Population 2023." https://worldpopulationreview.com/us-cities/delphi-in-population

simply capture the beauty of the untouched nature that surrounds it.[8]

After the murders, the town was shocked, then distraught. Hundreds gathered to pay their last respects to Abigail Williams and Liberty German. That followed a day of mourning by the community, including a visitation attended by thousands at Delphi Community Schools. It was originally scheduled to be from four to eight p.m., but the hours were extended to ten thirty because of the huge number of people who showed up.

Earlier that day, a motorbike ride was held to raise money for the families of the two girls. Hundreds of bikers showed up paying twenty dollars per bike and five dollars per passenger to participate. All proceeds went to the families. Blue and purple ribbons hung across the square downtown in Abby and Libby's honor, along with pictures of the girls.

There was one common theme throughout the day. "This doesn't happen in Delphi." The innocence of this town has been lost forever.

David McCain, whom we will talk about more, is a member of the Deer Creek Township Advisory Board and long-time advocate for the preservation of Monon High Bridge, told *Indianapolis Monthly*, "the slayings represented 'a loss of innocence' for the community. 'For me, it was overwhelming, because as a kid, I did the same thing that Abby and Libby did: I walked out there and enjoyed good days on the bridge,' he says. 'That area is the cradle of Carroll County history. People have gone there for over a century to enjoy the beauty.'"[9]

8. WRTV. "Delphi Daughters: A 360 tour of the Monon High Bridge." April 27, 2017. https://www.wrtv.com/longform/delphi-daughters-a-360-tour-of-the-monon-high-bridge

9. Koryta, Michael. "Halfway Across: The Delphi Murders." *Indianapolis Monthly*. October 13, 2021. https://www.indianapolismonthly.com/longform/halfway-across-the-delphi-murders

Abby and Libby were both active and played a lot of sports, Libby was really into softball. In April 2017, Delphi announced they were going to build a sports complex to honor the lives of the girls called Memorial Park.

People are still going to remember; people are still going to have a sense of loss. That feeling won't ever go away.

"It's not easy," German's grandfather Mike Patty said during an interview in early 2019. "We go through the highs and lows every day. You see something that is maybe a reminder of Libby. You open up a drawer or a cabinet and pull something out and have a tear or maybe even a chuckle and a tear. She was just a teenager. They were both just young little teenagers, doing all the corny and happy things they like to do. And that sucks that it's gone."[10]

10. Dunlap, Kim. "Delphi deaths, 4 years later." *Kokomo Tribune*. February 12, 2021. https://www.kokomotribune.com/news/local_news/delphi-deaths-4-years-later/article_cc393ef4-6c90-11eb-b65c-a7ed37df1dca.html

# Monday, February 13

There has always been a lot of speculation if the person responsible, known as Bridge Guy for most of the investigation, if he knew the girls were going to be there at the bridge and trails that day or if this was a random act of senseless violence?

We know what he did, but what did he want? Was this just a coincidence they were all in this isolated area at the same time? Was he at first just going to say a friendly hello and walk on by to parts unknown? Then did something change? Did something happen?

Or was he focused on them all along?

Were they followed? Was he somewhere on the trails and just somehow saw them walk past him? Two girls, best friends, oblivious to his presence, laughing and talking about their day, what was to become of it and what they would do together.

Or was it just the worst of all possible coincidences— was he just hoping to find two young girls to abduct and murder, then suddenly, they were right there in front of him? Did he watch them walk down a trail and onto the bridge and only then decide today was the day to do the unspeakable things that had been brewing in his mind, his soul, for decades? Did he feel emboldened by no one else being around?

Or did he already know they were going to be there? Did he contact one of the girls prior to this fateful day—pretending to be someone else and not the monster who he truly was, who they were about to meet?

We know so little about his motives, but also his methods. Where did he enter the trail system? Did he bring a vehicle, did he bring a bike, did he walk the creek?

I can't keep my mind from wondering about so many things. Often, I feel like I can crawl inside of a situation and see it as it was, how things played out in almost real time and logically put together a series of events. It's almost as if I can astral project myself into the body and mind of both the killer and the victim. Why did he do what he did? Why did she do what she did? Was this controlled? Was this all by design? What did the victim do or say to change the behavior and actions of the perpetrator?

Most importantly to me: what mistake did the perpetrator make? No one has ever, to my knowledge, committed the perfect crime. You would have to be Gandalf, schooled in wizardry, to do so. Sure, some have done it on television or in the movies, but in real life, humans make mistakes. They make errors and have fallible memories and actions. Plenty of people unfortunately have committed a crime, even murder, and gotten away with it. Some have even been so successful that they committed murder, gotten away with it, and someone else got locked up in the process. But no one has ever committed the perfect murder. They just didn't have the right detective working the case.

Here is a timeline of much of what I do know from that day. Much of this information is according to the *Scene of the Crime* podcast, which is put together by two of my long-time podcasting friends, Mike Morford and Jessica Bettencourt. Some of the information is from the Uncovered.com website run by several great people, some whom I have gotten to know a little over the last two years.

## FEBRUARY 12

Abby slept over at Libby's house

## FEBRUARY 13

**2:45 a.m.** (approximately)

After watching movies with Kelsi and her friends. Abby and Libby stayed up listening to music, talking, and doing "girl stuff." It was noted by Becky Patty that they made several videos of themselves. Were these videos taken on Libby's phone? Were these videos shared with anyone? If so, how? Via Snapchat or some other form of social media or social sharing?

**9 a.m.**

Libby's mother Carrie Timmons sent Libby a Snapchat message simply saying, "Good morning." Details like this break your heart. Carrie lived in another state and just wanted to say hi and wish her daughter a good morning. Libby received the message. We know this because she replied to her mother by sending a selfie of herself in bed.

**1:26 p.m.**

A sixteen-year-old witness sees Bridge Guy. This girl is with a group of friends near the Freedom Bridge. They are getting ready to leave. The sixteen-year-old took a picture on her phone and at 1:27 p.m. she sends the photo to her mother. This timestamp helps her to note the timing of seeing the suspect.

**1:30 p.m.**

The same witness is near some benches near the Freedom Bridge and notices a man who matches the description of Bridge Guy and says hello to him. In response, he gives her a look that frightened her as she passed him on a narrow trail. The witness said Bridge Guy was her height (5'6") or maybe an inch taller. Law enforcement says he is likely 5'6" to 5'8". The witness described Bridge Guy before seeing Libby's video, yet she gave law enforcement a description that matched Libby's picture and video. She describes his clothing as blue jeans, blue coat, and a hoodie pulled up over a billed hat. She said he was wearing some sort of face covering over the lower half of his face. According to at least one source, this witness is one of two who described the short, billed cap that was on the sketch released in July 2017.

**1:38 p.m.**

Libby and Abby arrive at the trailhead. They are dropped off by Libby's older sister Kelsi at what is commonly referred to as the Mears lot. This is because it is located across the street from the Mears property. It should be noted that this is more of a local entrance to the trails and not considered to be the "main entrance" to the trail system, which is formally titled the Mary Gerard Nature Preserve. The main entrance is located at the Freedom Bridge.

**2:07 p.m.**

Libby takes a picture of Abby walking on the Monon High Bridge and posted the photo to Snapchat. This is the last known communication from the girls. No one is on the bridge, but you can get a feel of what it looks like. It's a good photo. There is some artistry to it.

The cell phone has changed murder investigations forever. We are all walking around with a tracking device on us all the time, and a way to call for help if trouble arises. This makes the actions of Bridge Guy even more brazen.

From the first photo Libby took, we know that twenty-five minutes after she was dropped off, nothing has happened. This is when we start to not know the times of things. At some time after 2:07 is when she decided to record the guy coming across the bridge.

## 2:15 p.m.

Using her phone, Libby films Bridge Guy walking toward her and Abby on the Monon High Bridge.

## 2:45/2:50 p.m. (approximately)

Cheyenne Melissa Engles says she entered the trails at about this time. Cheyenne then walked the trails, heading in the direction of the Monon High Bridge.

Cheyenne says that she took a picture that she would later post on social media at 2:50 p.m. to 3 p.m. of Monon High Bridge while standing on the south end. She says she walked across the bridge from north to south. This is very important, as this would place Cheyenne on the same side of the bridge where Bridge Guy likely intercepted the girls and then led them down the hill. If everything went down the way I think it did, Bridge Guy was likely still around where he killed the girls or was in the process of fleeing the trail area.

Cheyenne says she does not remember hearing or seeing anything once on the south side of the Monon High Bridge. She later said she was on the trails between 3:45 and 3:50, claiming she saw a guy when she first got there and saw another couple of guys once she got to the bridge. This is either a typo, a mistake, or a lie. In a later Facebook post, she said she took the picture around 3, clarifying the correct time. In this post, she explained that she saw a woman there that she knew as well as a couple she knew, arguing.


## TIME UNDEFINED

A witness in his twenties arrived at the Mears lot with his girlfriend. They walked slowly along the 501 Trail towards the Monon High Bridge.

Bridge Guy walked past them heading west towards the Freedom Bridge. The witness said that Bridge Guy's hat was exposed. He did not notice a hoodie. His girlfriend says that she did not notice Bridge Guy at all. The couple is arguing at this time. Later when the witness saw a photo of Bridge Guy released to the public, he called in and told authorities that the image of Bridge Guy from Libby's phone is "the man I saw."

The sixteen-year-old female witness and the male witness in his twenties, according to online reports, are the sources of the first suspect sketch that shows Bridge Guy wearing the "newsboy" cap. According to online reports, neither witness was very happy with the sketch.

To clarify, both witnesses said that Bridge Guy was wearing a hat but not the newsboy-style cap shown in the composite sketch. They said that Bridge Guy was wearing a painters cap. The male witness said painters cap; the female witness said a short brim hat. The male witness says that a second sketch that came out later of a young-looking man not wearing a hat is not the man he saw that day. He says the man he saw that resembled the man as seen in Libby's video was a much older man than what is depicted in the second sketch.

It is interesting to note two very similar details in each of these two witnesses' sightings of Bridge Guy. Both witnesses say that Bridge Guy was wearing a scarf or a face covering over the lower part of his face. Both were with other people at the time and in both cases, they were with people who did not notice Bridge Guy.

The female witness said that Bridge Guy was wearing a hoodie over his hat. The male witness said he noticed the hat but no hoodie. Note that if these witnesses did see Bridge Guy and that their memories are correct, the female witness saw Bridge Guy before the murders took place and the male witness saw Bridge Guy after. There are several inferences that one could make based on this information. The hood could have come off at some point during the commission of the abduction and murders, and he—for any number of reasons—did not put it back up again. It also was possible the hoodie was damaged or bloodied and he discarded or concealed the hoodie when witnessed by the male.

**3:11 p.m.**

Derrick German called Libby's cell phone to tell her he was "almost there" but Libby does not answer her phone. Derrick says that the call went to voicemail, and he left a message. It has been reported online that this time is believed to be the same time or about the same time that Bridge Guy is seen by the male witness and that Bridge Guy was heading in the direction of the Freedom Bridge.

**3:13 p.m.**

Derrick arrives at the Mears lot. He calls Libby and again, she doesn't answer. Derrick sends a text to Libby's phone.

**3:13—3:24 p.m.**

At the Five Trail Intersection, Derrick encounters a man wearing a flannel shirt. This person has often been referred to as Flannel Shirt Guy/FSG/Flannel Shirt Man /FSM. We will call him Flannel Shirt Man to better distinguish him from Bridge Guy, as they are not one or the same. This man is reported to be David McCain. It is questionable if Derrick has positively identified McCain as the man he encountered as Flannel Shirt Man. It does appear that law enforcement fully believes that David McCain is indeed Flannel Shirt Man. David McCain is considered a possible witness and is not a suspect.

McCain was walking west on the 501 Trail coming from the bridge. When Derrick asked him about the girls, McCain told Derrick that he had not seen the girls but saw a couple down by the bridge. According to several online sources, the male witness in his twenties is one part of the "arguing couple" that McCain / Flannel Shirt Man tells Derrick about when the two encounter one another at the Five Trail Intersection.

At the time, David McCain was a member of the Deer Creek Township Advisory Board and an advocate for the preservation of Monon High Bridge. A few months after the murders, McCain and about one hundred other locals took part in a walk and prayer near Monon High Bridge. "It was quite moving for me," he says. "There were so many kids. You could see that they wanted to reclaim their trail."[11]

As we already know the video of Bridge Guy did not come from a trail camera but was taken by Libby with her phone. What is seen on the video footage recovered from the victim's phone is as follows. The man that is on the bridge is seen taking a few steps during the short video. His right leg appears crossed over his left leg, he is looking down, and his hands are in his pockets.

Here is where I must start speculating. It seems certain to me that he is looking down to make sure he is stepping on the bridge ties. People say he is walking funny, but we

---

11. Koryta, Michael. "Halfway Across: The Delphi Murders." *Indianapolis Monthly*. October 13, 2021. https://www.indianapolismonthly.com/longform/halfway-across-the-delphi-murders

only see him take two steps. He could be dodging a broken tie, moving to the side to be sure-footed. Also, in my mind, it appears he is walking funny; this might be because he is almost jogging, walking on the bridge as fast as he can.

But I also think we are seeing something else. He isn't walking perfectly straight; I think there is a decent chance he is drunk or has been drinking. He went there with bad intentions and might have had to build himself up to that a little bit.

One thing we know is, they were abducted. At some point, they were going where he said, where he told them to go. They wouldn't be taking these photos at 2:07 if they were already abducted. They were not under his control at this point. We will later hear the audio snippet of saying, "Down the hill." He is directing them. He is telling them where to go. This was not their choice; he had taken over.

If Bridge Guy was looking for a victim, why did he pick these two rather than anyone else? There were other people on the trails and on the bridge. What made him pick them over the others? Even if they are young and naïve, if one of them got away, it's all over.

**10:29 p.m.**

Law enforcement knew that the girls' cell phones were either dead or turned off. At this point, there were first responders on the scene, firefighters, other members of law enforcement, employees of the department of natural resources, and numerous family members from both families.

People were starting to panic.

Mike Patty was interviewed by the local news. Abby's mother Anna was as well. They were becoming concerned: it was getting late, it's dark, it's a warm day for February but still cold. They weren't entirely in panic mode yet, they were still hopeful, still expecting a good outcome.

They might have even been a little angry. But they were not thinking their girls were murdered. It was possible they were lost, even more possible they were someplace they weren't supposed to be and made up an alibi to fool their parents. Murder wasn't something that happened in Delphi.

Some people have insinuated this situation was caused by poor parenting, that someone should be watching these girls, they never should have been there, which is ridiculous. They were killed by someone who targeted them, or by a stranger. That bridge was part of their community, where kids went to walk around and be by themselves. It was just a mile and a half from downtown. They weren't abandoned in the middle of nowhere.

This was the act of an evil person, not the fault of the parents.

It is human nature to want to blame other people, especially when children are involved. Everyone wants to find someone to blame. It's natural anger. This case has brought out negative emotions in millions of people. But blaming the parents in any way is still wrong.

## MIDNIGHT

The official search was called off by law enforcement. A lot of people remain angry about this. Some conspiracy theorists think they delayed finding the girls on purpose, which is ridiculous. It was pitch black; searchers were going over rough terrain that is heavily wooded. When you don't know the worst has happened, it would seem riskier having all sorts of people out there looking for the girls. I don't think we would have learned any more if they were found at 12:01 a.m. as opposed to when they were found.

Sadly, I believe the murders were committed by around three o'clock. When officials later said it was all over by five, it means to me they have reason to believe the girls were killed and Bridge Guy was gone by that time.

When news of the murders came out, the community was in shock. It wasn't just that two little girls had been killed, it had happened on a trail, in the middle of nature. Murders on hiking trails are rare, but not entirely uncommon.

On November 15, 2001, Louise Chaput, a fifty-two-year-old psychologist, was murdered in the White Mountains while off for a solo hike. Her body was found with multiple stab wounds on Thanksgiving Day. Her death was ruled a homicide. The killer has never been found. In May 1996, Julianne (Julie) Williams, twenty-four, and Laura (Lollie) Winans, twenty-six, decided to go backcountry hiking in Virginia in Shenandoah National Park. The next evening, on June 1, 1996, rangers found their bodies at their campsite They had been sexually assaulted; they were found stripped, bound, and gagged with their throats slit. Their murderer still walks free.

In both cases, it seems certain that the killer was a random attacker. What of Bridge Guy? There were other women on the trails all alone that day. Why didn't he choose them? Was he looking for a victim of this age type? Was he seeking two victims rather than one?

Was part of his strategy the bridge itself? He would have to know he had the element of surprise in his favor. I think he waited for them to go across the bridge and waited until they were at the end before he started to act.

Libby had to have known something was off. When she filmed him, she wasn't trying to capture the moment of the man coming towards them over the bridge, she was documenting it because she could tell something was wrong.

When you get to the end of the bridge, that's it, you turn around and walk back. There is nothing there on the other side. Bridge Guy used this to his advantage. I don't think it was his first time walking it.

Picture the scene. The girls are ready to go back and get picked up at the parking lot and suddenly, this weird guy is coming towards them. They have two options. Either stand there and wait for this creepy dude to get close to them and see what he is up to or go back and try to walk past him. It's a little bridge with no rail, perched way up high. He could push them off, he could grab them. They are essentially trapped. They must stand there and wait for the Big Bad Wolf to get to them or walk straight at him.

They felt vulnerable, they were caught. He created a fictitious net, and he swooped in. As soon as he got to the end of the bridge, they were abducted in that moment.

The official search continued the next morning around six. By this point, it was a big deal. Two young girls had been out all night in the woods. Entire families were out searching. People were taking the day off work to help.

Kelsi German was in the woods searching when she heard someone out in the distance call out—they had found a shoe. Kelsi yelled back, asking what type of shoe it was. The description of the shoe sounded like Libby's.

Shortly after that, the bodies were found, around 12:15 by a man in the search party. He saw two deer and was looking at them on his phone, trying to take a picture. When the deer eventually bounded away, he moved his phone a bit and saw the bodies. Kelsi was close enough to run over to where the bodies were, but another searcher stopped her and prevented her from doing so. She has said, looking back on this day, she is grateful someone stopped her from seeing the crime scene.

Within twenty to thirty minutes of finding the bodies, police set up roadblocks and checkpoints, looking for witnesses on the Hoosier Highway. They asked drivers questions like, "Do you travel daily? Were you here yesterday? Did you see anyone? Perhaps someone hitchhiking? Any cars that seemed strange?"

They weren't incompetent, they did the best they could.

They didn't know much at the time, but they had to give some info to the public. In front of the cameras was Kim Riley, one of the public information officers for the Indiana

State Police; Carrol County Sherriff Tobe Leazenby; and Delphi Police Chief Steve Mullins. It had the vibe of something very hastily put together, a few guys just sitting there looking uncomfortable on folding chairs having microphones shoved in their faces.

Leazenby has given the impression that he wanted to provide more information right from the jump but was taking a back seat to others who didn't want him to talk. But every time he was interviewed, he let another small piece of information out.

I get the impression he really wanted to get this solved before he is out of office. This was to be Tobe Leazenby's last term as the sheriff of Carroll County. After a campaign ending with an election in November 2022, there would be, as they say, "a new sheriff in town." A new sheriff taking over is weird—sometimes the new guy cleans house and brings in his buddies and people he used to work with, and everyone else is gone on day one. Often times, all outstanding homicide cases are reviewed in great detail when the new boss takes over.

There was no real info in the initial press conference. In fact, Kim Riley pointed out the wrong spot where the body was found. All the public was told was two bodies were found, but they didn't even give identities. They said that they expected foul play; when asked why, it was "because of the way the bodies were found." For the most part, when someone says foul play is suspected during a law enforcement press conference, there would be a detailed explanation as to why they thought that, but none was forthcoming.

Of course, this strategy isn't unheard of. This is a well-known method of releasing info when it comes to criminal cases. Law enforcement will often hold back information, especially when it comes to cases with a lot of press. People often come out of the woodwork and either accuse people of being the killer, confess, or offer other sorts of information.

It makes it easy to confirm if anyone had intimate knowledge of the crime because of the information that has been held back. At the least, it's a way to get rid of people quickly who are cranks.

It was interesting, and infuriating, to hear they knew it was foul play because of the way the bodies were found. Remember, it still hasn't been released how they died. What was the way they were killed? This would be obvious to law enforcement right away if they knew it was a homicide and not a suicide or an accident.

Were they killed with a gun? A knife? Were they strangled with a rope? Strangled with someone's bare hands? Was one killed one way and the other girl another way?

We don't know.

We can infer from the discovery that they were not buried. Were their bodies staged or posed in some way? We learned that they were later, but not then. Was there debris or leaves or sticks placed over the bodies?

This is when the crazies started spreading rumors. Even Doug Carter, the supervisor of the state police, has been accused online of being the killer. Sure, he is the highest-ranking law enforcement officer in Indiana but in his free time, he kills children.

No one was immune. Some started saying Leazenby was acting odd at the press conference; in fact, if you thought hard about it, his demeanor was almost suspicious. I mean, come on, you know he is guilty, just look at him. One person pointed out Leazenby seemed nervous and was breathing heavily, which meant he killed her. Others said if you watched the way the other two officers on stage looked at him that means one, or both, suspected he is the killer. Even the mayor of Delphi has been accused of being the murderer.

People said things online or on social media that made little to no sense at all. Bridge Guy had a puppy dog in his coat pocket. You can see this in the picture. Some suggested that baby dolls purchased from a local thrift store were hanging from the trees surrounding where the bodies were found. It just made no sense, but some didn't care. They would read or hear of these suggestions and then later pass them off as facts when gossiping with their friends. There is no end to the insanity.

Mike Patty has been accused online of killing his own granddaughter. When Patty called AT&T asking them to ping Libby's phone, they were unable to because the Find My Phone feature was not working. This was because the week before the girls were killed, the family did a factory reset on the phone. Libby requested this; she told her family the service provider recommended the reset but who knows? It's possible she was doing something on the phone her family wouldn't like and she wanted to hide that from them. Some act like this means the Pattys had something to do with her disappearance. Yes, there was a factory reset but it wasn't done in secret, so if she was up to no good, it doesn't make sense she would approach her grandparents about it.

If Mike Patty killed two girls, he is not asking AT&T to ping his granddaughter's phone or trying to get the story on the news. But people still talk. "Oh, he looks like Bridge Guy" or "he sounds like Bridge Guy."

The factory reset was one of many ways Bridge Guy got lucky. All the apps that were on her phone before the reset had to be reinstalled. Libby never downloaded the Find My Phone app after the reset. There is a chance if it was working, the girls could have been found right away when it was still daylight. The family was trying to use Find My Phone by three p.m. While it is unlikely the girls were still alive, they still could have found Bridge Guy.

I've reviewed hundreds of cases over the years and have never seen a case where the victim gets lucky. Of course, there are cases where a victim gets away because of luck, but sadly, those aren't the types of cases I am usually working on.

When it comes to Delphi, there is not a ton of info out there so people tend to make things up, which means they get things wrong, sometimes almost comically so. But if you say something often enough, other people hear it and later what gets wrong is put out there as fact.

I have always tried to address this on *True Crime Garage* when this happens, but there is so much of it out there, a lot of it slips through the cracks, but let's face it—the squeaky wheel gets the grease, only a few people throw out these crazy theories but they get all the attention.

As much as these people anger me at times, I get it. Even I start to see things that aren't there sometimes, and I start getting confused and making no sense. I am not a detective or some Sherlock Holmes who can find the final solution that everyone else missed. But I work hard at it. When it comes to Delphi, I find myself reviewing other cases where a killer was found, asking myself how did they catch this guy, and could we apply that in Delphi? I have had to put this case down and tell myself I won't look for any info or listen to *anything* about Delphi for at least a month because I've reached a high level of insanity. This case seeps into my dreams. If I am not careful, it can affect my emotions in my daily life.

It becomes unhealthy for me. Then I start to wonder if *I* feel this way—frustrated, hopeless, and obsessed—what is it like for the investigators working the case?

A detective once told me two heads are better than one, which of course is a cliché. But he continued by saying, when it comes to detective work and a homicide investigation, four shoulders are better than two. This is also because it is simply unbearable for one person alone to shoulder all the mental and emotional trauma that can come with being in charge of a murder investigation.

So many people think they are incompetent or they're covering for one of their own. The notion of there being a police officer cover-up is ridiculous. I am certain there is no cover-up and I don't see incompetence either.

What I see is Bridge Guy got lucky. Libby went out of her way to take a photo which could potentially piss off this guy but he was lucky enough to be looking down the whole time, probably just so he is sure-footed on the trestle.

It's a forty-three-second video, but we only see a few seconds. Why don't they release the whole thing? What could it hurt? Carter says there is nothing else on the video or audio that would help identify Bridge Guy, but still, wouldn't it be better for witnesses to see all of it? Mike and Becky Patty and Abby's mother Anna are on record as having viewed the whole video. Her mother said she could still hear audio when the video was over, leading one to believe she could have hidden the phone in her hand or pocket while still recording.

Some people wonder why they didn't release a better photo, but the answer to that is obvious. It's the best one they have. When talking about the case on *True Crime Garage*, I have often said about suspects, "Well, he doesn't not look like Bridge Guy." The photo from Libby's phone is terrible. You can't pick anyone out of a crowd with it.

Soon, the Indiana State Police released a sketch of the murder suspect. The person depicted was described as a white male between five-six and five-ten, weighing one hundred eighty to two hundred twenty pounds, with reddish-brown hair and eye color that is unknown. In the July 2017-Bridge-Guy sketch, he is wearing a flapjack hat and a hoodie. He is sporting a thin goatee, with hair sticking out on the sides of his hat by the ears. The picture from Libby's phone was so pixelated, we must assume that law enforcement had some other kind of information to come up with such a detailed composite sketch of the killer. Some speculated that law enforcement was able to clean up the picture released to the public or that they were able to pull a better image of Bridge Guy from Libby's phone.

We can conclude something very different by looking at this aspect of the case in its simplest form. Law enforcement is asking the public for our help. They want us to help them to identify the man standing on the bridge. The man who shortly after that image was captured, confronted, abducted, and murdered two children. It would only stand to reason that the authorities are providing us with the best picture that they have for the public to provide them with the best possible information. Anything else would be a huge mistake on their part.

My conclusion was later confirmed by the words of law enforcement personnel closest to the case. The image they released was the very best that they had. They brought in tech experts to clean and clear it up as much as technologically possible. NASA and other heavy hitters even assisted in this process.

Bridge Guy almost certainly went there that day with the idea of sexually assaulting a victim or victims. Most crimes of this nature have a sexual component; sadly, this holds true even more so when talking about children. We know at least one of the girls was partially unclothed because of the statement about the missing item because they state the rest of the clothing was recovered. This alludes to the fact the killer might have even taken the item with him.

Moving the bodies or staging the bodies would either be to conceal or to pose them in some degrading fashion because it turned him on in some way. I think he memorialized this scene somehow.

If he took photos of his victims, I don't think he did that digitally. Attorney General Robert Ives said he submitted several subpoenas to obtain all cell phone records from phones within a five-mile radius of the trails to determine who was in the area that day. I question the accuracy of that. It's easy for me to believe some cell phones slipped through the cracks. But in theory, all owners of cell phones that pinged in the area of the bridge were contacted regarding their activities and asked about what they had seen. Investigators paid special attention to phone records of anyone who was new to the area or had spent several hours in the area during the time in question. Could Bridge Guy have been savvy enough to not bring his cell phone or even to have turned it off?

Even though there were no visible signs of struggle, there was probably some sort of fight. I am sure these two wouldn't have given up easily. Family and law enforcement have pointed out numerous times how much they loved each other. There was probably an opportunity at one point for one of them to run away from the other, but they didn't, which is proof of how tight they really were.

Law enforcement is on record they were killed where they were found. This was not an abduction, crime scene, and body dump. I think they were moved in the sense they were posed, but we are talking feet or inches rather than a significant amount of distance. The statement was the bodies of the girls were found in a wooded area approximately a half mile upstream from the bridge.

The location of the crime scene is fourteen hundred feet from the residence of Ron Logan, who quickly became a suspect. Fourteen hundred feet doesn't sound very far, but if you look at a football field and add the end zones, that's three hundred sixty feet. It would be 3.88 football fields from the back of his house, and of course, much of it was wooded.

A tip line was set up on February 17, the same day a public visitation was held for the girls at Delphi Community High School. There were a lot of rumors going around saying the girls' necks were covered up while in their caskets, leading people to believe their throats were slit.

On February 19, law enforcement told the world what most already knew; the man in the photo is a suspect.

The following day, the police ramped it up even more, announcing a statewide manhunt, urging people to come forward.

On February 22, Doug Carter held a press conference. The most important thing we found out was Libby had video and images of the suspect on her phone. This was when they also released the audio of Bridge Guy saying, "Down the hill." The public was told there is a reward of twenty thousand dollars for information leading to an arrest.

Of course, the old pervert roundup began as well. It would be incredibly naïve to not believe there was a sexual component to this crime. The easiest thing for law enforcement to do in a situation like this is to hit a few buttons on the computer and print out a list of local sex offenders, many of whom were on probation or at least must report in from time to time. In most states, your probation officer doesn't need a search warrant, they can just knock on the door and walk right in.

This has been fruitful in many investigations. A lot of times, these perverts can even be cooperative. If they are innocent, they are going to be cooperative because they want you to leave them alone. They're going to say where they were, they are going to give you alibis. Usually, you can move on from these people quickly.

Five days later, the reward increased to one hundred three thousand dollars and law enforcement had received ten thousand tips. Jim Irsay, owner of the Indianapolis Colts, along with retired punter Pat McAfee, put up another ninety-seven thousand dollars to make it an even two hundred thousand dollars.

Members of the public eventually added to this reward, and it continued to grow over time. When a murder happens, one never knows how a community is going to react. In this case, the public joined together in a way I have never seen.

# THE MAN ON THE BRIDGE

July 17, 2017, five months after the murders, police released a composite sketch ostensibly based on witness tips. Two years later, on April 22, 2019, they released another composite that looked much different.

During the press conference announcing the new sketch, Doug Carter looked and sounded like he was holding back tears. He almost gave off the vibe he wanted to choke Bridge Guy to death in front of everyone. It was very powerful. He was up there as a human being, not a cop. He had a pulse. He had life.

The press conference is as follows.

SUPERINTENDENT CARTER: I wasn't sure quite what to expect when I walked out, but I got to say to the Delphi Community, um, I got to say to the Delphi Community how grateful I am. You inspire people you don't even understand when, you don't even understand why. Information is being released today is the result of literally thousands and thousands of hours of extraordinary investigative efforts by Delphi, Carroll County, the FBI, the Indiana State Police, and countless other agencies.

This community surrounded us some twenty-six months ago. And you did everything you could to support us, but most importantly, you surrounded the family of these two little girls. Gosh, I'll never forget it! After you hear what we're going to release today, I'm going to ask for your continued support, your continued understanding, your empathy and compassion as we move forward to find out who did this. And we will.

We're seeking the public's help to identify the driver of a vehicle that was parked at the old CPS/DCS welfare building in the city of Delphi that was abandoned on the east side of County Road 300 North next to the Hoosier Heartland Highway between the hours of noon to five on February 14, 2017 [Note: It has been updated that the date was misspoken—it should be February 13, not 14]. If you were parked there or know who was parked there, please contact the officers at the command post at the Delphi City Building.

We're releasing additional portions of the audio recording from that day. Please keep in mind the person talking is one person and is the person on the bridge with the girls. This is *not* two different people speaking. Please listen to it very, very carefully.

We are also releasing video recovered from Libby's phone. This video has never before been previously released. The video shows the suspect walking on the bridge. When you see the video, watch the person's mannerisms as they walk. Watch the mannerisms as he walks. Do you recognize the mannerisms as being someone that you might know? Remember, he is walking on the former railroad bridge. Because of the deteriorated condition of the bridge, the suspect is not walking naturally due to the spacing between the ties.

During the course of this investigation, we have concluded the first sketch released will become secondary, as of today. The result of the new information and intelligence over time leads us to believe the sketch, which you will see shortly, *is* the person responsible for the murders of these two little girls. We also believe this person is from Delphi. Currently, or has previously lived here, visits Delphi on a regular basis, or works here. We believe this person is currently between the age range of eighteen and forty, but might appear younger than his true age.

Directly to the killer, who may be in this room: We believe you were hiding in plain sight. For more than two years, you never thought we would shift gears to a different investigative strategy. But we have. We likely have interviewed you or someone close to you. We know this is about power to you, and you want to know what we know. And one day, you will. A question to you: what will those closest to you think when they find out that you brutally murdered two little girls., two children? Only a coward would do such a thing. We are confident that you have told someone what you have done, or at the very least they know because of how different you are since the murders.

We try so hard to understand how a person could do something like this to two children. I recently watched a movie called *The Shack*, and there's also a book that talks so well about evil, about death, and about eternity.

To the murderer: I believe you have just a little bit of a conscience left. And I can assure you that how you left them in that woods is not, *is not* what they are experiencing today. To the family: I hope that you all will give them some time, because we're going to be asking that there is no media inquiry or no media response for at least the next two weeks, and I hope you understand why. The family found out about this, this information this morning. I just want the family to know that when I take my last breath on this earth, I'll be thinking about them. There's going to be a tremendous amount of questions. I know that, I know that. Never in my career have I stood in front of something like this.

Please be patient with us, please. We are just beginning. We are just now beginning, and I can tell you on behalf of the sheriff and the police chief, so many other partners that have stood with us over this period of time, that we will not stop![12]

Carter said a lot of interesting things here, such as they were taking the investigation in a new direction and releasing a new sketch of a considerably younger suspect than in the first sketch.

When he said, "We believe you are hiding in plain sight," and addressed the killer during the press conference, saying, "To the killer, who may be in this room," you could hear people gasp. There was a lot of debate around trying to figure out if he was looking at someone when he said it.

They announced days prior to the event they were having the press conference, so who knows, maybe he was there. I thought it was intriguing. The girls were killed on a Monday. A lot of these press conferences happen on a Monday, including this one.

This is kind of Profiling 101. Maybe the killer had Mondays off from their job. Maybe he was available on Mondays. Some killers want to be close to the investigation, they want to know what the police know. Maybe the police gave so much notice so the killer would show up. Maybe the Monday he killed two girls was a day he was off work, maybe he still is off on Mondays two years later, and maybe he had the opportunity to be in the room for the press conference. I don't think any of that was coincidence.

---

12. WFLITV. April 22, 2019. "Delphi Homicide News Conference: ISP release video, additional audio and a new sketch of the suspect." https://www.youtube.com/watch?v=WfJQINVMWPE

It seems possible they were pushing Carter out as the face of the investigation to create an adversary for Bridge Guy. The FBI used this kind of technique when it came to the Unabomber and the BTK killer. Certain killers want a worthy adversary, it brings out their competitive nature, which might cause them to slip up and make a fatal mistake.

They wanted Bridge Guy to have the chance to be there in person and look his enemy in the face. Bridge Guy versus Doug Carter. The hero. The single person who will lead us to the promised land. We all have an enemy. Bridge Guy needs an enemy too. Now he had one, someone he could identify by his face, by his title, by his name. They wanted to make Doug Carter the adversary. We have a shadowy face of evil, but we need the face of justice too, the guy who is going to be there until the cuffs are slapped on.

There will not be a safe place for this criminal to hide. You want this fucker on edge until he confesses, tells someone he knows, or eats a bullet.

I analyzed every damn word spoken at this press conference. The public was obviously confused by the new sketch. Law enforcement was upfront, telling people not to worry about the first sketch, just concentrate on this one.

This sketch looked nothing like the first, which obviously was and still is confusing. Now, he looked younger, a lot younger. His mouth is different. Even his eyebrows are different. Once again, law enforcement was inundated with calls saying, "It's my ex-boyfriend, it's the guy that mows my lawn, I think I saw this guy at a bar on Tuesday."

There has been so much debate over why there has been more than one sketch. The first sketch appeared to be based on witness statements, at least in part. Obviously, the video of Bridge Guy is not good, but it has often been argued the first sketch was based on the video. It's almost certainly somewhere in the middle; the video must have influenced the final drawing but it's probable there were some witness statements involved too.

They had to release the sketch because it could ultimately solve the case, but at the same time, you know they didn't want to because it was confusing and it made them look bad. The definition of a catch-22.

And then the age aspect is vexing. The suspect is believed to be between eighteen and forty but "might appear younger." Both a clear statement and a confusing one.

Profilers say the hardest thing to predict is age. They get ages wrong with serial offenders quite often. Profilers study the type of crime, the type of victim, methods used, circumstances of the crime, among many other things. A lot of that has to do with the intellectual and emotional makeup of the perpetrator. There can be a natural immaturity when it comes to offenders such as these. Oftentimes, a much older offender has impulse control issues that make them seem younger, and a lot of these guys have spent time in prison, which can lead to arrested development and stunt one's maturity and growth.

Saying he is eighteen to forty is very odd to me. He even said *currently,* meaning he thought it was possible Bridge Guy was sixteen when he murdered them. The guy we saw walking over the bridge was not a teenager. Sure, it's a bad photo but the guy I see doesn't look like he could be possibly sixteen years old unless the dude has led a hard life, and I mean really hard.

Carter said later he expanded the age range because he was worried it might leave Bridge Guy out. Someone could be thinking, *My uncle, who I kind of suspected, he wasn't around that Monday and has been acting odd ever since, but he is four years older than the age range so it couldn't be him.*

At this press conference, they let out that Bridge Guy said, "Guys, down the hill" instead of just "Down the hill." When you're relying on the public to help solve the case, it seems odd to hold so much stuff back. It makes no sense to me—maybe they have a good reason, but I can't imagine what it could be. The longer you wait to release evidence, the colder the case becomes.

The talk of the vehicle at the CPS building is odd. It could be just an FBI tactic, where a fictitious witness or vehicle is put out there to try to get someone to come forward. This is just bait. They say they want to talk to the driver, but they don't give a description of the vehicle. How would anyone possibly remember if a vehicle of any sort was parked there all those years ago?

If Bridge Guy is going to the trails and murdering some people and leaves, then parking there makes no sense. It's not close to the crime scene. Asking people if they remember seeing a vehicle twenty-six months ago parked next to the road didn't seem like a good strategy.

The way Bridge Guy walks was discussed. As I have said, I think he was drunk or ingested something to get his courage together.

I believe he grew up in the area or he lived there when the murders happened. How well would people know the bridge outside of the area? Many of the local teenagers went there but it was not well known in general, certainly not a tourist spot of any sort. His being local ties into a theory that I started to consider early on in the investigation. A theory about how he made his way to and from the crime scene. I think there is good reason to consider that he went in through the graveyard. Maybe the guy and his buddies used to hang out there in high school and waste time and party, and he knew it would be a good hunting ground.

Lunatics like this write the script of their fantasies, but they need to find the people to play those roles. If we need milk, we go to the grocery store. If you're looking for a blonde sixteen-year-old white girl, you go to the mall and pretend to be a photographer. These guys have plenty of time to figure out their plans. Because it's all they think about.

There is a good chance the killer tricked the girls into being there that day, under the guise of being someone else. But if it was some sort of random encounter, I think he knew it was a good strategic location to find what he wanted. I think he knew his ideal victim would probably be there— probably because he had been there before. We know what kind of victim he wanted. We know this because of whom he chose. He saw others. He selected these two.

When Carter said, "Directly to the killer," they were trying a Hail Mary of sorts. If he was in the room with them, they were obviously trying to get a reaction from him. The "hiding in plain sight" was letting the public know to be aware he could be your mailman, gym teacher, some guy you work with at the factory. Anyone.

"You want to know what we know. And one day, you will." They are trying to shame the killer, trying to let him know they're confident he slipped up and told someone too much, or at the least, people in his life knew he's different in some way.

While he may be terrified that he is going to get caught, the odds are the killer is getting some satisfaction doing this, having this secret that he got away with it, probably reliving his crime sexually in some manner. The serial killer Joel Rifkin said his mind was like a VCR; he could put in the tape of what he did and play it whenever he wanted. In some odd way, this may be a good thing because it may prevent some people from being killed, that monsters like this can replay what they did as opposed to looking for new victims. But sooner or later, it's not enough anymore and most of them need more.

Bridge Guy may have posed the girls' bodies and left them in a certain way, but the way he left them is not who they are or what they're experiencing today. They aren't being degraded and humiliated anymore, no matter how often he plays it back in his mind.

The FBI released behavioral clues to help the public find the killer. Were there changes in a daily routine? Was he sleeping more? Sleeping less? Has he been increasing his use of booze and drugs? Has he missed work or school? Does he have an excessive interest in the case? Did he spend time cleaning clothes or shoes, or dispose of those items? Maybe he's acting paranoid, or recently sold or trashed a vehicle.

When Ed Kemper killed his grandparents, he sat on the porch and waited for the police to come to arrest him. When they didn't come, he went inside, and called his mother and the police: he told his mother what he had done; he told the police to come and get him.

Dennis Rader, the BTK killer, killed a large portion of the Otero family as his first murders. Four members of the Otero family—the mother, father, and the two youngest children—were murdered and subjected to different forms of torture while the three oldest children were at school. He thought the police were coming to get him for sure afterwards, but no one came.

Bridge Guy must have felt this. When were they coming for him? His photo was all over the news. How did he even go down to the store and get a cup of coffee without being terrified about being caught?

When it comes to trying to solve a crime, lots of times people have valuable info and don't say anything simply because they don't know it's valuable. And then there are others who have more nefarious reasons for not dropping a dime. I think there is someone out there who is pretty sure they know the person who did it, but they never turned in a tip.

My suspicion is someone might even be providing a false alibi for Bridge Guy. 2:13 was the last communication from Libby's cell phone. Because of this, we know we are looking for someone who is unaccounted for from approximately two to five o'clock, who had the means and the ability to be on the bridge that day. The police have likely interviewed someone who knows him, maybe even someone who was involved.

Most likely it was someone covering for their husband, friend, boyfriend, father, or son. Someone who wasn't around that day or wasn't where they said they would be, and they don't want to say because they know he couldn't have been the killer. Or maybe they know he could have done it but they don't want to admit it to themselves, let alone to the police department.

I believe he didn't go there with the intention of killing anyone. I think he wanted to kidnap and abduct, but at some point, he couldn't control them. One of them fought back and he either lost his temper or tried to quiet them. He panicked and freaked out, like the loser he is, and this is the result.

He isn't important or significant. He is weaker than they were. He reacted to what they did and killed them. Murder is the biggest temper tantrum someone could throw. Like a three-year-old crying and kicking the floor. He is a nobody who can't control himself.

There were single women there that day. Why did he pick girls? He was sexually attracted to little girls almost certainly, but I believe he was picking two to abduct because when he got them to where he was taking them, there was someone else there waiting. We know they were killed on the trail that day, so while we don't know if he was planning to kill them, we know he was prepared to.

Maybe Bridge Guy had a helper who was in a vehicle nearby waiting for his partner to arrive with the girls. Or maybe he helped with an alibi.

One thing we know for sure, he was someone who wasn't accounted for from two to five on that day. How many people were in that area that day can that be said about? Either the guy is a total loner or someone knows something.

The recording from Libby's cell shows he coerced them to leave the trail, "down the hill." Is "Guys, down the hill" a complete sentence, or is "guys" the end of another sentence? We know Anna Williams viewed the entire video and audio and said there was more audio than what was released, meaning Libby must have concealed the phone at some point.

Anna said one of the girls said, "Well, where are we going to go?" during the video, as well as there being a variety of regular chitchat between the girls. I assume the girls' chatter was before the threat. Maybe Libby was filming before they realized he was a threat, or maybe much of the chitchat was around things like, "Do you know that guy? What do you think he is doing?"

My assumption is this snippet of audio is after Bridge Guy directed the girls. My guess is he either directed them through a wooded area or toward the creek. His voice sounds frustrated, almost like they aren't being cooperative.

Supposedly there was a transcript made of the audio which was leaked. The portion I heard went something like one of the girls saying, "I am not talking to him, you talk to him," like she was too afraid to speak to him or look at him, or maybe she is even blaming her friend for the predicament they're in. I should clarify that this was from an online source. I have no way of knowing how credible it is.

How did he get away? How did he get there? He had to leave somehow. He must get to the trail, abduct, and murder, then he must leave. Did anyone spot him leaving? Were his clothes covered with blood? Were his clothes wet from the creek? Looking at the map, it looks likely he would have to cross at some point.

We don't know if he had a vehicle. He could have gone on the Freedom Bridge and walked back to town, he could have gone through Logan's property, or he could have left through a cemetery that is rather close to where the girls were found.

As I have stated, I believe he wanted to kidnap them and take them elsewhere because the crime was sexually motivated. There is no way he would go about attempting to abduct two people without having a vehicle nearby. He would need some form of privacy. Maybe he was going to move them to a house on someone's property.

This type of predator will fantasize for days, months, even years before they act. Often, fantasies don't go the way they want in real life. This was scripted in his mind for a long period of time, to the point it became something he had to act on. This fantasy owned him, and it cost two girls their lives.

But it didn't play the way he wanted it to, the way he needed it to. There are other variables now, real people are involved, it isn't just a fantasy. He can't control everything in real life. People aren't puppets and the world is not this creep's stage. Therefore, a lot of criminals re-offend because they still haven't had their perfect fantasy come true. I have never believed he approached them by happenstance. This was planned out. I think the vehicle he needed to get them to was placed on the other side of the bridge. He set things up to his advantage and their disadvantage.

If you look at a map, you can draw a straight line from the cemetery to the bridge, and there is rough terrain where they would have to go down a hill. One can come off the main road and drive into the cemetery from one of two entrances. He could have parked his vehicle far from the road along the tree line by the cemetery where no one would see. He would just have to pop out of the woods and load them into his vehicle; most of the time would be spent bringing them through the woods, out of sight from prying eyes.

If it were me trying to carry out this plan, I would have parked in the back part of the cemetery. If you have a van or a covered truck, you could back into a space and not even have to walk around to open the door.

I think he started to have problems once he got them across the water. The further they go under his control, the more of a chance is that one of them could cause a scene or make a run for it. The two girls loved each other and probably wouldn't leave the other behind. I think something went down. He either decided to just kill one and take the other, or one decided to turn on him and fight back.

When it comes to a crime scene such as this, DNA and fingerprints are paramount. We all know what fingerprint recognition is. It's the verification of a person's identity by comparing their fingerprints with previously recorded samples. For more than a century, it has remained the most used forensic evidence in the world. DNA evidence became common in the 1980s and has long been known as something that can be collected from blood, hair, skin cells, and other bodily substances.

Touch DNA, also known as trace DNA, is a newer forensic method for analyzing DNA left at the scene of a crime. It only requires very small samples; for example, from the skin cells left on an object after it has been touched or casually handled, or from footprints. With this form of evidence, investigators can even find DNA on a victim who has been strangled, for example.

We don't know if law enforcement has any DNA, fingerprints, or hairs and fibers. We don't know if they are looking for animal fur; perhaps Bridge Guy had dog hair on his person and he left it behind. or he could have unique fibers in his vehicle that were transferred to the crime scene. We have never been told the manner of death or the results of toxicology reports or whether either girl was sexually assaulted. Basically, we know next to nothing.

It was a complicated crime scene because it was outdoors, not a controlled environment. Bodies found in the woods present a much bigger problem when it comes to collecting evidence, unlike a manager being shot in a back room at a convenience store.

There was a recorded and leaked radio call between two police officers where one said they found girl's undergarments underneath the bridge, away from the crime scene. It can't be said they were a part of the crime; they could have been there for years. But they could have been taken as a trophy and Bridge Guy could have just discarded them in a panic.

When it came time for the old pervert roundup, it turned out there were twelve sexual offenders in Delphi, and many more in surrounding areas, all of whom were interviewed by police. If you're a detective, you never want to do all the talking when you interview suspects. You want to throw out a question or two, and get the suspect talking, let them do all the work. Sometimes the awkward silences get the suspect to talk more. A lot of detectives like to play dumb. If they come off dumb, the suspect can overexplain things, or even offer their own opinions of what could have happened.

Many of them agreed to take voluntary polygraph tests. They collected a lot of DNA from these ostensible suspects, which makes one wonder if they actually had some DNA from the crime scene.

A state law went into effect in 2018, which requires all individuals arrested for a felony in Indiana to submit a DNA sample. In theory, if Bridge Guy had scrapes with the law before in Indiana, they have his DNA. I will never believe he woke up that day and decided to go out and murder two children and had never done anything else like that in his life. That doesn't mean he was caught and arrested before for a sexual crime, but people like this usually leave at least some trail of antisocial behavior.

There are several untested rape kits in Indiana. There is currently a backlog of over five thousand in the state, roughly the same number of untested rape kits as there were in 2017.[13] If a rape victim chooses to, they can have a medical professional conduct an exhaustive examination of their entire body for DNA evidence left behind by the attacker. That evidence is collected and preserved and commonly referred to as a rape kit. It's not out of the realm of possibility that one of these untested rape kits could solve the whole case.

Even if they don't have a DNA match through a rape kit, they could potentially connect it to an unknown offender, maybe for a rape in Gary, Indiana, in September 1995. At least then you can start to put together a timeline of your unknown assailant. Suddenly, a detective might realize a guy he just interviewed as a suspect was in Gary, Indiana, in '95 and can start looking at him a lot harder.

Robert Ives has said things on record that fascinate me. One thing he said was the crime scene was very odd. Then he followed that up by saying, "Any murder scene is odd." He told the host of the *Down the Hill* podcast, in Chapter 5: Signatures, "All I can say about the situation with Abby and Libby is that there was a lot more physical evidence than at that crime scene. And it's probably not what you would imagine, or what people think that I'm talking about, it's probably not. And so, because of unique circumstances, which all unique circumstances of a crime are a sort-of 'signature,' you think, 'Well, this unusual fact might lead to somebody, or that unusual fact might lead to somebody.'"[14]

This statement got a lot of people worked up. People started saying insane things, like the killer strung doll babies in the trees. Some say he brought a giant teddy bear and if

---

13. Indiana—End the Backlog. https://www.endthebacklog.org/state/indiana/#:~:text=*%20According%20to%20a%20media%20report,kits%20in%20Indiana%20in%202017

14. *Down the Hill: The Delphi Murders.* "Chapter 5: Signatures." (HLN. February 26, 2020.) https://podcasts.apple.com/us/podcast/down-the-hill-the-delphi-murders/id1494167201

you look at aerial photos of the area, you can clearly see the outline of it. I mean, *come on*. He would have to string up the babies in advance or carry a huge teddy bear down the trail to the murder scene. You really can't make this stuff up.

Sadly, most of the time, people kill people they know. They fight with their spouse, their boss, or their next-door neighbor. The murder happens because of a burst of anger or energy. There is a difference between what is "odd" at a murder scene of a husband killing his wife or a guy killing another guy in the bar, and what is "odd" thinking about a sexually driven homicide of a stranger.

I don't feel the need to go out of my way to know details of a story that only degrades the victim who has already been degraded but it is not uncommon for victims to be posed. It could be for shock value; it could be for the killer's own sexual gratification. Doug Carter, almost on the verge of tears, said, "I promise you they are not how you left them there that day."

It would not surprise me in the slightest if one or both were posed in a degrading fashion, especially surmising at least one was missing undergarments. It also wouldn't surprise me if he concealed the bodies with debris from the woods to give him time to get away. Time is the killer of evidence.

Often when these types of rapes or murders take place in a public area, the perp inserts things into the victims, such as sticks, rocks, or leaves. A victim can be raped with other things other than a man's penis or digits. This is to inflict pain and to humiliate. But it is also often because these offenders can't perform at the crime scene and will use something else to simulate their fantasy.

I think those are some of the things we might be thinking about when it comes to an "odd" crime scene.

There have been some awful rumors about the victims, such as one was pregnant and was going to have a baby and that is why she was killed, or the murder was a hit because someone owed drug money. If there was such an easy connection, I think we would have found this killer a long time ago. If at any time the girls speculated or said who the man was by name on the audio, this would be released to the public.

That doesn't mean the perp doesn't know them, even if they don't know him. BTK, as well as many other serial killers, would often identify and stalk his victims before killing them.

But it will always be my belief that these girls didn't know this guy. He was either a stranger or someone who tricked them into meeting him there, thinking he was someone else.

# Anonymous Letters

When it comes to Delphi, there are a lot of people who have been brought up as suspects in the case, all of whom have something in common. They all look like some version of what we believe Bridge Guy looks like, and they all reside, or did at one point, somewhat close to Delphi.

The reason most of these guys are on the radar is the crimes they committed after the girls were killed, not before. To me, the before aspect of things is more important because once Bridge Guy's image and voice are on TV, he might shut down, or at least go cold for a bit before he attempts something again. A lot of criminals run amok, but once their crime hits the press and there is a sketch of them out there, they chill out—for a while anyway. Others don't have the ability to stop, even for a little while.

There is still reason to believe justice will be served. I have seen other cases before that seemed hopeless where the killer was found.

*True Crime Garage* covered the murder of April Tinsley in December 2015. It was a cold case and included some anonymous letters from the killer. I am a sucker with anything that has to do with killers communicating with police, public, or media. The Captain says if it weren't for him, the whole show would be about Ohio cold cases or those involving a letter.

April Marie Tinsley had just turned eight, when on April 1, 1988, she left one friend's house to pick up an umbrella she had left at another friend's house. She never returned.

Her mother filed a missing persons report at three that same afternoon. Police started searching for her daughter almost immediately but to no avail.

Three days later, a jogger in Spencerville, Indiana, found April's body in a ditch on the side of a rural road in the eastern part of Indiana. An autopsy revealed she had been raped and strangled to death. Years later, *America's Most Wanted* covered the case and reported there was some sort of sex object left with the body. Her underwear contained the suspect's semen, but it was too small an amount to create a DNA profile at the time.

The residents of Fort Wayne lived in fear, knowing a murderous lunatic lived amongst them. This guy didn't just wake up one day and say, "Hey, I'm going to go abduct a girl!" I think this was planned out. I don't know if she was being watched. There are some people that speculate that she was, there are others that speculate she was just a crime of opportunity.

The case grew cold until May 1990, when an apparent confession was found written on a barn wall in nearby Grabill, Indiana. "I kill eight-year-old April Marie Tisley. I will kill agin."

In 2004, the FBI and the Fort Wayne police announced the writer of the barn note found in 1990 was the same person who killed April Tinsley. They don't say why, so we have to speculate how they could come to that conclusion.

My theory at the time was DNA was left at the barn where the note was found that matched DNA found on the victim. It was also possible there was a note left with the body. They waited years to tell us about the sex object, maybe they never disclosed that there was a note either.

The note on the barn also asked, "Did you find her shoe?" One of April's shoes was found later and away from the body. At the time that the barn note was authored, the killer knew of the other shoe. This was eventually disclosed to the public before the killer was apprehended but years after the crime.

On Memorial Day weekend in 2004, Emylee Higgs found a plastic bag on her pink bicycle. The seven-year-old girl brought it to her mother, who was blown away by what she found: a used condom and a threatening letter which read, "I am the same person that kidnapped, raped and killed April Tinsley. You are my next victim." The Higgs family immediately notified the authorities, who quickly realized that the note's handwriting was similar to the one scrawled on the barn.

Shortly afterwards, three similar packages were found by little girls in Fort Wayne, each containing similar information as well as similar misspellings and threats. There was a used condom in three of the missives that was ejaculated into. The fourth note had a polaroid picture of a man holding his dick in his hand, with his legs also visible. You can't see his face. It said, "Hi Honey I been watching you I am the same person that kidnapped an rape an kill Aproil Tinsley you are my next vitem." The police and FBI speculated that these grammatical errors were purposely done to try to throw people off from figuring out the identity of the person who wrote the letters.

Some people speculated the person could have taken the pieces of paper and turned them upside down to write, which would basically be writing the letter backwards, which might explain why sometimes he's kind of jumping a letter or skipping a letter. I didn't think that was the case. I also heard that maybe he is righthanded and he's writing it with his left and or lefthanded and writing with his right hand to throw people off so they can't identify his handwriting. I don't think that's the case either.

When testing the condoms, they found DNA and compared it to the DNA that they found at the crime scene. It was the same.

They know that the suspect is white from the photo where his legs are visible. There is a bedspread in the background of the photo. It was paisley patterned, blue-green almost. The police went to a lot of local hotels to check the bedspreads because it appeared to them to be something typical of a cheap hotel.

You know this is somebody familiar with the area because it was predetermined where he was going to leave these letters. I almost wondered if this guy wanted to witness the intended little girl finding the letter. I could see him getting some kind of kick out of seeing the shock on the face of this little girl, or seeing her reaction to finding these disturbing things—whether it be nude photos, used condoms, whatever. The letters were in Ziplock bags, so again he's fully intending for people to find these letters. He doesn't want them destroyed by the weather or the rain.

The FBI created a profile of the killer. I include it below.

The one significant advantage criminal behaviorists had in looking at this case was the sheer volume of offender behavior we must consider. This behavior had been demonstrated over the course of sixteen years from 1988, when April Tinsley was abducted, raped, and murdered, through 2004, when the same individual left messages claiming responsibility for April's death, as well as forensic evidence tying him to that crime.

Two tremendous clues he provided are his age range and his race. ... Age and race are important because they give the police and the public a way to narrow the pool of possible suspects. However, the greatest benefit of being able to see the variety of behavior exhibited over a sixteen-year period is the way it begins to inform our opinion of the kind of offender he is, as not all child sex offenders are the same. It also gives us insight into the underlying personality which drives the decisions he makes, including the way he interacts as a member of a family, a neighborhood, a community, and a workforce.

We call this type of individual a preferential child sex offender. One would surmise that Bridge Guy may be one too. By that we mean he has a long-term and persistent sexual desire for children. In this case, the offender has demonstrated a specific sexual interest in little girls who have not yet reached puberty. In other words, he is attracted to hairless, undeveloped girls. This interest will not go away. Girls between the ages of five and ten would greatly appeal to him. This does not mean he cannot interact sexually with adults or even older children, but his overwhelming sexual fantasies and desires focus on young girls. He may be married; however, the vast majority of preferential child sex offenders are not. If he has a long-term intimate adult partner, that partner will almost certainly have an idea that this individual has a sexual interest in little girls but may be in denial regarding the extent of that interest or his ability to act on it.

This offender may establish relationships that give him access to little girls; for instance, he may date or befriend someone in the little girl's family. Perhaps he'll seek employment or volunteer activities that give him proximity to little girls. He will be drawn to places where children congregate—playgrounds, swimming pools, parks, etc. Wherever he goes, if a little girl is nearby, his eyes will follow her. He may go out of his way to interact with her. In an unguarded moment, he may even make a casual sexual reference about a little girl which, if overheard, would strike someone as very inappropriate.

Most of us do not associate adult attention toward a child with sexual attraction. People noticing his interest in little girls may simply interpret it as someone who just loves kids. This offender prefers the company of children to the company of adults, and he may be socially awkward or inappropriate when interacting with adults.

A preferential child sex offender tends to collect things that serve to support his fantasies and are consistent with his sexual preferences. In this case, since our offender's preference is for little girls, he may collect images of little girls, perhaps clothed, candid pictures or even child pornography, and probably both. He may take these pictures himself or he may find them through other sources. He may also collect other items that are arousing to him and remind him of the little girls he wants. These other items could range from articles of clothing to advertisements depicting little girls to Hello Kitty items or any toys that little girls find appealing.

The public tends to think that once a person kidnaps, rapes, and kills, he will always kidnap, rape, and kill. A preferential child sex offender can engage in a lot of different behaviors that satisfy his sexual needs but do not rise to the level of the prior offense. The offender may substitute nuisance sex offenses like peeping, indecent exposure, and leaving obscene notes or sexual items for a child to find. If the item is left in a mailbox or on the front door, the resident may think it was intended for the adult female in the home rather than the little girl who lives there. Oftentimes, these incidents are not reported because the significance of the offense is not recognized by citizens at the time. If the offender has a criminal history, it is more likely to involve sex offenses against children.

After 2004, there was no known activity by this offender, but we've seen gaps of years in his activity before and this could be explained in several ways. He could be institutionalized in hospital or prison. He could have ongoing access to a victim that satisfies his desire for a child partner through a relationship with their adult caretaker. He could have relocated, or he could have died.[15]

The FBI profile indicated this offender has demonstrated that he has strong ties to northeast Fort Wayne and Allen County. This is where he likely lives, works, and/or shops. If you lived in this area, you may have been standing next to him in line at the grocery store, sitting beside him in the pew at church, or working beside him on the production line.

The profile also suggested that the perpetrator was a white circumcised male, whose current age was in his forties to fifties. It suggested he frequented places where children were likely to be and was of low to medium income who either owned or borrowed a Polaroid camera in 2004 and had hair on his lower legs. In 2004, he possibly owned/borrowed a forest green pickup truck having a matching camper shell with dark tinted windows.

While the letters left on bicycles and in mailboxes were all undeniably unsettling and creepy, law enforcement had DNA from the semen. Testing confirmed it matched the DNA from the killing of Tinsley. They found two possible matches in its genealogy database.

One of the matches was John D. Miller, who lived in a trailer park very close to the barn where the first letter was written on the wall.

Investigators went through his trash and found used condoms that matched the DNA of the murderer. When

---

15. FBI. "Tinsley Killer Profile." https://archives.fbi.gov/archives/news/stories/2009/may/april-tinsley-murder-pt.-3/tinsley-killer-profile

detectives came to his house and asked him if he knew why they wanted to talk to him Miller said: "April Tinsley."

The FBI's profile was spot on except he owned a blue Mercury Lynx.

Miller told police he was "trolling down the street" when he came across April Tinsley. He pulled up a block in front of her and waited outside his vehicle for her then ordered her to get in the car. He took her to his trailer in Grabill, raped her, then strangled her to death. The next day, he disposed of her body in the ditch.

On July 19, 2018, he was charged with felony murder, child molestation, and criminal confinement. He was sentenced to eighty years in prison.

In July 2018, police announced they caught April's murderer. We were doing a presentation on Sam Shepard in Columbus; at the end, we did a little question and answer session. There was a woman in the crowd who asked if there were any updates on April Tinsley. I told her I had reason to believe it would be solved soon. Twenty-four hours later, the police announced they solved the case. She must have thought I was super connected, but I just got lucky. I knew they had DNA and fingerprints and his writing, so I was just spit balling.

After John Miller was in custody, he told authorities that he used to fondle a little girl that his mother babysat. John was like twelve or so and the girl was around five. He kept the little girl's panties. His mother found them, and she stopped babysitting the child.

When *America's Most Wanted* covered the case and showed the bedspread asking people if they knew someone who had something that looked like it, John's mother asked him if he still had his bedspread and if so, he should get rid of it. She died before he was caught so we cannot know for sure if she knew.

Miller has come up as a suspect in Delphi but in theory, has been disqualified.

The serial killer Samuel Little, who has confessed to ninety-three murders, once said of a victim, "She was fighting for her life, and I was fighting for my pleasure."

Tinsley had her whole life in front of her but that didn't matter because some evil monster was willing to trade her life for his good time.

# Who Would Take Two Girls?

In the summer of 2012, Elizabeth Collins lived with her parents and siblings in Evansdale, Iowa, a small midwestern town of 4,700 residents and a suburb of the Waterloo-Cedar Falls metropolitan area. Evansdale is a blue-collar town. Many residents are involved in agriculture production in some manner. Elizabeth was described by her mother as a "bubbly little person" who was always active and busy. She was eight years old and loved typical girl stuff like having her nails done, but also liked playing softball and hockey and riding her bike. One of her best friends was her cousin, Lyric Cook, age ten, who lived just minutes away in Waterloo. Lyric went to Kingsley Elementary and was also an active, outgoing girl, who loved bowling, cheerleading, gymnastics, and being outside.

Lyric and Elizabeth's mothers, Misty Cook and Heather Collins, are sisters. Heather is married to Drew Collins. They seemed to be a very typical American family, hardworking, religious parents raising a bunch of children. Heather had her hands full as they had several young kids and had some undisclosed health issues. Consequently, her mom, Wylma, came over for four or five hours daily to help.

Misty was married to Dan Morrissey. But in 2012, Misty and Dan were estranged and had been separated for years. In fact, Dan was out on bail pending trial for four separate criminal cases from 2011, which included assaulting Misty and significant drug charges, including manufacturing meth. Misty got into trouble for drug charges in 2003, to which she plead guilty and was incarcerated for a time. She was released in 2006. In July 2012, when our story takes place, she was still on federal supervised release.

Misty and Dan's daughter, Lyric, lived with Misty and Heather's mom, Wylma Cook, in Waterloo. Wylma had permanent custody of Lyric. Lyric and her cousin Elizabeth played together nearly every day.

On Friday, July 13, 2012, Misty Cook Morrissey was staying with her mother and Lyric in Waterloo. She left for work at 8:30 a.m. for a new job at a convenience store. Misty worked about two miles away from the Collins' house in Evansdale. After Misty left, Wylma took Lyric over to the Collins' house. Both Heather and Drew Collins were going to be gone for the day, so Grandma Wylma was going to be watching the kids and brought Lyric, as usual.

Lyric and Elizabeth set off around 11:30 for a bike ride. This was something they routinely did; they always stayed within yelling distance of the house and would check in about every fifteen minutes.

Often, Elizabeth's older brother Kelly went with them. But not on this day. The girls were last seen by a family member at 12:15, and Heather arrived home shortly after that.

At one p.m. or so, Heather sent out Kelly to scout the area and tell the girls to come home. But he returned, reporting that he could not find them. At this point, Drew stopped home, which he often did during the day. Heather told him she was going to look for the girls, got in the car at 1:20, and started driving around. Misty says Wylma called her at work around two to tell her that they could not find the girls. Misty called her ex, Dan. Dan, his mother, and his fifteen-year-old son all headed to Evansdale to help look. Misty left work and went over to her sister's house. By

2:30, all these people were out driving all over Evansdale looking for the girls.

At 2:45, members of the search party were at Meyers Lake. This is a popular recreation area about one point six miles from one of the girls' homes. The home where they were being watched by grandma was located at 166 Brovan Boulevard in Evansdale. Once at Meyers Lake, the search party began asking people whether they had seen two little girls on bikes. One man told the family he saw two little girls on bikes going west on the bike trail, but the time was unclear. Meanwhile, Heather went to the Evansdale PD at around 2:48 p.m. According to the *Cedar Falls Courier*, "Within minutes of authorities learning of the disappearance of Lyric Cook Morrissey and Elizabeth Collins, three Evansdale squad cars were scouring the area and checking the home. Within half an hour, the search mushroomed with four Black Hawk sheriff's deputies and Evansdale firefighters joining the effort."[16]

Around four p.m., a firefighter found the girls' bikes lying on the Evansdale Nature Trail at Meyers Lake on the paved bike trail at the far southeastern corner of the lake. Investigators also found Elizabeth's purple purse and cell phone (this phone did not have service, it was just used for games) thrown over the fence onto the lake side.

Meyers Lake covers twenty-seven acres and is about twenty-five feet deep. The lake is a major recreational area for the people of Evansdale: it is stocked with fish for anglers, it has a boat ramp, bathrooms, a playground, picnic areas with grills, and a scenic, paved bike path winding its way around the lake.

The Collinses lived about a mile and a half from Meyers Lake. The Evansdale Nature Trail, on which the girls'

---

16. *Cedar Falls Courier*. "Timeline of events: The search for Lyric and Elizabeth." December 10, 2012. https://wcfcourier.com/news/evansdale_search/timeline-of-events-the-search-for-lyric-and-elizabeth/html_c8ef29ca-d077-11e1-8635-001a4bcf887a.html

bikes were found, starts at Lafayette Road in downtown Evansdale, a block away from the Collins' house. There are few areas where a vehicle could be parked close to the trail. Some that are wooded.

What were the girls' bikes doing by Meyers Lake anyway? This was not exactly close to home. Heather and Drew Collins told the media that they did not believe the girls would have biked that far on their own, as the lake was not an area they frequented.

Heather pointed out that both girls were good swimmers. To the family, the fact that the girls' shoes weren't sitting at the water's edge was definitive proof that the girls had not decided to go for dip on this eighty-degree summer day. And even if they had, the chances that both would drown seems very limited.

The following was provided to the media by Kent Smock, who was, at the time, the police chief of Evansdale, based on notes he maintained of the investigation.

By 4:40 p.m. on Friday the thirteenth, emergency calls went out to Evansdale residents to notify them of the missing girls. Officers began canvassing the lake neighborhoods, and the media was notified by 5:30 p.m. Boats were put into the water on Meyers Lake to begin scanning the surface, and divers with a local search and rescue organization were called in to search the lake. Surrounding city police and firefighters, Black Hawk County Sheriff's deputies and Iowa State Police joined Evansdale PD in searching wooded areas. A plane was brought in to search from the air, and the National Center for Missing and Exploited Children (NCMEC) was notified of the girls' disappearance by eight p.m.

The NCMEC had a representative on the ground in Evansdale by the next morning and began emailing and faxing photos of the girls to businesses, truck stops, and retail locations within one hundred miles. The Iowa Division of Criminal Investigation (DCI) and FBI both arrived and began interviewing people as well as looking into registered sex offenders in the area. Thirty FBI agents and fifteen DCI agents joined the search. The FBI's Child Abduction Response Team also was on site.

A nearby creek, surrounding woods, and a city campground were all searched in the coming days. These large-scale searches included corn fields and farmland, rivers, ponds, abandoned buildings, wooded areas, and other public places. Cars were stopped at police checkpoints in the days after the disappearance, police searching car trunks, and asking drivers to be on the lookout for the girls. For a full week, the nearly round-the-clock searches, interviews, evidence collection, and information gathering proceeded full steam ahead.

Within hours of the girls' bikes being found, the order was given to drag the lake. After two days of dragging, nothing was found. But investigators decided it was best to drain the lake, to be sure that they weren't missing anything.

On the seventeenth, FBI bloodhounds were brought in to track the girls' scents. Police refused to comment on the dogs' findings, but a family member said on Nancy Grace, "I watched the bloodhounds continue into this dense forest area, which is about four hundred yards. I watched them go into that area and they positively identified both girls were at that location."[17]

An FBI spokeswoman said that the dogs' detection of the girls' scents indicated a "strong possibility" that the girls had been there, meaning that it was likely that the girls had been at the lake, rather than their bikes and possessions being planted there by their abductor. The bikes were processed for prints and other evidence, but police won't say if anything was found.

Police quickly started the time-consuming task of interviewing all the family members. The family was

17. Nancy Grace: No clues in disappearance of two Iowa cousins. July 17, 2012. https://transcripts.cnn.com/show/ng/date/2012-07-17/segment/01

initially completely cooperative. Investigators were granted permission by both families to search any houses they were living in or had lived in without having to obtain search warrants. Computers were taken by police. Their cell phones were searched. But as police dug deeper, they did not ignore the criminal pasts of Misty and Dan, who was a known meth manufacturer and dealer out on bail when the girls went missing. On the day before the girls disappeared, Dan appeared in court and instead of taking a plea, he opted to proceed with a trial.

Dan and Misty put on a united front, holding hands, and even staying together in a motel rather than going to their respective homes to try to avoid the media—despite a restraining order Misty had against Dan and the fact that they had been separated for years. But then things changed. It seems that Evansdale police suspected that Dan could harm his daughter and niece. Or at least that he might know who was responsible. In fact, according to his sister-in-law Tammy Brousseau, the girls' aunt, who spoke with ABC News, gave statements to the effect that Dan Morrisey felt he was being treated like a suspect. Tammy says, "I can see Dan becoming very defensive after he's being told, you know, you killed your daughter and niece. You know you did it. We have proof. We have evidence that you did this."[18]

UPI reported that Dan abruptly ended a police polygraph session after investigators accused him of injuring the girls and knowing where they were. After this debacle, Dan and Misty hired an attorney, who advised them to stop talking to police or the media, and not to take any more polygraph tests.

On Tuesday the seventeenth, Chief Deputy Rick Abben of the Black Hawk County Sheriff's Office held a press conference saying that authorities had been "grasping for

18. Jaffe, Alex Perez and Matthew. "FBI Believes Missing Iowa Girls Are Alive." ABC News, July 23, 2012. https://abcnews.go.com/US/fbi-believes-missing-iowa-girls-alive/story?id=16827922

straws" in their search for the girls, but it was as if they had just disappeared into thin air. "It wouldn't be proper for me to stand here and tell you we have a theory because we don't," he said. "We have two missing girls, and we have no idea why." He stated, "We have no reason to believe there was any foul play at this time." He also said, "Everyone is a suspect until we find something."[19]

Wylma Cook last saw the girls riding their bikes behind Lederman's Big and Tall at 3524 Lafayette Road at about 12:15 p.m. Surveillance camera footage from a business called Cornbelt Auctions at 3520 Lafayette Road captured the two on their bikes riding at 12:11 p.m. But the business owner said the cameras were eight minutes behind, making the sighting more likely being at 12:19 p.m. This was less than a block from the Collins' home. The girls were biking in a direction away from the lake at the time the footage was shot. According to *Iowa Cold Cases*, the girls were next seen at 12:23 p.m. on Brovan Boulevard, and then again sometime between 12:30 and one p.m. on Gilbert Drive, not far from Meyers Lake.

Six days after the girls were last seen, police were still not calling their disappearance an abduction. The day after the girls went missing, Chief Smock told the media that the case was being treated as a "suspicious disappearance." Media outlets theorized that a double abduction—one in which two little girls were taken at once—would be very unlikely. And Smock told the media that it is so rare for an abductor to take two children at a time.

Deputy Chief Abben said that no weapons had been found, although some evidence had been sent to the DCI crime lab for analysis. He said, "Investigators are confident the girls are not in Meyers Lake and this case is being

---

19. *Cedar Falls Courier*. "Timeline of events: The search for Lyric and Elizabeth." December 10, 2012. https://wcfcourier.com/news/evansdale_search/timeline-of-events-the-search-for-lyric-and-elizabeth/html_c8ef29ca-d077-11e1-8635-001a4bcf887a.html

handled as an abduction. If they were lost in that area, they would have been found by now."[20] He reiterated that they had not cleared anyone. "Everyone is a suspect until we find these young girls," he said. Abben announced that a fifty-thousand-dollar reward was being offered for information leading to the arrest and conviction of anyone involved with the abduction of the girls.

In a weird turn of events, the FBI released a statement saying that it was likely that the two girls were still alive. An FBI spokeswoman told ABC News this being based on "evidence" that had been found on Friday the twentieth, but she would not elaborate. *The Des Moines Register* reported that officials "have some things that we can't discuss that lead us to believe they [the girls] are alive."[21] She went on to say: "Cooperation with law enforcement is the key factor in discovering the whereabouts of Lyric and Elizabeth. Unfortunately, law enforcement have not received total cooperation from all family and close friends."[22] She specifically said that the family's failure to cooperate was a "hindrance" to the investigation. Officials would not elaborate on who specifically was holding back, but it seems likely that the comments were aimed at Dan and Misty because they stopped talking to police and giving interviews on the advice of their lawyers.

According to CNN, both Misty and Dan passed polygraph exams and police cleared them based on this and their alibis—Misty was at work, and Dan was at home with his son, and this was backed up by his mother.

20. KCCI. "Missing Girls update: 'case now handled as abduction.'" July 20, 2012. https://www.kcci.com/article/missing-girls-update-case-now-handled-as-abduction/6870649

21. UPI. "FBI: Missing Iowa Girls Likely Alive." July 21, 2012. https://www.upi.com/Top_News/US/2012/07/21/FBI-Missing-Iowa-girls-likely-alive/UPI-31831342918680/

22. UPI. "FBI: Missing Iowa Girls Likely Alive." July 21, 2012. https://www.upi.com/Top_News/US/2012/07/21/FBI-Missing-Iowa-girls-likely-alive/UPI-31831342918680/

It seems that police might have had a working theory that the girls' abductions were somehow related to Dan's drug connections. Aunt Tammy said, "The children weren't exposed to those people. They were pretty much, for the most part, kept away from there."[23] But that did not stop the rumors from flying that maybe the girls were taken by someone connected to Dan, someone involved in his shady drug underworld.

*The Daily Mail* said the girls could have been abducted by drug dealers as "payback"[24] for Dan's snitching. The *Mail* article said that Wylma told them "it's possible"[25] her son-in-law made an enemy through his cooperation with police. Many were wondering about Dan suddenly deciding to go forward with a trial rather than taking a plea deal the day before the girls were taken; this could be seen as suspicious. It was easier for many people to believe that there was a known suspect or reason that the girls had been taken than to believe the alternative, that the girls were kidnapped at random by a stranger.

Well, it was time for the old pervert roundup. And that is exactly what law enforcement did. Investigators tracked down approximately ten registered sex offenders living in Evansdale, and all were cleared by police. But according to CNN, there were two hundred registered sex offenders in

23. UPI. "Lyric Cook-Morrissey, Elizabeth Collins: Iowa Girls' Family Downplays Past Issues - UPI.Com." July 19, 2012. https://www.upi.com/Top_News/US/2012/07/19/Iowa-girls-family-downplays-past-issues/UPI-42611342727658/

24. *Daily Mail*. "Missing Iowa Cousins Lyric Cook and Elizabeth Collins 'May Have Been Abducted by Drug Dealers.'" July 28, 2012. https://www.dailymail.co.uk/news/article-2180143/Missing-Iowa-cousins-Lyric-Cook-Elizabeth-Collins-abducted-drug-dealers.html

25. *Daily Mail*. "Missing Iowa Cousins Lyric Cook and Elizabeth Collins 'May Have Been Abducted by Drug Dealers.'" July 28, 2012. https://www.dailymail.co.uk/news/article-2180143/Missing-Iowa-cousins-Lyric-Cook-Elizabeth-Collins-abducted-drug-dealers.html.

a ten-mile radius.[26] Which is kind of messed up, when you think about it.

Investigators had a hard time figuring out exactly how the girls were abducted. Where the bikes were left was quite far from the house and was not an area car could travel on. Further, the girls' scents had seemed to lead into the woods. How had a predator, or predators, managed to get control of two girls, silently, and sight unseen, in broad daylight? Had the girls been lured to a vehicle, perhaps by someone they knew and trusted? Had they been grabbed from another location, perhaps along a road, and the bikes left by their abductor on the trail and the dogs were just mistaken or confused? Had someone been watching Lyric and Elizabeth, and planned the attack carefully, being sure to take the girls from Meyers Lake where they would not be expected to go, and leaving no footprints or tire tracks?

There were a rash of child abduction attempts throughout Iowa in 2012. The following reports appeared in various media publications:

May 19, 2012: Authorities were looking for a man suspected in the attempted abduction of three girls on the west side of Perry, Iowa. Perry police say the man stopped his car about eight p.m. Friday and asked the girls, ages eight and nine, for directions to a convenience store. He then tried to get the girls into the car, asking for them to show him the way. Police say the girls ran to a neighbor's house.

June 6, 2012: Metro police teamed up following a string of attempted child abductions in the Des Moines area. The most recent happened in Pleasant Hill on May 23. Police say a man in an SUV tried to lure a young girl into his car.

In June, parents in Forest City, Iowa, were notified of two abduction attempts. In one of them, the driver of a tan panel/work-style van stopped three children on bicycles on

---

26. CNN.Com. Transcripts. http://edition.cnn.com/TRANSCRIPTS/1207/19/ng.01.html

North Eighth Street and told them he was going to get them. The children ran away, and the driver drove off.

In March, the police department investigated a possible attempt to abduct a ten-year-old boy. The boy, who was in front of his home, said he was approached by an Asian male, approximately fifty years old and with a thin face. The suspect was driving an older grey van, possibly bearing Iowa license plates. The man reportedly tried to lure the boy into his van after asking directions to a church.

Whether any of these attempted abductions could have been the same person who took Elizabeth and Lyric is certainly something that police in Evansdale would have considered.

On the four-month anniversary of their daughters' disappearances, a letter appeared in the newspaper. It read:

> To Whom it May Concern: We would use your name, but we don't know who you are. Or maybe we do? Maybe you are someone who knows the girls? Maybe you are someone who just acted upon an impulse? Maybe you planned to take them? We don't know, because we don't know who you are.
>
> But we can sort of imagine that you must not have had the things you needed to grow up feeling safe and loved. Because only someone who hurts inside would hurt another person and their family. We've all heard the saying, "Hurt people, hurt people." We believe that is true.
>
> We are so sorry for whatever happened to you, when you were growing up. Certainly, all children do not receive all the love and care they deserve. Some are even abused by those who are supposed to have taken care of them. When that happens, it is very wrong.
>
> Taking the girls from us has caused much pain, pain for them, pain for us and our families. Since the

time you took them, maybe you've wondered more than a few times, how you could ever make it right. How to be a hero, not a monster. Things probably look pretty hopeless for a good outcome.

We want you to know that we are praying for you to do the right thing. By releasing the girls, everyone wins. Even you. The person who took them.

Imagine how it will feel to have everyone remember that you were the one person, in all the missing children cases, the one person who cared enough to let the girls go! You will not be remembered as the one who took the girls, but as the one who let them come home.

Our lives have not been the same since July 13. Please, let our girls come home to us.

Do the right thing. Be a hero.

Sincerely

Drew and Heather Collins

Dan and Misty Morrissey-Cook[27]

Heather Collins said in interviews that she and Drew met with authorities every day for months. They barely slept and spent every day hoping for word and praying that someone would just drop the girls off somewhere.

On December 5, 2012, came the phone call they dreaded. The families were told that two bodies had been found that were believed to be the girls.

Three hunters found two small corpses in Seven Bridges Wildlife Park in Bremer County, north of Evansdale, an off-the-grid, 166-acre wildlife area about twenty-two miles from Meyers Lake. The area was not one that someone would just stumble on. It was frequented mostly by hunters,

---

27. *Cedar Falls Courier.* "Missing Cousins' parents write open letter to kidnapper." November 13, 2012.
https://wcfcourier.com/news/evansdale_search/missing-cousins-parents-write-open-letter-to-kidnapper/article_1abbb67a-2d7e-11e2-9bbe-001a4bcf887a.html

ATV riders, fishermen, canoers, kayakers, and campers. Locals were known to dump used appliances, and there was even the occasional old meth lab in the brush, brambles, and woods. Some locals also used the area as a party spot, particularly high school-aged kids.

The hunters were making their way through the brush near a river. The area where the bodies lay was accessible only by one road. 270th Street. This road had a dirt road off it that went a short distance to a dirt parking area and turnout near the riverbank. The bodies were found about one hundred fifty feet from this turnout. The whole place is incredibly desolate: the kind of place where you could go and not see any other humans for weeks, maybe months.

The Iowa State Medical Examiner's Office confirmed after the autopsies the remains were Lyric and Elizabeth. The ME was able to determine a cause of death, but this has never been released by law enforcement. Law enforcement made statements to the effect of details surrounding the cause of death would be known only to the killer. And Evansdale Police Chief Kent Smock said investigators had "an idea"[28] of how much time passed between the girls' disappearance and when they were killed. However, he would not release that detail to the public. Investigators have also never addressed whether they have the suspect's DNA in this case, although given that the bodies were exposed to the elements for five months, DNA recovery could be difficult. Drew Collins has stated that he was never informed whether DNA of anyone other than the girls was found. The family has chosen not to learn how their girls were killed.

In 2013, the year after Lyric and Elizabeth were murdered, Iowa investigators were alerted to another double abduction of two girls. On May 20, twelve-year-old Desi

---

28. *Globe Gazette*. "Murder suspect was probably familiar with park." February 3, 2015 https://globegazette.com/community/mcpress/news/local/murder-suspect-was-probably-familiar-with-park/article_bf357231-0593-5492-b0c1-29741a534d7c.html

Hughes and her fifteen-year-old friend Kathlynn Sheppard were abducted while walking home from school around four p.m. in Dayton, Iowa. They got into a vehicle with a man who offered to pay them to mow lawns, but then just kept driving, subduing them by waving a "gun" that was actually an instrument used to euthanize livestock. Their abductor, Michael Klunder, drove around for about ninety minutes, and then took the two to a hog processing facility where he worked, and zip tied their hands. He then left Desi in his truck while he dragged Kathlynn off to places unknown. Desi bravely escaped the vehicle and hid out in the woods before approaching a nearby home to call for help. Around eight p.m., police located Klunder's truck at a nearby rural property; Klunder had hung himself. Kathlynn Sheppard was nowhere to be seen, although significant amounts of her blood were found on the truck. Her body was found a few days later by fishermen about fifteen to twenty miles down the Des Moines River. She had been stabbed and beaten to death by a sharp instrument.

Michael Klunder—who was a six-foot-six, forty-two-year-old farmhand—had already served time in prison, from 1992 to 2011. This was half the sentence he received for the 1991 kidnapping and assault of a young woman, whom he grabbed, hit, and pulled into his car. In an unrelated case, Klunder abducted three-year-old twin girls, who were found alive in a trash receptacle. These were the daughters of a female acquaintance. Klunder said he was angry with one of the girls, so he kidnapped them, drove fifty miles with them in the trunk, and left them in the garbage. One of the girls showed signs of having been choked. Klunder completed a sex offender treatment program in prison and registered as a sex offender upon his release.

Police in Evansdale and Dayton thought that Klunder could be connected because of some of the similarities between the abductions. Two girls, taken in daylight from a public place. Klunder had spent some time in Bremer

County, where Seven Bridges was located, in the nineties. But eventually, investigators in Evansdale ruled Klunder out. His movements on the day of their abduction were accounted for, they said. He had been at home in Stratford, which is one hundred miles away. They also noted that there were forensic differences between the cases.

On August 21, 2014, more than two years after Lyric and Elizabeth were killed, Evansdale police held a press conference announcing a new website dedicated to the girls' case and discussing the likely characteristics of their killer. They had developed a profile of sorts with the help of the FBI's Behavioral Analysis Unit, who believed the killer was a single individual who was familiar with both Meyers Lake in Evansdale and Seven Bridges Wildlife Area in Bremer County. According to the profile, the offender blends in with the community at large and may be a resident of Black Hawk or Bremer Counties. He likely used "quiet coercion" to subdue the girls and coerce them into leaving with him, using a ruse or threats of violence. The cousins were possibly the victims of opportunity, seized by someone who had expressed interest in underage girls, and possibly had attempted abductions in the past. Finally, the suspect likely altered his appearance and/or cleaned, painted, or disposed of his vehicle after the abduction.

In 2015, Chief Smock asked for the public's help naming people who were familiar with the area where the girls were found. He said, "I think you will all agree with me that Seven Bridges is extremely remote. We have no doubt that the person or persons responsible for this crime are very familiar with Seven Bridges."[29]

In late 2016, Iowa authorities received a report of an attempted abduction. A man pretending to be an undercover

---

29. *The Gazette*. "Investigators Focusing on Bremer County Wildlife Area in Evansdale Missing Cousins Case." February 3, 2015. https://www.thegazette. com/news/investigators-focusing-on-bremer-county-wildlife-area-in-evansdale-missing-cousins-case/

police officer tried to lure a young girl into his car. The girl told her parents, and the child's neighbor and brothers chased the suspect's silver vehicle until police got there, even confronting the driver about his attempt to kidnap the child.

This pervert was fifty-eight-year-old married father of two Jeff Altmayer. He was arrested and charged with enticing a minor and impersonating a public official. Once police had Altmayer in custody, they started to connect other abductions and attempted abductions on him. It turned out that Altmayer had been trying to lure kids into his vehicle for months, if not longer. His M.O. was to entice children by offering them one hundred dollars to get in his van. Once they did, he would molest them, or attempt to. He eventually succeeded in sexually abusing at least two girls. Altmayer worked as a traveling automobile damage field inspector; he spent a lot of time in his vehicle driving around areas of the Midwest. All in all, police were able to link Altmayer to nineteen such incidents in nine different counties. As stated in the *Des Moines Register,* "Between May 31, 2016, and November 16, 2016, Altmayer is suspected of trying to entice at least 19 children; he sexually abused two of them, police say. His victims were all girls, with an average age of 10. But he went after kids as young as 6 and as old as 13."[30]

The Iowa DCI agent who eventually filed a criminal complaint against Jeff Altmayer for one of his attempted abductions in Jasper County was also the lead agent in the Lyric/Elizabeth investigation. One of the reasons that Altmayer was interesting to this DCI agent and other investigators was that he had tried to lure two children at once, multiple times. Evansdale investigators would

---

30. *Des Moines Register.* "A stranger with $100 bills: How an Iowa man tried to kidnap at least 19 kids across the state." May 26, 2018. https://www.desmoinesregister.com/story/news/crime-and-courts/2018/05/26/jeff-altmayer-iowa-child-abductions-how-he-sought-lure-kids/483420002/

acknowledge only that Altmayer was "one of our leads," but refused to elaborate.

In February 2018, Jeff Altmayer was sentenced for first-degree kidnapping, second-degree sexual abuse, and two counts of enticing a minor in Jasper County District Court. He got life in prison and his wife of several decades divorced him.

As previously mentioned, Dan Morrissey had been supposed to plead to the 2011 meth charges the day before the girls went missing. But he changed his mind and opted for a trial instead. The judge pushed it back a little out of sympathy for what Dan was going through with his daughter's abduction, but eventually the trial was scheduled for March 2013. Dan had been out on supervised pretrial release until February 2013, when he was sent back to prison for missing appointments with his pretrial officer and testing positive for meth. Dan decided to avoid a trial after all, and pled guilty to several meth-related felonies, which included intent and conspiracy to manufacture meth; after Dan's guilty plea, the judge sentenced him to ninety years in prison, where he still sits today.

The drug angle of the Lyric and Elizabeth investigation does not appear to have led anywhere, but it is still a working theory in the case. In 2015, an article in the *Des Moines Register* said, according to Chief Smock, "Investigators have not ruled out that the killings could be connected to drug activity involving Cook-Morrissey's parents."[31]

Misty still can't bear to look at pictures of Lyric. "Somehow, through this whole thing, my drug history became such a focal point in people's eyes in relation to

---

31. *Des Moines Register*. "Slain Evansdale girls' case to focus on wilderness area." February 3, 2015. https://www.desmoinesregister.com/story/news/2015/02/03/murdered-iowa-girls-case-focus-wilderness-area/22794367/

their disappearance. It was absolutely crippling and it's really, really hard to get over."[32]

Lyric and Elizabeth's case is one that has often been discussed in the context of the Delphi double murder. The two cases share some startling similarities, and although investigators seem to believe that they are not related, many true crime followers believe that the similarities are too numerous to be coincidental.

Both cases involve the abduction and murder of two young girls in Midwest towns (four hundred miles apart). Both cases occurred on or near recreational trails, but also in areas where the girls were not supposed to be. Both cases occurred in the middle of the day, in broad daylight. Both cases occurred on the thirteenth of the month. In both cases, the bodies were found in remote areas that investigators believe required familiarity on the part of the killer. Both sets of investigators stopped short of declaring the offender a local. In both cases, a close family member had ties to the drug world, and rumors flew that drug connections were responsible; in both cases, the older of the two girls was being raised by her grandmother because her parents were involved in drugs.

In neither case is the cause or manner of death of the victims known to the public, nor is it known whether there was sexual assault. Because of this, we can't compare some of the more important aspects of the killer's M.O. And of course, there are significant differences between the cases, the most obvious of which is that in Delphi, the girls were murdered very close to where they were taken, whereas in Evansdale, the girls were transported twenty-two miles away via vehicle. As we said, investigators have concluded

32. *Des Moines Register.* "New family helps revive Misty Cook after daughter's death." July 13, 2017. https://www.desmoinesregister.com/story/news/crime-and-courts/2017/07/13/new-family-helps-revive-misty-cook-after-daughters-death/474101001/

that it is unlikely that the cases are related, but for some, the similarities outweigh the differences.

As of 2017, authorities had interviewed over one thousand people in Lyric and Elizabeth's case. Nonetheless, the murders of Lyric and Elizabeth remain unsolved. The deaths of the girls wreaked havoc on their families. And people in Evansdale say that the town has never been the same. Drew Collins said in an interview that the deaths of the girls devastated the town. Drew continues to assist in cases of missing children, reaching out to Mike and Becky Patty in Delphi to let them know he was there to help.

# THE USUAL SUSPECT

It was a warm Thursday morning in September when Tim Watkins, age sixty, set out on his regular bike ride in Palmer Lake, Colorado. Palmer Lake is about twenty miles outside Colorado Springs, a conservative, military-oriented city that is home to the US Air Force Academy.

Tim was an extremely experienced mountain biker. Tim's life was mountain biking. At one time, Tim owned and operated a well-known bike shop in the area, and he helped to create and maintain the bike trail network that carved through the rugged, hilly terrain of Mount Herman, connecting Monument, Palmer Lake, and the surrounding woodlands and canyons. He and his buddies even felled trees to create makeshift bike bridges over Monument Creek. Tim was the person responsible for drawing the most popular map of the bike trail network, and some of the trails bore his name.

On this day, Tim set out up the steady, ascending Mount Herman Road, an unpaved two-lane road. At some point on Mount Herman Road, in the hills above Monument, his phone butt-dialed a friend and he had to stop his ride and say hello. This is the last known conversation anyone had with Tim Watkins.

Tim was born on November 17, 1956, in Fort Collins, Colorado, and moved to Palmer Lake when he was very young. At college, he earned a degree in education, and afterward, he worked in the ski patrol at some of the nearby mountains. Tim loved adventure and everything outdoors. He spent a lot of time learning survival skills, hunting, and fishing. Tim started his bike shop, Balanced Rock Bike and Ski, in Monument, around the year 2000, with his second wife. It ran for several years, but he was a bike man, not a businessman, so the shop eventually closed, and he and his wife divorced. Tim then married his third wife, Ginger, whom he'd known since they were kids in Palmer Lake.

In September 2017, Tim and Ginger were having some problems. They loved each other, but Tim's lack of steady income caused tension in the marriage. She told Tim she needed a break and she asked him to move out for a while. He took to sleeping in his car at various trailheads and living in a tent. At some point, he told his son Isaac that he was very depressed, and that if it weren't for his kids, he might contemplate suicide. On the day before he disappeared, Tim asked Ginger if he could come home; the next day was her birthday and he wanted to spend it with her. Ginger said yes and he spent the night at the couple's home. The two made plans to celebrate their upcoming anniversary. The next morning, Thursday, September 14, Ginger left for work and Tim set out on a bike ride.

Ginger returned from work around 8:30 p.m., expecting a small birthday celebration with her husband. She noticed that Tim and his bike were gone, but his car was in the driveway. Knowing that Tim would not still be riding, as he had notoriously bad night vision, she texted him but got no response. Assuming he was with his parents or Isaac, Ginger fell asleep, and woke at six the next morning to find that Tim was still unheard from. After sending yet another unanswered text, she left for work. Around ten, she called the Old Town Bike Shop in Colorado Springs to see if he had shown up for work. He hadn't. Ginger knew that this was extremely unlike Tim. A few hours later, she called the Palmer Lake Police Department but was told by Chief

Jason Vanderpool that Tim's disappearance didn't rise to the criteria for a missing persons report until Saturday, after forty-eight hours had elapsed.

Isaac began searching the hills above Palmer Lake, worried that his father may have carried through on his thoughts of suicide. On Saturday, Ginger made a public plea on Facebook for help finding Tim. Sixty people gathered at the Palmer Lake Town Hall and organized grid searches among the network of trails. From there, eleven private search parties set out, fanning out over several square miles of forest.

Around two p.m., a searcher spotted a shoe near the entrance to the popular Limbaugh Trail into Limbaugh Canyon, one of Tim's favorite places to ride and a trail that he helped construct. It was Tim's size.

Later, other volunteers spotted some items scattered up Mount Herman Road, about a half mile northwest from the shoe. These were some of the contents of Tim's wallet. Then, another team spotted Tim's bike off a trail. This titanium bike was specially designed for Tim by a friend and was immediately recognizable to those who knew him.

After the bike was located, law enforcement began searching for Tim. The assumption was that Tim was injured somewhere, possibly due to a bike accident or even an animal attack. He had once had a very close run-in with a mountain lion, and there are bears in the area. El Paso County Search and Rescue used bloodhounds to comb the area for his scent. A local group of drone operators pitched in, providing aerial coverage. Through Saturday night, searchers and volunteers found nothing else.

The next morning, on Sunday, around 11:45, Tim was found dead. They found the body not fifty feet from where his bike was found and forty yards west of the mouth of the Limbaugh Canyon Trail. Tim's body was found lying in a shallow four-foot-by-three-foot old mineral prospector's hole, his body covered up with branches and leaves. Some of Tim's items were missing, such as his hydration pack, jacket, helmet, phone, socks, and one of his shoes.

At first, police did not publicly reveal the cause of death, leaving the townspeople to speculate and leading to rumors and gossip spreading. Stories circulated about animal attacks and car-versus-bike collisions. In fact, Tim's autopsy results have never been released. We don't know any details as to specific injuries Tim might have sustained. But we do know something very important: Tim Watkins was shot.

Police on the scene discovered that Tim's beloved mountain bike had a flat tire: it had been shot through by a bullet. CBS's Denver station reported on September 19 that Tim had been shot "several times;" other news sources stated it was "multiple times."

*Outside* reported the following in November 2018:

> According to sources familiar with the investigation, Watkins had been shot in three places and buried beneath logs and branches in a shallow depression 40 yards west of the Limbaugh Canyon Trail. Bullets had grazed his ear and injured his hand; the likely fatal shot, from a .22 caliber, entered near his ribs and never exited. Closer examination of his front tire later revealed that it had also been shot. Watkins is the first mountain biker known to have been murdered during a ride.[33]

Additionally, a long story in *The Gazette* about the case interviewed a friend of Tim's who observed his body and described it as "pockmarked" with bullet holes. The El Paso County Sheriff has never confirmed the number of bullet holes or that a .22 was used.

---

33. *Outside*. "Murder on a Mountain Bike." November 25, 2018. https://www.outsideonline.com/outdoor-adventure/exploration-survival/murder-mountain-bike/

The bullet that went into Tim's torso was removed and examined for potential ballistics matches, but it was determined that the bullet was too mangled to be usable. Since the shooting occurred in the great outdoors, it was difficult for investigators to find any shell casings. But what investigators saw was enough for Tim Watkins' death to be declared a homicide.

The community around Mount Herman was shocked and terrified by the news that one of their own had been gunned down while doing what he loved—riding his bike.

Mount Herman is a very big hunting and gun community. Most people in the area own guns, and open-air sport shooting at makeshift ranges was rampant and completely unregulated. As a result, bullets often were whizzing around in the air in public recreational spaces. Locals voiced concern that accidental shootings were inevitable in this kind of situation. Tim and his son, like many in the area, had firsthand experience with this. About ten years before Tim was killed, he and Isaac were backpacking and suddenly bullets whistled by Isaac's head and ricocheted off a boulder. Near misses like this were fairly common. Other mountain bikers told stories of bullets hitting the trail in front of them as they navigated a narrow mountain bike trail. In 2014, one couple reported that while they were picnicking, their Jeep was hit with gunfire. Stories likes this, about close calls with unregulated gunfire, caused the Forest Service to finally ban recreational shooting in the Mount Herman area later in 2014. The ban cited weekly complaints of bullets barely missing people, and 911 reports of trail users being pinned down by gunfire. According to *Outside*, within days of the ban's implementation, signs announcing it were peppered by gunfire, likely from protesting shooters. Within weeks,

Forest Service personnel issued about eighty warnings to people found shooting in defiance of the ban.[34]

While some in the area say that the ban did cut down on random shooting, others say it largely went unheeded and unenforced. One state senator, who was a friend of Tim's, describes biking with his sons and seeing a dad and his kids shooting right at a No Shooting sign and menacing him and his sons when he reminded them of the ban. And in 2015, a sixty-year-old grandfather named Glenn Martin was killed by an errant bullet while camping with his family, roughly twenty miles from where Tim was shot. Martin's killer has never been found.

Tim's friends and family say that while he was not confrontational and was always friendly, he often stopped and asked people firing their guns to be more cautious, warning them that there were biking and hiking trails in their bullets' range. His family believed it possible that Tim had approached the wrong person with his simple request to stop shooting and been shot. The fact that he was shot at least three times and his bike tire also shot ruled out an accidental shooting in the minds of most people.

There were dangers in the woods of Mount Herman other than haphazard shooting. There were pockets of homeless, transients, and drifters who often descended on the unsettled areas of Colorado. Tim was one of the people who took it upon themselves to clean up the broken TVs, old couches, and other trash left by the homeless who lived in the campsites. Human waste was a problem, as these camps were often not near sanitary facilities. Often, these homeless encampments would be littered with used needles. Tim's family said that he was not one to take violations of the law, dangerous behavior, and destroying of his beloved natural environment lightly. If he saw cars driving recklessly

---

34. *Outside*. "Murder on a Mountain Bike." November 25, 2018. https://www.outsideonline.com/outdoor-adventure/exploration-survival/murder-mountain-bike/

close to cyclists on Mount Herman Road, he'd be likely to flip them the bird. He probably would say something to campers or homeless who were littering. Is it possible that Tim Watkins ran into someone he may have confronted, and this person shot Tim?

Within days of Tim's death, reports circulated that a man was threatening people with a hatchet on the trails near where Tim's body was found. On September 25, police in Woodland Park, which is twenty miles down Mount Herman Road from Monument, announced an arrest of a transient. Police spotted the vehicle, which matched the description of the one driven by the Hatchet Man, in an Arby's parking lot. They waited to see who got into the car, and then pulled the car over for expired Indiana plates and a broken taillight. Driving the red Chevy Prism was thirty-one-year-old Daniel Nations. They arrested him for "unrelated weapons charges."

Mount Herman residents took notice when the sheriff's office also charged Nations with felony menacing. According to the arrest affidavit, "Nations accosted and threatened a passing dirt biker with a hatchet at his campsite on Mount Herman Road after placing logs in the road that forced the rider to stop."[35] Nations blocked off the road with logs, seized a hatchet, and brandished it at the dirt bike rider, saying his bike was too loud. The rider turned around and sped away and reported the incident. Officers searched Nations' car and found a hatchet and a .22-caliber rifle, possibly the same caliber bullet that killed Tim Watkins, although this has never been confirmed by law enforcement.

In addition to these formal charges, it seems that there were several other reports of threatened violence and menacing against Nations: for example, Detective Jason Darbyshire of the El Paso County Sheriff's Office told

---

35. *Outside*. "Murder on a Mountain Bike." November 25, 2018. https://www. outsideonline.com/outdoor-adventure/exploration-survival/murder-mountain-bike/

*Outside* that Nations had acted aggressively during a road-rage incident in Monument around the same time. Nations "got out of his vehicle, confronted another driver, and ended up kicking and breaking their windshield," Darbyshire said, adding that the incident "escalated very quickly."[36] In addition, the media reported that several complaints had been filed about a man menacing mountain bikers with a hatchet.

Nations' wife and two young children were with him at the time of his arrest. A background check on Nations revealed that he had a criminal record, including felony convictions for domestic battery in front of a child and a sexual offense—both in Morgan County, Indiana. Nations also has convictions for indecent exposure and habitual drunk driving in South Carolina. The report also notes that Nations was charged multiple times with domestic violence. Because of his felony history, Nations cannot legally own a firearm, so police charged him with felony possession of a firearm. And since the threats against hikers and bikers took place in El Paso County, police there charged him with felony menacing, reckless endangerment, assault, and trespassing. Finally, on October 10, final charges on suspicion of failing to register as a sex offender were filed against Daniel Nations.[37]

Daniel Nations' possible involvement in the Tim Watkins murder case quickly led to suspicion that he could have been involved in the Delphi murders. Unfortunately, the Watkins case remains unsolved. As to his possible involvement in the Watkins case, it is anyone's guess but given the nature and similarities when comparing what

---

36. *Outside*. "Murder on a Mountain Bike." November 25, 2018. https://www.outsideonline.com/outdoor-adventure/exploration-survival/murder-mountain-bike/

37. *The Gazette*. "TIMELINE: Daniel Nations' major life events, criminal history." October 21, 2017. https://gazette.com/news/crime/timeline-daniel-nations-major-life-events-criminal-history/article_d170d19c-c469-5eda-984a-c37e06172d12.html

Nations was charged with and the facts of the Watkins case, it is understandable that he remains a person of interest as far as the public is concerned. A person as reckless and possibly dangerous as Daniel Nations is, flying way under the radar in somewhat remote recreational spaces filled with people is most certainly a recipe for disaster.

At the time of Daniel Nations' arrest in Colorado, this left many of us to ponder the following. What do we know that could tie Daniel Nations with Libby and Abby's murders? For one thing, his last known address in Indiana is not far from where the girls were found, about sixty miles. The girls were taken on a trail used for hiking and biking, like the case with Tim Watkins and the people Nations threatened with his hatchet. Libby and Abby and Tim were all found in relatively inaccessible areas located off trails.

We don't know if they were shot, or whether a hatchet might have been involved, but in combination with the mugshot/composite similarities, and Daniel Nations' former residence in Indiana and criminal history, it was enough to make investigators in the Delphi murders fly to Colorado to interview Nations. It emerged in the media that Indiana State Police had actually been looking for Nations in connection with the Delphi case, starting around July 2017, when it was noted that he had failed to check in as a sex offender in Carroll County for more than two months (he left for Colorado in May and failed to notify anyone).

In response to all the tips the ISP received about Nations based on his mugshot, they released the following statement:

> We are aware of the arrest of the person in Colorado and are investigating to see if he could be a suspect in the Delphi double murder investigation. Please keep in mind the Indiana State Police has received more than a thousand photos of persons alleged to be similar in appearance to the composite sketch of the Delphi person of interest. Each and every one of these tips are

investigated for any potential connection to our case. We will give the same attention to the person arrested in Colorado, but right now there is nothing that definitively connects this person to our investigation.[38]

Spokesperson Jackie Kirby with the El Paso County Sheriff's Office admitted "many similarities" in the Watkins case and the Delphi murders and was not denying a possible connection. She said police in Indiana have requested no further information be released to the public. "They have asked us not to speak on their case. So, I'm not at liberty to elaborate on anything that's related to what happened in Indiana,"[39] said Kirby.

Daniel Nations was born on October 18, 1985. His life has been plagued by violence and disfunction. He never knew his father, who is in prison for child molestation, and was raised by his grandparents in Chesnee, South Carolina, with visitation to his mother Rebecca Smith on weekends and holidays. In November 2002, when then seventeen-year-old Nations was staying with her, Rebecca was murdered by her brother, James Junior Cummings. Her body, naked but for underwear and a cast on a broken arm she suffered in a fight with her boyfriend, was dragged into the woods and covered by leaves. Rebecca's autopsy revealed that she had cocaine in her system, had been stabbed twice, and had a broken jaw and nose that looked like they had been hit with a hammer.

Nations' grandmother says she asked Nations and his wife to move off her property years ago, and hasn't spoken to him since. It's unclear where Nations was between the ages of seventeen and about twenty-two or -three, but at

38. ABC News. "Man Arrested in Colorado May Be Suspect in Unsolved Murder of Indiana Teens, Police Say." September 29, 2017. https://abcnews.go.com/US/police-indiana-man-suspect-delphi-double-murder/story?id=50148510

39. ABC News. "Man Arrested in Colorado May Be Suspect in Unsolved Murder of Indiana Teens, Police Say." September 29, 2017. https://abcnews.go.com/US/police-indiana-man-suspect-delphi-double-murder/story?id=50148510.

some point, he became a marine. He was dismissed after about four years for "general under honorable," meaning that his performance was satisfactory but that he failed to meet all expectations of conduct for a marine. During his service in the military, Nations claims to have developed PTSD and a severe anxiety disorder. It's possible that these mental afflictions are likely why he would end up being treated leniently by the judge in the hatchet case. But the hatchet case was far from his first run-in with the law.

Nations has a long criminal history. He has convictions for public indecency in North Carolina that stem from two 2007 incidents where he was masturbating in public, deliberately exposing himself to more than one victim, including a woman and her child who were biking. And according to Heavy.com, he had already racked up five indecent exposure charges prior to these most recent transgressions. For these 2007 offenses, Nations served two years in prison and was required to register as a sex offender. After his release, he moved to Indiana, where he was required to register as a sex offender and did so in Carroll County. But he failed to resister as a sex offender in Johnson County as required, had no fixed address, and was living under bridges and at camp sites, although we don't know if that was still the case during the timeframe when the Delphi murders took place.

In 2015, Nations seems to have really started into a downward spiral.

He was arrested in 2015 on a marijuana charge, for pleasuring himself, and peeping in the stall of a women's restroom at a gas station in Indiana, and for domestic battery for an incident where he punched his wife Katelyn in the face, breaking her nose, in front of their children. He served ninety-nine days in jail.

In 2016, Nations managed to be arrested only once, for possession of marijuana and drug paraphernalia, and driving without a license. In early 2017, Nations initially checked in with law enforcement weekly as required by his sex offender status. He checked in on February 14, as scheduled, the day that Abby and Libby's bodies were discovered. He was arrested and jailed for four days in February 2017 for a failure to appear in an earlier eviction case. He was released, and continued to check in, notifying of a change of address to the Greenwood Motel in Indiana on April 12. He was arrested again on April 25 for marijuana possession and a driver's license violation, and he failed to appear in court as required in July 2017. This is because on May 12, he checked out of the Greenwood Motel and, he says, went to Colorado.

When Abby and Libby were killed on February 13, Nations was working for a construction company in Zionsville, Indiana, about an hour's drive from Delphi. During his time living in Indiana, he rented various apartments, and people who interacted with him had some choice words to say about him. Nations, Katelyn, and their kids were evicted by Berniece Riggs after racking up a thousand dollars in property damages. Another landlord, Randy Hamilton, rented Nations and his family a house in Martinsville. Hamilton said about Nations, "He's a damn nut, I'll tell you that. He's the weirdest person I've met in my life. He had a zero-tolerance temper. He chopped trees and a chair with a hatchet" in a fit of anger.[40] A woman who employed Nations on her farm in Martinsville, Suella Ferrand, told CBS in Denver, "He was definitely not a good guy."[41] He trashed the apartment she rented him, frequently became violent, destroyed property, and even threatened one of her family members with a hatchet. Ferrand says it

40. *Journal & Courier.* "Colorado Hatchet Suspect Has 'zero-Tolerance Temper,' Landlord Said." September 29, 2017. https://www.jconline.com/story/news/crime/2017/09/29/colorado-hatchet-suspect-has-zero-tolerance-temper-landlord-said/717253001/

41. CBS Colorado. "Hatchet Suspect Charged, More Charges Likely To Come." September 28, 2017. https://www.cbsnews.com/colorado/news/daniel-nations-hatchet-el-paso-county/

got so bad, she had to get police and the courts involved and have him forcibly removed by court order.

On July 18, 2017, the Indiana State Police begin investigating Nations because he had failed to check in since April, and departed from his known address, the motel. At the time of Tim's murder, Nations, his wife Katelyn, and their two little kids were living out of their car and at camp sites throughout Colorado. Nations' brother, Edward Lyles, had been assaulted and murdered in Colorado Springs in early 2017. He was kicked in the head by steel-toed boots. Edward's murderer, Matthew Stroker, was sentenced on the same day that Tim Watkins was killed. This murderer's lenient sentence of only sixteen years, some speculate, could have caused Nations to go off the deep end and lash out at the first person who happened by—i.e., Tim.

Things weren't going that well for Daniel Nations. He was being looked at by Colorado law enforcement for the Tim Watkins case, as well as the hatchet menacing allegations, and in connection with the murder in Delphi. Although investigators questioned Nations about Watkins and, they say, thoroughly investigated him, they never named him as a suspect. Nations denied threatening anyone with a hatchet, saying he just yelled at people and shook his fist. But the hatchet found in his car and multiple witness reports were clearly enough to bring charges. Three months after his arrest, prosecutors cut a deal with Nations that allowed him to plead guilty to one felony menacing charge and the weapons possession charge and receive no jail time. He got three years probation. In the plea deal, no mention was made of Tim Watkins. Detectives told Tim's family that they had no evidence to link Nations to the murder scene: ballistics tests were inconclusive because the bullet inside Watkins was too deformed to match its striations to the murder weapon, and, according to local media, DNA tests were also inconclusive, though it's unclear whether Nations submitted DNA or what DNA might have been found, if any.

In any event, Nations was released from jail in Colorado in January 2018 with just probation.

Nations was extradited back to Indiana in February to face charges in three counties for, among other offenses, failure to register as a sex offender and possession of marijuana. He pleaded guilty and served some time in multiple jails. In early July, he returned to the Colorado Springs area to try to regain custody of his children, who were taken by child services and were now the subject of a custody dispute between Nations and Katelyn, who had divorced him. Nations gave a lengthy, sorrowful interview to the *Colorado Springs Gazette* in August in which he called the Watkins allegations "preposterous" and said, "I'm not what they made me out to be."[42] He told the paper that he wants to clear his name, that he is a victim of all the rumor and speculation about Delphi and the Mount Herman incidents. He said he took the plea deal in the hatchet case just to avoid jail time, and that he did not threaten anyone with a hatchet.

Nations said he has too much self-respect as a former marine to dress sloppily, carry extra weight, and have longer hair like the Delphi composite sketch suspect. He also said he has an alibi—he was at his wife's ultrasound on the day of the Delphi murders, and that he gave his DNA to the ISP. Now, it is worth noting that Katelyn did apparently have an ultrasound appointment that day, but she says she "thinks" Nations was with her but cannot be certain.

Nations also told the newspaper that his children are his life and that any run-ins with people in the Colorado woods he may have had were because he was trying to protect his kids. Mountain bikers were zooming by too close to their tent, so he placed logs on the path and had a confrontation

42. *Colorado Springs Gazette.* "Back in Colorado Springs, Daniel Nations says 'I'm not what they made me out to be.'" August 20, 2018. https://gazette.com/news/back-in-colorado-springs-daniel-nations-says-i-m-not/article_90e13f08-9c15-11e8-8eee-afc825d25419.html

with one rider while he happened to be holding a hatchet. The episode on the road, he said, was when another car almost ran them off the road, endangering his family. He admits to having "anger issues" driven by his PTSD but says that he would never attack anyone. But we know he attacked his wife Katelyn, who has said that she is afraid of him.

Was Nations involved in the deaths of Abby and Libby? Until there is someone convicted of the murders, to some, Nations will remain a person of interest in the case, but Carter said that they've talked to many persons of interest identified in thirty thousand tips and "we feel confident there was no involvement."[43] For those who believe that Nations' resemblance to the sketch is uncanny, this is hard to swallow. We can only surmise that there was DNA found in the Delphi case, and that it excluded Daniel Nations. But the ISP has never stated that any DNA was found, so this is just speculation.

We also know that Nations lived quite far away from Delphi, and that he shared a car with his wife. Katelyn says that he could not have taken the car for the day to get to Delphi, because she needed it for her prenatal appointment. She also says he did not own a blue jacket like the one the perp is wearing in the bridge photo. Finally, Daniel Nations' voice in interviews is not as deep and resonant as the perp's voice on the Delphi recording.

On October 3, 2017, Indiana State Police stated that they could not "specifically include or exclude Daniel Nations as a suspect in the Delphi homicides." But on the anniversary of German's and Williams' deaths, February 13, 2018, Indiana State Police Superintendent Carter announced

---

43. WRTV. "ISP: Daniel Nations 'Not Someone We Care a Whole Lot about at This Time' in Delphi Investigation." https://www.wrtv.com/news/local-news/carroll-county/isp-daniel-nations-not-someone-we-care-a-whole-lot-about-at-this-time-in-delphi-investigation

Nations was "not a person that we care a whole lot about at this point in time."[44]

44. WISH-TV. Delphi Officials Hold Press Conference on Year Anniversary of Teens' Murders. February 13, 2018. https://www.youtube.com/watch?v=ThmnNQk4o2E

# Photos

February 15, 2017 - Indiana State Police released a picture of a man they want to speak with. Four days later Indiana State Police name the man seen in this photo as the prime suspect. (Source: www.in.gov)

July 17, 2017 - Law enforcement agencies
working the Delphi double homicide case
released this composite sketch of the suspect.
(Source www.CarrollCountyComet.com)

April 22, 2019 – Indiana State Police announced a "new direction" for the Delphi Murders investigation. With that announcement ISP released a new composite sketch of the suspect. (Source www.in.gov)

Indiana State Police seeking information about murder suspect. (Source www.in.gov)

Liberty "Libby" German (Source www.in.gov)

Abigail "Abby" Williams (Source www.in.gov)

Suspect Richard Allen's booking
photo (Source www.in.gov)

Sig Sauer P226 40 handgun, similar to the one owned
by Richard Allen. (Source www.sigsauerarmory.com)

# REWARD

## UP TO $5000

**FOR INFORMATION LEADING TO THE ARREST OF
THE PERSON(S) RESPONSIBLE FOR THIS FIRE**

*Somebody
Knows*

Keyana Davis, 11    Keyara Phillips, 9    Kerriele McDonald, 7    Kionnie Welch,

**Killed in their Flora, Indiana home on November 21, 2016.
This was determined to be an arson fire.**

## 1-800-382-4628

or write: P.O. Box 80132 - Indianapolis, Indiana 46280
YOU DO NOT HAVE TO GIVE YOUR NAME

Reward provided by
The International Association of Arson Investigators, Indiana Chapter #14
in cooperation with the Indiana State Fire Marshal
and the Property Insurance Companies Operating in Indiana

The amount of the award is dependent upon the value of the information as determined by
the International Association of Arson Investigators, Indiana Chapter #14

www.iniaai.org

Reward for information leading to the arrest of
the person(s) responsible for the Flora fire.

# MURDERERS ROW

There are numerous people who have been rumored to be Bridge Guy over the years. I could write a whole book about them, but to be honest, I would be kind of worried about anyone who wanted to read it.

Here are the guys that have had the most attention from law enforcement and armchair sleuths alike.

You almost have to start with Ron Logan. He is the reasonable doubt for any potential defendant, especially since he has passed away. If you're a defense attorney representing the real Bridge Guy, you love Ron Logan. He looks like him, he lives near where the bodies were found, and he asked someone to make up an alibi for him on the day of the girls' deaths.

On March 17, 2017, a search warrant was executed at Logan's home. In the written warrant, an FBI agent stated, "I believe there is probable cause to believe that RONALD LOGAN has committed the crime of murder and evidence of that can be found on RONALD LOGAN's property."[45]

Logan was a drunk driver on probation during the murders. According to the conditions of his probation, he couldn't drive or be in a bar. But they discovered he was drinking and driving that day. The original search was around a probation violation. Logan was facing a probation

---

45. Logan Warrant. https://interactive.wthr.com/pdfs/logan-warrrant.pdf

violation because of his driving and creating a false alibi. This is talked about in the warrant. On March 6, they searched his home looking for firearms in his main residence, which they found. He was a habitual drunk driver, which means he was not allowed to drive or own guns.

Let's face it. The prime goal of this document is to get a search warrant. Law enforcement needs a judge to sign off on it, so the FBI is going to give the judge every reason to do so. They are going to make Logan look as bad as possible. If I am an FBI agent and I thought this guy was like a five or a six, I am still going to make him look like a ten. Because one of two things is going to happen if I get to execute my search of his property, he will go from a five to a ten and we can arrest him, or go to a one and we can move on from him. So either way, it works for the investigation.

It's obvious they didn't find a whole lot when they searched his home or they would have arrested him and charged him. A lot of the points made that make him sound guilty are really to obtain the warrant. When you look at the FBI search warrant for his house, the first thing that jumps out to me is they are searching everything this dude has. One thing good though is we get more facts through this warrant, the type of things they wouldn't say in a press conference.

The description of Bridge Guy is interesting. There has been much debate over whether he wearing a hat, is there no hat, is his hood up? Law enforcement thinks he is wearing a hat, for sure; as the warrant says the suspect was "wearing a cap."[46]

The fact the FBI is the one seeking the warrant is key when analyzing the investigation. There is something going on, I don't know what; my guess is there might be infighting among agencies. There is a good chance the FBI liked a

---

46. Logan Warrant. https://interactive.wthr.com/pdfs/logan-warrrant.pdf

suspect and ISP liked another, which could have caused issues.

According to the warrant, the last contact by "cellular device" was at 2:13 p.m. This is very important. The FBI says the last ping of the phone was at 5:30, meaning it either died or was turned off at that time.

The warrant goes on to say the suspect is a "white male wearing a blue jacket, with a heavy physical build wearing a cap and blue jeans."[47] The cap and blue jeans are the only items of clothing that appear to be certain. Many online say it's a camo hat, or one with natural colors. I think that holds some weight.

The FBI also confirms in the warrant the video Libby took was forty-three seconds long, but there are rumors they had much more than that.

The document says, "Victims LG and AW were found dead from wounds caused by a [redacted] weapon."[48] The information is blocked out, in theory, so the killer could possibly incriminate himself down the road because the general public has no idea what really happened.

What could it be? People don't say a *gun* weapon, maybe a *sharp* weapon or a *blunt* weapon. I always thought it was likely he had a gun; he abducted them and needed a way to control them and chose two victims instead of one. So, a gun would be easier to control them, but when it came to killing, he was either lucky enough or smart enough to not use it.

It appears to be a five-letter word that was redacted; my guess is *blunt* or *sharp*. One wouldn't say *hand* weapon, *gun* weapon, or *rope* weapon. A rope or a knife he could have just carried in his pocket. He had to know he would be witnessed by other people at some point. He didn't want to stand out too much. He needed to get close to them to

---

47. Logan Warrant. https://interactive.wthr.com/pdfs/logan-warrrant.pdf.
48. Logan Warrant. https://interactive.wthr.com/pdfs/logan-warrrant.pdf.

corner them. He wasn't going to want to be so obvious to be carrying a shotgun, a chainsaw, or an axe. Sometimes the earliest rumors have the most truth. One that has been a constant is that toward the end of the audio, there is a noise believed to be a gun being cocked or the sound of a bullet being chambered to threaten the girls, then the recording stops. Does this warrant mean law enforcement knows a gun was involved?

The warrant states, "A large amount of blood was lost by the victims at the crime scene. Because of the nature of the [victim's] wounds it is nearly certain the perpetrator of the crime would have gotten blood on his person/clothing."[49] The large amount of blood being lost is definitely new information, something no one has been told before.

The warrant states, "It was also discovered that the [redacted] of one of the victims was missing from the crime scene while the rest of their clothing was recovered."[50] Because of the way this was worded, we know it's clothing. It's a very long area that is redacted. My guess would be "undergarments."

The warrant goes on to say, "Victims LG and AW were found dead with wounds caused by a [redacted] weapon."[51]

We also find out a "large amount of blood was lost by the victims at the crime scene. Because of the nature of the [victim's] wounds it is nearly certain the perpetrator of the crime would have gotten blood on his person/clothing." Bridge Guy being covered in blood and going back through the trail system makes no sense. If people saw him covered in blood, we wouldn't be talking about this now. Bridge Guy would be in prison.

The warrant says, "it appeared the [girls] bodies were moved and staged"[52] and "it is common for perpetrators

49. Logan Warrant. https://interactive.wthr.com/pdfs/logan-warrrant.pdf
50. Logan Warrant. https://interactive.wthr.com/pdfs/logan-warrrant.pdf.
51. Logan Warrant. https://interactive.wthr.com/pdfs/logan-warrrant.pdf.
52. Logan Warrant. https://interactive.wthr.com/pdfs/logan-warrrant.pdf.

of this nature to take a 'souvenir' or, in some fashion, memorialize the crime scene." This suggests Bridge Guy took something of the girls with him or took a photo of the scene which is part of the reason for the search warrant.

*Moved* and *staged* don't necessarily mean moving the bodies a great distance. It could mean five feet. It could also mean a victim was killed where she laid but the killer could have moved her legs or posed her.

It goes on to say "LG" and "AW" had "no visible signs of a struggle or a fight,"[53] which is really concerning. You would hope at least one of them scratched him or fought in some way.

We find out that Logan has a receipt from a business called Aquarium World that day stamped 5:21, which gives him plenty of time to kill the girls. Logan had this to say about his visit there that day. "Monday afternoon, I was in Lafayette Aquarium World getting tropical fish for my aquarium so when I came home one of the neighbors asked for permission to come back here and search for the missing girls and that's the first time I heard anything about it."[54]

An acquaintance of Logan gave him alibi, saying he was with him that day and drove him to Aquarium World. But that person later admitted he lied. Not only that but the acquaintance said, "Logan had never asked him to lie for him in the past."[55] Earlier that day, Logan went to the dump and threw things away the same day the girls died. But he didn't ask him to lie for him then.

One of his ex-girlfriends claimed Logan was physically abusive, to the point he once dragged her out of her car by her hair. She related that after they broke up, he stalked her and told her that he could "kill her and no one would find her body."[56] We don't know the dynamics of the relationship,

53. Logan Warrant. https://interactive.wthr.com/pdfs/logan-warrrant.pdf
54. Logan Warrant. https://interactive.wthr.com/pdfs/logan-warrrant.pdf.
55. Logan Warrant. https://interactive.wthr.com/pdfs/logan-warrrant.pdf.
56. Logan Warrant. https://interactive.wthr.com/pdfs/logan-warrrant.pdf.

we know people sometimes embellish or lie after a messy breakup, he was a bad person, he was a monster. That could be happening here. Or this woman could just be trying to help her community.

I've been in heated discussions. I have yelled things at people that I regret. I've been in bar fights, I've beaten people up, and I've been beaten up. I have never said to anyone, even my worst enemy, *I could kill you and no one would find your body.* If he really said that, then he is a different kind of person. He clearly had a drinking problem, it's possible he could have said something of this nature when he was drunk out of his mind, but I've been drunk too, just a couple times, and saying something like that never comes to mind.

The warrant mentions Logan "carried a gun everywhere he went,"[57] often in a fanny pack. The level of concern they have over a firearm is odd, especially in an area where most people have them. With that said, Bridge Guy has been thought to be possibly wearing a fanny pack. I suggested on *True Crime Garage* it might even be a field dressing kit.

We also learn through the warrant that one woman said when she saw the photo of Bridge Guy, "she thought the police were looking for Logan because she thought the photograph was Logan."[58] This is very interesting, but if she thought that, then why wasn't that taken more seriously by law enforcement?

The warrant goes into a lot of detail about his phone being near the crime scene at 2:13, but come on. He lives there. It simply means his phone was near his home at 2:13. Any sentence that says his phone was in the proximity is true, but he could have been sitting on his couch watching *Jeopardy*!

---

57. Logan Warrant. https://interactive.wthr.com/pdfs/logan-warrrant.pdf
58. Logan Warrant. https://interactive.wthr.com/pdfs/logan-warrrant.pdf.

The warrant then brings up the words of another ex of Logan, who said she once told someone, "If she ever ended up dead, Logan did it"[59] and she thought he must have been responsible for the girls' deaths when she heard the news. It goes on to tell us there were fifteen tips related to Logan. Obviously, they're receiving thousands of tips, so these could be good tips or just people calling up and saying, "I think it's Ron Logan" There were tips about Mike Patty, Tobe Leazenby, Doug Carter, and so on. That means nothing.

The warrant states they were looking for things like clothing, guns, and electronic devices, and even animal hair samples. I believe on the victim's body or clothing they must have found animal hair. Does Bridge Guy have a cat or a dog? Could its fur have been transferred?

Here is the thing about Logan. Yes, he lied trying to create an alibi, but he had a reason to do so, one that isn't all that nefarious. He drove to Aquarium World when he wasn't supposed to do so because he was on probation.

And yes, Logan dresses like Bridge Guy. Most middle-aged men in Delphi do.

Why would he leave the bodies on his property? One would think he wouldn't want that. He is going to go out and kill two girls and leave the bodies on his own land?

Libby was almost two hundred pounds. I am in pretty good shape, I am not seventy-seven like Ron Logan, I couldn't move two hundred pounds of dead weight any good amount of distance. If he was so worried about an alibi, you would think he wouldn't leave bodies on his property.

Three days before the FBI came out and said they wanted a search warrant, David Bursten of the Indiana State Police tweeted out that Logan's probation violations had nothing to do with the murder. This is where there is an obvious sign of a fork in the road—one month after the murders, ISP

59. Logan Warrant. https://interactive.wthr.com/pdfs/logan-warrrant.pdf.

says there is no connection while the FBI asks for search warrant. There is a disconnect here.

It's fascinating what they weren't looking for. Items such as ropes, handcuffs, zip ties, or duct tape. At no point are they telling the judge they think they will find any of that, which makes me think that none of these items were used in the crime. Bridge Guy picked two people to victimize but he didn't have these items. Does that mean he had another way of controlling them? Either a gun or another person to help him?

The thing that really makes him look innocent is he wasn't asking for an alibi for when the abduction happened at 2:13, he asked for one for his drive to Aquarium World. Obviously, if he were the killer, wouldn't he be asking for an alibi for when the murders occurred? I really think he just drove to the aquarium and asked someone to say they drove him and it was just him trying to cover up his probation violation.

Logan wore glasses; every time I have seen his face, he is wearing glasses. Neither sketch of Bridge Guy has glasses on, nor does he have glasses on in the photo. Walking that sketchy bridge without glasses if you need them to see would be a very odd thing to do.

I don't think that he looks like Bridge Guy. Ron looks older than what I think I'm seeing in that now infamous Bridge Guy picture. I also don't think that he matches the description—not only does he look older, he looks to be taller.

Logan has a prominent mustache. Neither sketch featured a guy with a mustache. He was interviewed two days after the murder with a full mustache so it wasn't like he shaved it.

Listening to him talk, he sounds nothing at all like Bridge Guy. If anyone said Logan sounded like Bridge Guy, I would say the person needed to get their hearing checked.

Ron Logan was later arrested and sentenced to two years for operating a vehicle as a habitual traffic offender. Two years is a long time to do in prison, and worth trying to put an alibi together to stave off that ending.

I've seen people who have said Logan has gone out of his way to do everything he can to make sure that everyone knows what he was up to that day and that he was not involved. I've heard other arguments that have said just that completely counter that, stating he has not been very forthcoming at all.

The FBI's search warrant resulted in no charges against Logan for the murders. All of that was probably due diligence to rule him out as a suspect.

But he is still everyone's reasonable doubt.

Ron Logan died in January 2022.

Another suspect, Thomas Bruce, is incredibly interesting to me. He was a former pastor and navy veteran who has moved around a bit and has been married a few times. He met his last wife in California, then moved with her to Missouri.

On November 19, 2018, he went into a Catholic religious supply store in Ballwin, Missouri, after having a few drinks at a nearby bar. Things hadn't been going his way as of late. He was out of work, the church he was running had lost its following. He was depressed and down and just not himself. Or maybe he was more himself than ever.

When he entered the store, there was a customer and two employees inside, all were women. After looking around for a bit, he went to the register to make some sort of minor purchase but when checking out, he said he forgot his wallet and went back to his car.

He came back in with a gun. He is no longer a customer; now he is a bad guy.

My guess is he had a rape kit in his vehicle; he scouted the place and made sure there was no threat to him and the women in there were to his liking. As a coward, he wanted to make sure no men were in the store. He wanted control. He wanted to victimize people who were vulnerable.

He forced them into a back room, then sexually assaulted at least two of them. One victim, fifty-three-year-old Jamie Schmidt, who was the customer in the store and the mother of three children, refused his sexual demands. He shot her in the head, killing her.

She was there buying items to make homemade rosaries. It just shows one isn't safe anywhere. She was at a church store during the day, in a suburb, during the middle of the week. You go from being a regular person living your everyday life to being corralled into a back room by a sex maniac with a gun.

After his spree of murder and rape, Bruce went home and chilled out for a bit waiting for his wife to come home from work. She is a good woman, he is a bad guy. She is working, doing the best she can, and he is spending his days drinking and scheming and raping. He had dinner on the table for her when she came home, and they watched the evening news together. When news on the rapes and murder came on, his wife was shocked and said, "Who could do such a thing?"

Bruce replied, "You never know in the world we live in these days."

Law enforcement had two good witnesses. They saw Bruce before he got the gun, when he was pretending to be normal, so they were calm and had a good sense of what he looked like. They were able to give law enforcement a good description of him.

The cops started going to local businesses in the area, to see if they had any information on who could have done this. There happened to be a sports bar near the Catholic Supply store where Bruce sat and boozed before he raped and killed. He was a regular there. The police gave the bartender a description of the suspect. It turned out someone matching the description had given one of the bartenders his business card, which she promptly threw in the trash. Police went through the trash. Suddenly, they had a name.

Police arrested Bruce on November 21, 2018, at his trailer park home after watching it for nearly eleven hours. I once heard a detective say you can't swing a bat without hitting a sexual offender in a trailer park. Bruce would have been a good one to hit.

Police seized cars, clothing, guns, and ammo that matched a shell casing found at the store. Police also found Bruce's fingerprints on Christmas cards and other items he took to the Catholic Supply's checkout desk before the attack. He was indicted on seventeen charges including several sexual assaults, illegal possession of firearms, murder, and kidnapping.

Bruce's internet search history included queries for child pornography and violent, forced sex acts. A search of Bruce's computer revealed at least thirty sexually explicit web searches, eighteen of which were made the day before the attack, two on the morning of the attack.

But this wasn't all Bruce had been up to. After he was arrested, law enforcement got a call from a seventy-seven-year-old woman who was raped in her home. According to her, Bruce showed up and told her he was a worker for AMVETS and talked his way into her house. Then he forced her into the bedroom and raped her, took her cell phone, and went back to his regular home life. The woman told police she was one hundred percent sure her rapist is the same guy they just arrested.

Because Bruce committed this murder in the daytime, and he doesn't look unlike Bridge Guy, he became a Delphi suspect.

Shortly before the murder, he purchased two guns without his wife's knowledge. He told her he won them in a raffle. This was in part because he didn't want her to know he was planning to use them for nefarious reasons, but also, she was working and he isn't, and he doesn't want to tell her he's spending his money on guns.

One day a pastor, then a rapist, then a murderer. Did he just go off the rails once he hit the other side of fifty or had he always been capable of this stuff and just kept it hidden until now? It seems that alcohol played a part in these actions as Bruce had been spending a lot of time day drinking prior to the crime.

Did he just snap or did he do other things we weren't aware of and he just never was caught? A month or so before the murders, he was involved in a minor auto accident and was extremely belligerent with the responding police officer.

Given his crimes, then his argument with the cop, it looks to me like this guy was pretending to be depressed all day but really was out trolling for victims and sitting in a bar getting drunk, trying to get enough courage to victimize people. The bottom line is, Bruce is just a psychotic manipulator who conceals his true self.

Bruce plead guilty and was sentenced to life in prison. Did he plead guilty just so he wouldn't be looked at too hard for these other crimes he was suspected of committing?

On January 8, 2019, our next weirdo, Charles Andrew Eldridge, age forty-six, who happens to be one ugly bastard, was arrested in Randolph County, Indiana, after arranging to meet with a thirteen-year-old girl for sexual reasons, was actually a police officer. Probably not his favorite day ever.

He faced multiple charges, including two counts of attempted child molestation. During news coverage of his arrest, local Indiana residents noticed his mugshot and said he looked like Bridge Guy. The Indiana State Police tip line started blowing up.

He, of course, denied involvement, but we already know he is attracted to adolescent girls. As soon as he was arrested, people in his circle said a lot of bad things about him, like he always seemed like a sicko, weirdo-type of guy, and maybe even molested some girls who were close to him. Not only that, but people said he was into guns, and get this. He likes to spend time in the woods. Lock him up.

Another odd thing about Eldridge is he often shared stories of missing children's cases on his social media and even shared several posts relating to the murders of Libby and Abby. He posted public appeals and a story about potential DNA evidence, as well as the sketch of the suspect—which the public believes he looks like—bearing the tagline, PASS IT AROUND. [HE] COULD BE ANYWHERE.

There is no real true link to the case other than his looks and his charges. Some people say he is violent and has a temper, but he doesn't have any violence on his record.

Our next freak is Paul Etter, who kidnapped and sexually assaulted a twenty-six-year-old woman who pulled into his driveway on June 22, 2019, after she got a flat tire. Etter came out of his house and asked if she needed help. Feeling more than a bit creeped out by his vibe, the woman declined and drove down the road. Etter then followed her until she pulled into a friend's driveway, where he abducted her. He then took her back to his home, where he sexually assaulted her before taking her back to her car.

I don't know what this guy was thinking. Of course, she can identify him by appearance and by where he lives. Not a very sophisticated criminal. In general, they are dumb and lazy, but this guy takes it to a new level.

The victim happened upon Etter, and he took advantage, then he did nothing to cover it up. One thing we know about Bridge Guy—he didn't let them go. And he was prepared to kill.

The police spotted Etter and tried to pull him over, which led to a vehicle chase and a five-hour standoff, resulting in Etter killing himself. There was a Delphi tip called in about Etter before he came onto the public's radar, so he was already known to investigators. After his death, they collected his DNA to make sure they had it on file. It isn't clear if they were able to clear him.

Out of all the suspects, Etter is probably the one I like the least.

James Bryant Chadwell III isn't the most ridiculous suspect out there, he looks a bit like Bridge Guy number 2, he has the same hair and same jawline. He also is a bit of a lunatic. He has a lengthy record of somewhat low-level criminal stuff such as reckless conduct and aggravated assault but in April 2021, he went completely off the rails.

According to a probable cause affidavit, a missing child was "located in the residence of James Chadwell on Park Avenue in Lafayette, Indiana." Which is really an innocuous way of describing what went on here. Officers were dispatched regarding a missing child report near Park Avenue in Lafayette on April 19. It states, "Upon arrival Officers took a report stating ... a female child approximately ten years old had left her residence at approximately 6:30 p.m. and could not be found. While officers were searching the neighborhood, they made contact with James Chadwell, who told officers the girl had been at his residence earlier but had left."[60]

Officers continued their search but later returned and asked for permission to check his residence. He allowed them in, and the officers checked the basement, which was secured with a chain lock, according to the affidavit. They "found a young girl who was visibly distraught and crying, with her clothing on the floor beside her." She was identified as the missing girl and said Chadwell tried to kill her. She was injured and taken to the hospital for treatment.[61]

The girl said Chadwell hit her in the head multiple times because she was fighting back. Chadwell was also choking her with his hands on her neck and put her in a headlock, to the point where she passed out. The victim said most

60. *Heavy.com*. "James Brian Chadwell: 5 Fast Facts You Need to Know." August 30, 2022. https://heavy.com/news/james-brian-chadwell/
61. *Heavy.com*. "James Brian Chadwell: 5 Fast Facts You Need to Know." August 30, 2022. https://heavy.com/news/james-brian-chadwell/

of her clothes were off when she regained consciousness and Chadwell took her into the basement. He repeatedly sexually assaulted her. When police found the victim, she was reportedly naked and had extensive bruising from a dog bite.

The lock on the door to the basement is so odd to me. What the hell is it doing there? He is setting up his home as a tool for what he wants to do. Abduct, sexually assault, and maybe even hold a victim captive and continually sexually assault them. In a perfect world, *maybe* he would even keep them forever.

Chadwell is a monster. He choked the girl repeatedly until blood came out of her eyes and ears. He bit her. He was going to kill her. It was only through quick police work that her life was saved.

He was forty-two when arrested. Doug Carter said Bridge Guy was eighteen to forty but may appear younger. Chadwell is one of these dudes I would guess to be less than forty-two. Maybe early to mid-thirties.

After the arrest, Chadwell's family immediately threw him under the bus, saying he is evil, and that he is more than capable of horrific violence. Ashley Chadwell, the perpetrator's brother, told the press James is a monster and capable of murder.

Some say he has a tattoo on his arm that resembles Liberty German. It doesn't look unlike Libby, but I did say on record I don't think it looked a whole lot like her; it appears to be more like gothic artwork. The girl in the tattoo has blood coming out of her eyes and she is smiling, which makes it even more creepy. I said on *True Crime Garage* it looks more like something from *Magic: the Gathering* than Libby, which of course caused many people to write me saying I am crazy and stupid. At times I'm certainly capable of being both.

This happens more than one might think. When you have hundreds of thousands of listeners, getting a few crazy emails a week is not a lot. When I get these mean and nasty emails, I think to myself, *I don't want to lose this listener or upset this person. I am just a guy in a garage, I am not going to be right about everything. I am not capable of it.* I don't usually respond to missives such as these because I am not going to change their minds and I don't believe in punching down. I value my audience more than anything. I know I am lucky, and hearing from fans is validation I do a good job and work hard. The moment you turn your back on that it can go away quickly. I set the bar high for the integrity of our show.

Many people in the true crime community have a theory and they know they're right. Some guy in a basement on a computer is not going to solve this crime. Even in my position, I am not likely to solve it either. If it's unsolved, it's unsolved for a reason—until then, let's band together and work on it rather than there be infighting.

There were things other than the tattoo to get internet sleuths on his trail. In one post on Facebook, Chadwell wrote, "I'm in love with a lil redhead. You make my soul smile. I'll chase you til I can't walk, then I'll chase you in my wheelchair." That really got some people going.

He also apparently spent a lot of time sleeping outside. Near bridges, even. In a June 2020 post on Facebook, he wrote, "Sleeping under a bridge for a while til work starts. Only ten days. Cool, dry, no neighbors, and the bridge is only six minutes from work. Be thankful for the little things."

All in all, not a bad suspect. He lived fifteen miles away from the scene of the murder. He was capable and he looks enough like the second sketch.

Chadwell ended up getting ninety years for attempted murder, two counts of child molestation, kidnapping, criminal confinement, battery with serious bodily injury, and strangulation.

Our next suspect is Garrett Kirts. The initial headlines in this case stated that a woman's body was found in a hunting shack. It appeared she had been tortured.

The victim was eventually identified as Nicole Bowen, a mother of two, thirty years old, from West Lafayette, Indiana. They found fingerprints at the scene. The owner of said fingerprints is Garrett Kirts, twenty-one years old, from Lebanon, Indiana. Eventually, five arrests were made in this case: Kirts, Ashley Garth, Christopher Matthias, Jasmine Parker, and Talitha Beckley.

Very early on, the newspapers reported police believed that Bowen was killed elsewhere and her body was dumped in or around the shack. The headline WOMAN FOUND TORTURED IN A SHED is very different from what happened. She wasn't tortured in that shed, she wasn't held captive in that shed after being abducted elsewhere and brought there. Kirts was just trying to conceal her body.

Nicole Bowen had a relationship with Kirts at one time, and Ashley Garth was going out with Kirts when all this took place. There was some kind of beef between Nicole and Garth. There was a meeting arranged between the two women, but what we can't confirm is if Bowen was going along with this meeting or if she was brought there against her will.

What we do know is she arrives at a trailer with Kirts. I've heard a couple different news reports, one stating that the trailer was owned by Garrett Kirts, the other saying it was owned by Ashley Garth. I can't say for certain who out of this batch of losers owned the trailer but anyway, Nicole Bowen is brought there. There is a small gathering going on, populated by the other defendants.

At some point, there is an altercation that quickly turns into a physical fight between Nicole and Ashley. As a quick aside, if there are two women fighting over Kirts, this isn't a world I want to live in. It's odd thinking Bowen was with him at all, but we all have peaks and valleys in our lives.

I am going to take a wild guess, going off mugshot photos and what appears to be happening here, that all these individuals are involved in drugs, very likely meth. So, while this dispute could have been over Kirts, it very well could have been over something else. But we do know there was an issue between Nicole and Ashley.

So now we have Nicole Bowen and Ashley Garth in the middle of a physical fight. Kirts jumps in the fray, puts Nicole in a headlock, wraps his arm around her neck, tightens his arm until she goes unconscious, and he puts her on the floor. He then goes through the trailer and finds implements to help him choke, strangle, and suffocate her.

At one point, he used an extension cord to strangle her with a bag over her head. It is no wonder when her body was found it appeared that she had been tortured. Meanwhile, all these other disgraces standing around in the trailer do not stop Kirts from killing this woman.

After Nicole is killed, Kirts gets his car, backs it up to the trailer, places her body inside, and calls his buddy Christopher Matthias and says, "Hey, I got a body here, can you help me?" and of course, Matthias will very quickly agree to help Kirts dispose of this body because that is the kind of friend he is. They drove around until they found what they thought to be the perfect place to dump her body, the aforementioned shed.

Soon, all five of these terrible people are eventually arrested. This is a horrible personal tragedy but a good case for law enforcement. It's a "sexy case" in law enforcement lingo, one that has leads and detectives have leverage on the people they're talking to.

These people started turning on each other, "He did it, I was there, but I didn't have anything to do with it" and so on.

I don't like Garrett Kirts for the Delphi Murders as much as many people do, mostly because it is difficult for me to believe he killed two girls in public and got away with it. I don't think he could organize a two-car parade let alone get away with a double homicide.

One of the reasons people like Kirts so much is the 2019 ISP press conference where Doug Carter goes off script and talks about the movie *The Shack* and how it tells of eternity and good and evil. So many people connected the dots and suggested this wasn't a coincidence; this was a subliminal way of Carter telling us the person who left the woman in the shack is Bridge Guy.

A few weeks before Nicole Bowen was killed, forty-nine-year-old Ray Hanish was strangled to death. No arrests have been made but Kirts is a suspect in the crime.

There is a theory Kirts may have killed the girls to seek revenge. Derrick, Libby's father, has documented drug issues and some contact with the police around them. These issues are possibly why Grandma has raised the kids instead of him. Life is tough, shit gets hard, addiction happens, this doesn't make Derrick a bad guy. At this time, he seemed closer to clean living than not.

The theory is Derrick got into some legal trouble with drugs and reported Ashley to law enforcement to save his own ass. This forced Ashley to give up custody of her child.

Many theorize that Kirts murdered the girls in an act of revenge for Ashley. Seems like a stretch, but there it is.

Kirts was sentenced to fifty-five years in prison. I am not pro-death penalty or against. I am a firm believer that every circumstance needs to be looked at differently. The victim's family wanted him executed; the prosecutor took a plea. I am not saying Kirts should be executed but I am saying I want justice for the victims' families, and they wanted an eye for an eye, a life for a life. They should have had that option.

When it came to April Tinsley, John Miller confessed and got eighty years, even though April's family wanted him executed. Miller is sixty-three years old: eighty years in prison is probably appropriate. I worry with Kirts that fifty-five years is not enough. Sometimes fifty-five years doesn't even mean forty. He is a horrible person who can't be in society. Having said that, I empathize with April's family. Miller admitted he wanted to abduct and kill again and the taking of a child's life should always come with the most severe of consequences.

# What is He Into?

As soon as one of these new suspects comes along, it quickly becomes the flavor of the month, everyone gets excited, this is the guy, he is the one. Then it tapers off. With a few, the stink has remained to the point people will go, "That's my guy and I am sticking to it." One of those guys is Daniel Nations, even though law enforcement has made statements that they aren't that interested, as well as James Chadwell and Garrett Kirts. These are the three, other than Kegan Kline, that we keep coming back to. We will get to Kline later.

Having audio and video of a killer is the rarest of situations in a double homicide. Regarding Chadwell, he not only looks like him, but he sounds like him. In the case of Kirts, it's similar. Many agree he looks like him, and he sounds like him. Chadwell and Kirts had social media so the public could do their own research and hear these guys talking. Personally, I think the one who sounds most like Bridge Guy is Chadwell. In Ohio and Indiana, some people sound like Texas or the Deep South, others sound like Yankees. Kirts sounds like he is from the South. I don't hear that with Bridge Guy.

While the public is concerned with audio and video, to law enforcement, it's just a small part of the equation. The people who like Kirts say he dressed like Bridge Guy who is wearing a blue jacket and jeans and boots. That doesn't narrow it down a whole lot. This is rural Indiana after all. Some say Kirts' body type matches the suspect, being heavy on top, with skinny legs. I don't disagree about this, but one thing I find interesting about Kirts, similar to Chadwell and Nations but not similar to other suspects, is that they are all younger, and have an appearance that they can look older and different if need be.

Ted Bundy was a master at that. He could naturally change his appearance quite well just by growing facial hair or getting a different haircut. He could look totally different month to month. All of these three suspects can look older or younger than what they are.

The fact of the matter is, we don't know anything as the general public. Some people are idiots, to put it kindly, who think Doug Carter is involved or the family is involved. Patty didn't kill his granddaughter; Carter doesn't kill children in his spare time.

People argue about potential suspects online all the time. They fight about things such as what Bridge Guy is wearing when the fact is, we do not know. I find it aggravating, funny, and sad all at once. Is he wearing boots? Is he wearing a hoodie? Is he wearing a fanny pack? The only real thing we know is he is a white guy with a blue/navy coat and wearing jeans. What kind of shoes is he wearing? Are they work boots? There is a pig farm nearby. He must work there because he is wearing boots. It goes on and on.

The hat thing is what is most argued about online. Reddit and YouTube are where one can find a lot of speculation. If you check the comments and replies, prepare for a migraine headache. Some say it's his hair, others say it's a flapjack-style hat. Some say it's a camouflage ballcap. When Covid hit, neck gaiters became fashionable, so some say he is wearing a neck gaiter or face covering. The neck gaiter is an interesting theory because he could have it around his neck and pull it up or take it down whenever he wants. There is something ominous about a man wearing a face covering on a warm day. So, a neck gaiter that he can pull up and down at his choosing might be a preferable method to conceal his identity but also have the ability to remove it to avoid standing out if necessary. You want to disguise yourself but not to the point that you draw attention. One person on the trails that day said they saw a man who had a face covering on.

The girls didn't know who Bridge Guy was because they never say his name. One of the victims knows she is recording, so you would think if it was John from the flower shop or Joey from down the street, she would say his name at some point. "John, I don't want to go down the hill" or "Joey, why are you doing this to us?"

While it is important to look for someone who committed a heinous act after the murders, it might be more importantly to look at people who may have done it before.

Which is why I mention Kevin Jameson.

An eleven-year-old girl was riding her bike on a quiet road near SR29 in Carroll County in Indiana, when she was approached by a man in his late twenties or early thirties driving a black Jeep with red doors. Now, that's got to be hard to track down, right?

The man in the Jeep offered the girl money if she would get in and help him with directions to a place nearby. She said no, and later told her parents, who then told police.

While police couldn't find the suspect immediately, many people reported seeing the suspect's vehicle. Turns out there was just one sexual predator in the area driving a Jeep like that around. It wasn't long before the police arrested the driver of the vehicle, Kevin S. Jameson, thirty-one, of Lafayette, who is a convicted sex offender and is listed on the Indiana Sexual Offender Registry with Tippecanoe County.

Consider the behavior this guy exhibited. He is a registered sex offender for life, pulling up to a young girl saying, "I'll give you some money to get in my Jeep and help me figure out directions."

This type of behavior mostly likely escalated over a period of time. Often, these guys, they evolve and do worse things and get locked up for good, or they get better at what they're doing and are more difficult to catch.

You might have a rapist who commits one rape and never does it again. Maybe he is fearful of getting caught, or even remorseful and horrified by what he has done.

On the other hand, a serial rapist could be arrested because one of his hairs was found at a crime scene, and once he gets out of prison, he starts shaving his head and body. With this kind of perpetrator, rape is what they do, this is who they are, and they will figure out ways to fulfil their fantasies.

Jameson has already been in trouble, and he has faced consequences, but he can't stop himself from doing it again. He jumps in his stupid black Jeep with red doors and tries to pick up a little girl.

I believe Bridge Guy falls under the same basic category. He has fantasized about doing some very freaky things and almost certainly committed an offense or two before, whether he was caught or was lucky and got away. A lot of times, guys like this will assault or mess with a loved one or a family member, maybe the child doesn't talk because of fear and embarrassment, or maybe he has a girlfriend or wife who is just completely under his power and doesn't have the ability to talk to anyone about what she suspects the man in her life is doing.

And what kind of things was Bridge Guy doing?

Most serial killers are clearly sexually motivated. Strangulation and sodomy are common with these types. When it came to the Boston Strangler—who was ostensibly Albert DeSalvo, although there was some doubt about if he was guilty in every case attributed to him—the victims had been raped and their bodies were left nude and posed.

Death was always due to strangulation and the ligature, usually a stocking or a pillowcase, was invariably tied into an ornamental bow and left around the victim's neck.

The Russian serial killer Alexander Pichushkin chose victims who were senior men, many were homeless. Pichushkin would bring them home with him to drink, then kill them with a hammer blow to the head and shove an empty vodka bottle in the wound.

What is Bridge Guy into? What he did that day is possibly less important than what he *wanted to do* that day.

Seasoned investigators will often ask the wife or girlfriend of suspects, "What is he into?" A lot of times, they might act at least part of their kink out with a consenting partner. This can give the investigators insight into whether this is their guy or not.

Bridge Guy has almost certainly done something—maybe it was a misdemeanor, or maybe it went unreported. Ted Bundy was a peeping Tom before he began killing. Serial killers don't always, or even often, just start out that way. They might begin by looking through someone's window at night, then they start breaking into homes, maybe even when the occupants are sleeping. Then it might escalate to rape before they start taking lives.

John Miller looked for a victim numerous times before he killed April Tinsley. Bridge Guy just didn't wake up that day and become a bad guy. He has committed other crimes or at the very least has spent a considerable amount of time fantasizing about committing a violent and horrific crime. There has to be someone suspicious of him. You take someone like Jameson: how would he have devolved after this experience if he had not been caught? We know he wanted the girl in his car. What would the endgame be? How would he adapt? We must keep that in mind when looking for Bridge Guy. It isn't just what happened after the murders; maybe he did some of these things before.

These types will move around. When it gets too hot where they are, they move to another hunting ground. We have to keep going back to the simplicity of this. The victims are children. It's clear that is his preference. He chose these two to be his victims. This is pedophiliac behavior, his sexual template for this crime are adolescent girls.

A lot of people have odd, even violent sexual fantasies, but they never consider acting on them. With this kind of monster, the fantasies overtake their entire life. Maybe some of these types can keep it casual and offend here and there, but for a good percentage, this is a lifestyle built around fulfilling their fantasies and gratifying their lust.

Dean Corll, who murdered a minimum of twenty-eight boys and young men before he was killed by an accomplice, built a whole life around feeding his need to kill. Unfortunately, he was rather successful with it.

Wayne Chapman was a card-carrying member of NAMBLA who molested around one hundred boys. Chapman made a lifestyle out of his deviancy; it was almost his occupation. He became part of a network of pedophiles ranging from someone who wanted still images of a child, to people who are sadists who want movies of victims being raped or even killed.

I would expect there to be something nefarious Bridge Guy did well before February 13. He didn't just wake up that day and become a murderer.

# THE SHERIFF

Leading up to the unfortunate four-year anniversary of the still unsolved double homicide, Carroll County Sheriff Tobe Leazenby and the *Carroll County Comet* invited readers to submit questions about the case. Sheriff Leazenby then chose questions to answer, which were printed in the following two editions of the newspaper.

Over the years, I noticed a shared opinion of Sheriff Leazenby from many of the looky-loos watching the case from afar. Most seemed to hold the FBI in high regard, offering up glowing reviews of the federal agents, but had a much different opinion of Leazenby.

I heard people comparing Leazenby to Barney Fife, a fictional deputy sheriff from *The Andy Griffith Show*. The character, while my personal favorite from the show, is certainly no Sherlock Holmes and most of the time, not much of a hero. Frankly, I found it absurd and incredibly disappointing that people would bother to say this or post this thought online. There is a fine line that separates those who want to help and those who are just getting in the way. I have never met nor spoken to Sheriff Leazenby directly, but from what I have seen and experienced, he appears to be a very capable and experienced leader.

Sheriff Leazenby takes time out of his busy schedule each week to contribute to the *Carroll County Comet* by writing a weekly column. I love this approach to community policing. It's informative to the community and reminds everyone this sheriff is here for you. He works for you. This also suggests that he is very approachable to the good residents of Carroll County as well, a man of the people. Further, the sheriff is an elected state government official and for persons watching the case from afar to call the sheriff incompetent is flat out rude to the good people of Carroll County who voted for the sheriff. I'm happy to go on the record stating that if I were a resident of Carroll County, he would have received my vote.

The Q&A with Sheriff Leazenby was several articles long, spanning two editions of the local paper. I have cherry picked some of the questions and answers and provided them here.

The sheriff's willingness to do the Q&A suggested to me what I had long suspected—that he is lock and step with how the FBI and the ISP want to handle the case. Leazenby is a team player, but I have always suspected that he may feel that if the public knew a little more about the case, the public could be more helpful. Read some of these questions and answers and decide for yourself.

Q. HOW WOULD THIS CASE BE HANDLED FROM THE BEGINNING HAD THERE NOT BEEN ANY AUDIO/VIDEO OF THE PERSON OF INTEREST?

A. Obviously we would have had to rely on other evidence gained, from all sources.

Q. DID ONE OR MORE THAN ONE SET OF FOOTPRINTS LEAD SEARCHERS TO THE AREA WHERE THE GIRLS WERE FOUND?

A. This speaks to an evidentiary aspect of the investigation and I would respectfully prefer not to answer.

Q. THE PUBLIC HAS BEEN GIVEN TWO SKETCHES, IS THE THOUGHT THERE IS MORE THAN ONE PERSON INVOLVED OR IS THE SECOND SKETCH THE SUSPECTED

KILLER? PLEASE CLARIFY THE TWO SKETCHES, THIS HAS BEEN A POINT OF CONFUSION SINCE THE SECOND SKETCH WAS RELEASED.

A. These were produced by information gained from witnesses near the area during time frame. The primary focus by investigators is on the second sketch.

Q. WHY HAVE NO OTHER PHOTOS FROM LIBBY'S PHONE BEEN RELEASED TO THE PUBLIC?

A. This is close to an evidentiary information question and I prefer not to respond.

Q. WHY HAVE YOU NEVER RELEASED THE FBI'S SUSPECT PROFILE TO THE PUBLIC?

A. It has been discussed with the FBI, but again, it is currently felt it is close to the evidentiary element.

Q. ARE THERE REGRETS ABOUT NOT SECURING THE MORNING HEIGHTS CEMETERY AS A POSSIBLE PART OF THE CRIME SCENE (I.E. POSSIBLE EXIT ROUTE OF THE KILLER(S)?

A. At the time, it was uncertain exactly what the "totality of the circumstances" were.

Q. DO INVESTIGATORS BELIEVE THE BRIDGE PHOTO AND VOICE BELONG TO SAME PERSON?

A. Yes

Q. IN THE PUBLIC DOMAIN THERE HAVE BEEN DESCRIPTIONS OF THE CRIME SCENE, DESCRIPTIONS OF ITEMS FOUND AND THE POSITIONING OF THE BODIES. DO YOU FEEL THERE WAS AN EXCESSIVE NUMBER OF PERSONS PRESENT ONCE IT WAS DETERMINED TO BE A CRIME SCENE?

A. Once secured by law enforcement as a crime scene, no. I would surmise that searchers did not immediately know what they had come upon.

Q. YOU HAVE SAID YOU RECOGNIZE THE VOICE ON THE VIDEO. DO YOU RECOGNIZE IT AS A JAIL INMATE, OTHER LAW ENFORCEMENT TEAM OR PERSON YOU KNOW OUTSIDE YOUR EMPLOYMENT SPHERE?

A. I still have not been able to pin it down. In my 30+ year career or even, as with most of us, we have heard certain voices but have difficulty in recalling exactly who it is.

Q. The families of the Delphi victims have appeared on countless shows and Internet videos for interviews. Libby's grandfather Mike Patty stated he called "cop buddies" and asked if they could ping Libby's phone. Were you, or one of your deputies, the "cop buddies" he called?

A. I would suggest he was referring to someone in law enforcement. And, it could have even been dispatch, initially. The ultimate decision was a law enforcement decision.[62]

Q. Libby's grandmother Becky Patty, with whom she lived and who is the mother of her (Libby's) biological father Derrick German, stated during an interview there were countless cars at the trails that day-not all of them looking for the girls. Did the Patty family post on social media the girls were missing before contacting the sheriff's department?

A. I do not recall. But, I know we were not immediately contacted because the family did not suspect anything negative and were simply conducting their own search.

Q. Has it been determined the girls were killed where they were found?

A. Based on information known, yes.

Q. Why did you and the prosecutor choose to do an interview with Headline News (HLN) yet ISP said there would not be a press conference this year? Again, who is leading the case? ISP,

---

62. Carrol County Comet. "County Sheriff answers double homicide questions from readers." February 17, 2021. https://www.carrollcountycomet.com/articles/county-sheriff-answers-double-homicide-questions-from-readers/

COUNTY SHERIFF, FBI OR COUNTY PROSECUTOR? YOU CAN SEE THE CONFUSION FOR THE PUBLIC AND THE MIXED SIGNALS, SO TO SPEAK. EXPAND ON WHO RUNS WHAT PARTS OF THE INVESTIGATION. WHO DETERMINES WHEN THERE IS A PRESS CONFERENCE?

A. In a general sense, the leading agency, is the agency who routinely patrols and responds to calls for police services in a given jurisdiction. In this case, my professional opinion is that this crime occurred "in the county" and we are considered the "lead" agency. ISP, FBI, Prosecutor's Office, Investigator, and all other agencies are considered "assist" agencies, coming on board to "assist" us. Being a small agency, we frequently rely on larger agencies who have many more resources (lab, manpower, technical assistance, etc.) to help with investigations. This is commonplace throughout the United States. Smaller agencies will sometimes "relinquish" an investigation to a larger, "assisting" agency, such as ISP, but I feel strongly that since this crime occurred in the county, I feel we are the lead but with many partners. Additionally, when decisions, which we feel are major to the case, are being looked at, our investigative partners are consulted, like a huge "think tank", and we all reach a decision which all agree upon.[63]

Q. THE PUBLIC HAS HEARD FOR FOUR YEARS, THE INVESTIGATION "IS ONE PUZZLE PIECE FROM BEING SOLVED." WHAT IS THAT ONE PIECE SPECIFICALLY? IS IT A NAME? IS IT JON DOE TOLD ME HE KILLED THE KIDS? OR, ARE YOU LOOKING FOR CONFIRMATION OF WHAT YOU KNOW- JON DOE WAS NOT AT WORK, HE HAS A BLUE JACKET, HE CUT HIS HAIR ON FEB 14 OR I SAW A GUY WITH A BLOODY JACKET AT 4 P.M. ON FEB 13 AT

63. Carrol County Comet. "County Sheriff answers double homicide questions from readers." February 17, 2021. https://www.carrollcountycomet.com/articles/county-sheriff-answers-double-homicide-questions-from-readers/

THE GAS STATION? YOU ARE NOT GIVING THE PUBLIC A LOT TO WORK WITH YET NO ARRESTS IN FOUR YEARS. AREN'T YOU WORRIED ABOUT MORE VICTIMS? IS THE SUSPECT DEAD OR INCARCERATED SO THAT IS WHY NO PRESS CONFERENCE OR ADDITIONAL INFORMATION IS BEING RELEASED?

A. The person specifically responsible for Abby and Libby's death. Our team of trained, experienced, and professional investigators will know that "one piece" when they see it.

Q. THE LACK OF COMMUNICATION ON THE PART OF YOUR DEPARTMENT AND LAW ENFORCEMENT IS A SIGNIFICANT CONCERN FOR MANY INDIVIDUALS. THE EXCEPTION SEEMS TO BE THE FAMILIES OF THE VICTIMS. WHY DO YOU THINK THIS IS THE CASE?

A. I respectfully disagree with this statement. As I have said since the beginning, much of what we "protect" and keep "close to the vest" is preserved for the courtroom and trial. To release too much information would, in my opinion, potentially "taint" a jury before a trial even begins. And, as most know, the "double jeopardy" clause exists in the US Constitution which means, in short, the Prosecutor only has one chance at prosecuting this case. I feel, as Sheriff, I have been very open and accessible, at least to main stream media, and answered most questions reasonably.

Q. DOES THE PROSECUTOR RELY ON YOU TO DETERMINE WHAT INFORMATION IS GIVEN TO THE PUBLIC OR DOES HE MAKE THAT DECISION INDEPENDENTLY?

A. As with me, as Sheriff, he is an elected official. He does not supervise me and I do not supervise him. He is part of the investigative team and is consulted frequently. But, as a Prosecutor, he is bound by a different set of rules which state specifically what he can or cannot state.

Q. THERE IS A SURGING MOVEMENT ACROSS THE NATION, FROM PROFESSIONAL INVESTIGATORS AND OTHERS, INSISTING THE POLICE RELEASE MORE DETAILS ABOUT THE CRIME SCENE AND THE INVESTIGATION, NOT TO MENTION THE ENTIRETY OF THE VIDEO AND AUDIO FOUND ON LIBBY'S PHONE. WHY ARE YOU NOT RELEASING INFORMATION? TEXTS WRITTEN BY SEARCHERS ON THE SCENE ARE NOW ON THE INTERNET FOR EVERYONE TO SEE (AND THEY ARE BEING WIDELY DISTRIBUTED). THERE IS ALSO DISPATCH AUDIO FROM WHEN THE GIRLS WERE FOUND ON THE INTERNET NOW. GIVEN THESE FACTS, HOW CAN YOU JUSTIFY NOT RELEASING MORE INFORMATION?

A. I respectfully disagree with this statement. As I have said since the beginning, much of what we "protect" and keep "close to the vest", is preserved for the courtroom and trial. To release too much information would, in my opinion, potentially "taint" a jury before a trial even begins. And, as most know, the "double jeopardy" clause exists in the U.S. Constitution which means, in short, the Prosecutor only has one (1) chance at prosecuting this case. I feel, as Sheriff, I have been very open and accessible, at least to main stream media, and answered most questions reasonably.[64]

Q. THERE ARE MANY RESIDENTS OF THE COUNTY THAT HAVE NEVER BEEN ON THE TRAILS, DESCRIBE THE TERRAIN OF WHERE THE GIRLS WERE FOUND? WHAT IS THE MOST DIRECT ROUTE OUT OF THE AREA THEY WERE FOUND? HOW LONG OF A WALK FROM WHERE THEY ENTERED TO WHERE THEY WERE FOUND?

A. Very similar to one of the state's parks. A lot of hills, brush, trees, etc. Directly south of the Morning

---

64. *Carrol County Comet*. "County Sheriff answers double homicide questions from readers." February 17, 2021. https://www.carrollcountycomet.com/articles/county-sheriff-answers-double-homicide-questions-from-readers/

Heights Cemetery but on private property. I do not recall the specific distance.

Q. RON LOGAN HAS STATED ON NEWS PROGRAMS THE ONLY WAY TO GET TO THE SITE IS OVER DIFFICULT TERRAIN AND PRIVATE PROPERTY. GIVEN THE DIFFICULTY GETTING TO WHERE THE BODIES WERE FOUND, MANY BELIEVE THE KILLER(S) WERE FAMILIAR WITH THE AREA. DO YOU AS A LAW ENFORCEMENT OFFICER BELIEVE THAT AS WELL?

A. Very much so. It is part of the reason why we continually feel it is a "local" or someone who was very familiar with the area.

Q. WHO MONITORS/SUPERVISES THE COUNTY INVESTIGATORS AND HOW IS THAT MONITORING DONE? ARE THERE WRITTEN RECORDS OF TIME SPENT ON INVESTIGATION?

A. As Sheriff, I am charged with that responsibility. But, also, our county investigators are professional and experienced. I trust their abilities. We talk frequently, a lot of times, daily. Granted, there are days there is nothing new to discuss. Records are kept, yes.

Q. IS THERE STILL A TEAM OF INVESTIGATORS? HOW MANY COMPRISE THAT TEAM AND HOW OFTEN DO THEY MEET?

A. Yes. Two county detectives, two ISP detectives, and from time to time, outside detectives from other police agencies, including the FBI. A portion of the team meets almost daily but with technology, meetings are not always "in person." Obviously with COVID, some meetings have been by Zoom.

Q. AS THE LEAD AGENCY, ARE YOU THE PERSON IN CHARGE OF THE TEAM OF INVESTIGATORS?

A. I supervise the county detectives. Outside agencies have their own supervisors.

Q. FORMER DELPHI POLICE CHIEF STEVE MULLIN STATED AT THE FIRST PRESS CONFERENCE "OUR PEOPLE

KNOW WHAT TO DO" AFTER BEING ASKED IF THE COMMUNITY WAS IN DANGER AND WHAT PRECAUTIONS SHOULD RESIDENTS TAKE. PARENTS OF SCHOOL-AGE CHILDREN WERE TAKEN ABACK BY THIS STATEMENT. AS THE COUNTY'S CHIEF LAW ENFORCEMENT OFFICER, ARE RESIDENTS, PARTICULARLY YOUNG GIRLS OF CARROLL COUNTY IN DANGER GIVEN THE UNSOLVED MURDERS OF SIX YOUNG GIRLS?

A. Comparing Carroll County to other jurisdictions and our annual statistics, I still feel Carroll County is one of the safest areas to live in. I would much rather raise a family here than say, a larger metropolitan area.[65]

Q. CARROLL COUNTY AND DELPHI ARE SMALL TOWN USA. YET THERE HAS BEEN A SIGNIFICANT NUMBER OF VIOLENT DEATHS IN THE LAST FOUR YEARS INCLUDING THE DOUBLE MURDER ON SR29 WHERE VICTIMS (MALE AND FEMALE) WERE SHOT AND BURNED, A MAN WAS SHOT AND KILLED NEAR DEER CREEK AND A DELPHI POLICE OFFICER WAS RECENTLY FOUND DEAD. FOR A COUNTY WITH UNDER 20,000 PEOPLE, THAT IS 2+ MURDERS PER YEAR WITH THE MAJORITY BEING FEMALE. ACCORDING TO NATIONAL DATA, MALES MAKE UP 78% OF ALL MURDER VICTIMS. IT APPEARS THE OPPOSITE IN CARROLL COUNTY. ARE FEMALES AT A HIGHER RISK FOR VIOLENCE IN CARROLL COUNTY?

A. In my professional opinion, I would say no. A lot of the situations, again, in my opinion, are coincidental.

Q IN YOUR PROFESSIONAL OPINION, WOULD YOU DESCRIBE THE DEATHS OF THE SIX FEMALES AS "PLANNED"?

---

65. Carrol County Comet. "County Sheriff answers double homicide questions from readers." February 17, 2021. https://www.carrollcountycomet.com/articles/county-sheriff-answers-double-homicide-questions-from-readers/

A. No. Rather, "victims of circumstance or opportunity." Additionally, ISP is the lead with the Flora investigation. Our agency is not actively involved with that investigation.

Q. THE DELPHI CASE HAS GARNERED ATTENTION ALL OVER THE WORLD. BASED ON YOUR PROFESSIONAL EXPERIENCE, WHY DO YOU BELIEVE IS IT UNSOLVED GIVEN THE SMALL NUMBER OF RESIDENTS, PHOTO, AUDIO AND LARGE REWARD?

A. Difficult to say. But I believe we have perseverance on our side.

Q. WOULD YOU CLASSIFY THE MURDERS AS "RETRIBUTION" KILLINGS?

A. Do not know until we have that opportunity to talk to the responsible party. [66]

Q. HOW MANY TOTAL TIPS HAVE BEEN RECEIVED? HOW MANY THIS YEAR? HOW MANY THIS MONTH?

A. Total throughout the investigation is approximately 50,000.

Q. WHEN A TIP COMES IN, TAKE US THROUGH THE STEP-BY-STEP PROCESS OF HOW THAT TIP IS PROCESSED BY THE TIP LINE OPERATOR TO HOW IT IS DISTRIBUTED TO THE "INVESTIGATORS." PLEASE DESCRIBE WHAT TIPSTERS ARE TOLD AND THE FOLLOW-UP.

A. Tips which come into the system are entered into a database. Each tip is then reviewed by investigators and prioritized. Emailed tips receive an automated response. If investigators need additional information from a tipster, they contact that individual directly.

Q. DO FAMILY MEMBERS RECEIVE UPDATES ON THE CASE? IF SO, HOW OFTEN AND IN WHAT FORM?

---

66. *Carrol County Comet.* "County Sheriff answers double homicide questions from readers." February 17, 2021. https://www.carrollcountycomet.com/articles/county-sheriff-answers-double-homicide-questions-from-readers/

A. Yes. Occasionally we meet with the families when it is felt it is needed. An open line of communication exists with them.

Q. WHAT WOULD IT TAKE TO CONVINCE YOU TO RELEASE MORE OF THE DETAILS OF THE CASE?

A. As I stated previously, the integrity of the investigation must be preserved and to release additional information may damage that integrity which must, in my opinion, be maintained for the courtroom.

Q. DOES A DATABASE EXIST THAT CONTAINS CARROLL COUNTY VIOLENT CRIME DATA? IF SO, HOW CAN THE PUBLIC ACCESS THIS?

A. Obviously we have extensive records of each jail booking which reflect each individual's particular arrest violation. It can be publicly accessed but the request must be specific to a person or their alleged arrest violation/crime.

Q. WHAT SORTS OF INFORMATION DO INVESTIGATORS CONTINUE TO LOOK AT FOR THIS CASE?

A. Several aspects specifically associated with Feb. 13, 2017.[67]

Q. DOES THIS INVESTIGATION NEED "NEW EYES"? WHAT REASON CAN YOU GIVE TO NOT CHANGE THE INVESTIGATIVE STRATEGY?

A. New eyes frequently occur within the core of investigators. The ISP, FBI and we have consulted often with experts and other agencies to provided us with their evaluation of the investigation to this stage.

Q. WHAT ADDITIONAL INVESTIGATIVE EDUCATION HAVE YOU AND/OR YOUR DOUBLE HOMICIDE DETECTIVES, TONY LIGGETT AND KEVEN HAMMOND, RECEIVED IN THE PAST FOUR YEARS?

---

67. *Carrol County Comet.* "County Sheriff continues to answer double homicide questions from readers." February 24, 2021. https://www.carrollcountycomet.com/articles/sheriff-leazenby-continues-to-answer-double-homicide-questions/

A. The investigation itself has been a learning process. To date, both detectives (Hammond and Liggett) have attended and successfully completed at least a half dozen trainings as they relate to homicide investigations. Additionally, our investigators have experts to their avail and are not above asking for assistance from those seasoned in investigations such as this one.

Q. Do investigators follow tips from social media? One person, a Shawn Harmon, posted that his father and son were connected to the homicides. Was this tip investigated fully?

A. The simple response is – yes. Information which is felt to be legitimate to the investigation is followed into. This is not the arena for speaking to a particular inquiry or tip.[68]

Q. How many people have been interviewed by the investigators? You have stated that you were interviewed three times yourself. Does it bother you that your employees are in the position of interviewing you? Does it bother you that other members of law enforcement, such as the State Police and the FBI, have spoken to you as a potential suspect in this crime?

A. Investigators are only conducting their due diligence in following up on anyone and everyone who has been mentioned in the case.

Q. What elements of this case make it so difficult to solve?

A. Several, however the presiding factor seems to be that whomever is responsible has never discussed it with anyone.

---

68. *Carrol County Comet*. "County Sheriff continues to answer double homicide questions from readers." February 24, 2021. https://www.carrollcountycomet.com/articles/sheriff-leazenby-continues-to-answer-double-homicide-questions/

Q. Do you know if the girls were found where they were killed or if they were moved post mortem?

A. Answered previously. Found where they were killed.

Q. Do you know how the murderer was able to gain control of both girls at once?

A. It is believed by manipulation and intimidation factors.

Q. In January 2019, you did an interview with a woman named Angela explaining that Ron Logan has been "covered" and not "cleared". Have you been able to clear Ron Logan yet?

A. No one is truly "cleared" until we have the alleged responsible party in custody and formal criminal charges are filed by the prosecutor.[69]

Sheriff Leazenby offered up a final thought and statement to the general public.

It has been intriguing and thought provoking to be able to engage in these presented questions the past two weeks. I realize not all agree with my responses. However, I have received responses of the affirmative aspect too. As Sheriff, the utmost importance, in my opinion, is the integrity of the investigation. The only way we will resolve to gain justice for Abby and Libby, for their respective families and our caring community, is to remain dedicated to the preservation of said integrity.

I believe we wholeheartedly owe that to these two wonderful young ladies.

---

69. *Carrol County Comet*. "County Sheriff continues to answer double homicide questions from readers." February 24, 2021. https://www.carrollcountycomet. com/articles/sheriff-leazenby-continues-to-answer-double-homicide-questions/

Thank you. [70]

Finding justice for the girls was close to my heart and to those of our *True Crime Garage* listeners. I decided to submit a few questions of my own for the good sheriff. I started out with a little ass kissing. I had seen the criticism online. I wanted him to know which side I was on. My letter submitted to the *Carroll County Comet* read:

> Dear Sheriff Leazenby,
> Thank you for your hard work and continued efforts on this very difficult case. I truly appreciate the dedication shown by you and the Carroll County Sheriff's Department.
> Is there any reason to believe the killer had some kind of help or assistance and this is making this difficult case even more complicated? By help or assistance specifically I mean a second perpetrator or maybe someone who dropped the man off or picked him up. Do you think someone is providing a false alibi?
> If the man on the bridge was totally alone, where do you think he parked his vehicle?
> Is there still reason to believe that the vehicle previously mentioned in news releases is involved? Or has that vehicle been cleared?

He didn't choose my questions to answer but my focus was on two primary aspects of the case. Does the evidence suggest that anyone else was involved in any form or fashion, and the perpetrator's vehicle or means of travel.

I was still hopeful, but my optimism was wavering. It was a depressing case from the start. Two little girls were

---

70. *Carrol County Comet.* "County Sheriff continues to answer double homicide questions from readers." February 24, 2021. https://www.carrollcountycomet. com/articles/sheriff-leazenby-continues-to-answer-double-homicide-questions/

senselessly killed but now my sense of despair when it came to this case was reaching its peak. If there wasn't going to be a break in the case soon, I was going to need to step away for a few weeks to compose myself.

# ANTHONY SHOTS

And then came anthony_shots. What follows is an Indiana State Police press release.

December 6, 2021

### DETECTIVES WITH THE DELPHI INVESTIGATION SEEK INFORMATION

While investigating the murders of Abigail Williams and Liberty German, detectives with the Carroll County Sheriff's Office and the Indiana State Police have uncovered an online profile named anthony_shots. This profile was being used from 2016 to 2017 on social media applications, including but not limited to, Snapchat and Instagram. The fictitious anthony_shots profile used images of a known male model and portrayed himself as being extremely wealthy and owning numerous sports cars. The creator of the fictitious profile used this information while communicating with juvenile females to solicit nude images, obtain their address, and attempt to meet them. Pictured on your screen, you'll see images of the known male model and images the fictitious profile sent to underage females.

We have already identified the male in these images that were used by anthony_shots. The male that is in the photos is **not** a person of interest in the investigation. Detectives are seeking information about the person who created the anthony_shots profile.

Investigators would like any individual who communicated with, met, or attempted to meet the anthony_shots profile to contact law enforcement by utilizing the tip email **abbyandlibbytip@cacoshrf. com.** Please provide as much information as you possibly can. For example, when you communicated with anthony_shots, how you communicated with the profile, what social media applications the account used, and if anthony_shots attempted to meet you or obtain your address. If you have saved images or conversations with anthony_shots' profile, please attach them to your email.[71]

Shortly after this was released, news broke that Kegan Kline was the man accused of being behind the catfish social media account anthony_shots. Police said the page was an example of elaborate catfishing that used a fake profile with a model's picture to contact juvenile females "to solicit nude images."

While it was known that Kline was a suspect almost immediately, a probable cause search warrant affidavit wasn't filed until August 2020 by David R. Vido of the ISP. Potential charges included child solicitation, possession of child pornography, child exploitation, obstruction of justice, and synthetic identity deception. On February 25, 2017—just twelve days after the Delphi murders—the ISP and FBI executed a search warrant at the home of Kegan Anthony Kline and his father, Tony Kline. The name on the warrant is redacted and the affidavit does not mention the Delphi murders, at least what is visible.

---

71. Indiana State Police Information Channel. "Indiana State Police Delphi News." December 6, 2021. https://www.youtube.com/watch?v=Ir4Z86LPwVo

The information from the FBI involved an adult male accused of "soliciting female juveniles utilizing the social media platforms, Snapchat and Instagram" and using the name anthony_shots. That man is named as Kegan Anthony Kline by authorities. The warrant says, "During Kegan's interview, he initially denied creating fake social media accounts and talking to underage girls. Later in the interview, he admitted to creating the anthony_shots profile and speaking to underage girls."[72]

And goes on to say,

Kegan told investigators he created the accounts approximately 6 months ago. Kegan stated he talks to girls he knows personally and girls he doesn't know personally. Kegan stated he meets girls on Instagram. He said he knows the age of the girls he communicates with because he talks to them. Kegan stated if a girl told him she was 16 or under he wouldn't care and would still talk to them. Kegan told investigators he finds girls on Instagram and then tells them to talk to him on Snapchat. Kegan admitted to speaking to approximately 15 girls that were underage and advised he probably received pictures from every one of them. He advised he saved their pictures to his gallery.[73]

Kegan "again admitted to creating the fake Anthony_ shots profiles and speaking to underage girls." They ranged from fifteen to seventeen years old, and he received

72. Warrant—State of Indiana Vs. Kegan A. Kline. Transcript. https://www. wishtv.com/wp-content/uploads/2022/03/Tx-statement-Kegan-Kline-10-19-2-FINAL-VERSION-Redacted-1.pdf

73. Warrant—State of Indiana Vs. Kegan A. Kline. Transcript. https://www. wishtv.com/wp-content/uploads/2022/03/Tx-statement-Kegan-Kline-10-19-2-FINAL-VERSION-Redacted-1.pdf

"approximately 100 sexual pictures form underage girls,"[74] the warrant alleges.

> The warrant affidavit also states,
> The user of this device communicated with female teens and shared media files depicting CSAM (Child Sex Abuse Material). Media artifacts were also found on this device. There were multiple CSAM and erotica media files which the user saved to the device or shared or received. There were CSAM files that depicted female children approximately 12 to 17 years of age, posing nude and/or partially nude; and/or performing a sex act on themselves.[75]

We eventually learn that Kline has been using this profile and another one, EmilyAnn45, to collect child porn material and chat with underage girls. EmilyAnn45 was a profile that was ostensibly a teenage girl; it was the fake profile he used first.

When it comes to EmilyAnn45, we don't know his intentions, although we can guess. He wants the person on the other end to believe they're speaking to an underage girl, maybe to befriend them and get compromising photos and videos that way.

But soon he figures out there was a better way. What if he started writing to these girls pretending to be a handsome young dude with a six pack, one who has access to sports cars and money?

I believe what may have led ISP to Kline was Ski-Mask Man. An adolescent girl named Alexis gave her address out to handsome, young anthony_shots, and next thing you

74. Warrant—State of Indiana Vs. Kegan A. Kline. Transcript. https://www.wishtv.com/wp-content/uploads/2022/03/Tx-statement-Kegan-Kline-10-19-2-FINAL-VERSION-Redacted-1.pdf

75. Warrant—State of Indiana Vs. Kegan A. Kline. Transcript. https://www.wishtv.com/wp-content/uploads/2022/03/Tx-statement-Kegan-Kline-10-19-2-FINAL-VERSION-Redacted-1.pdf

know, a fat guy in a ski mask is looking in her window. The police tracked the fake profile back to Kline.

When this traumatizing event took place, the girl told her mom and dad she gave this hot young guy their address, then this Ski-Mask Man shows up. She could tell by the physique Ski-Mask Man was *not* anthony_shots.

Alexis was a friend of Libby's. It turns out the Libby was also writing to, and flirting with, anthony_shots. The girls were killed on February 13, and Ski-Mask Man showed up on February 20. Police showed up at Kline's house February 25 in Peru, Indiana, where he lived with his dad, Tony. I am assuming Alexis told the police Libby was talking to Anthony and she was infatuated with him. It's hard to know how many dots the police connected at this point. Oddly enough, although they would tell you it was just coincidence, Kegan and Tony go out of town before the twenty-fifth; they went to Vegas of all places.

When police start questioning Kegan, he denied everything, but once he was shown proof and it was obvious they knew he was shots, he then admitted what he had done. He admitted just a little at first. "I used the account to talk to 17-year-olds," then it was, "I talked to some that were 16," then "maybe if I was talking to one younger than 16, I didn't stop talking to them, but it wasn't on purpose."[76]

Kegan lived with his father, who is mentioned in a lot of these online conversations. For example, messages were found where EmilyAnn45 says she has sex with Kegan and his father at the same time.

This level of predator is beyond scary. As parents, we keep kids close. We vet their friends, keep them out of harm's way, keep them safe at night, send them to a safe school. What Kline has done by pretending to be a girl or a young man online is something a parent can do absolutely nothing

---

76. Warrant—State of Indiana Vs. Kegan A. Kline. Transcript. https://www. wishtv.com/wp-content/uploads/2022/03/Tx-statement-Kegan-Kline-10-19-2-FINAL-VERSION-Redacted-1.pdf

about other than teach children about online predators. He crept into your safe home; not through the front door, he used his phone, his tablet, to get access to your underage daughter.

Another thing that is bizarre is the girls he was communicating with all lived near where he lived. If you're this kind of creep, you could do this to anyone, anywhere. You could be trying to get photos of girls from Alaska, Texas, Singapore—anywhere, really. That way, if Mom or Dad catches on to what you're up to, you don't get in any real trouble. But he was doing it with girls within driving distance of his home. Why? If he didn't want to see them, what would be the point?

Kline looks nothing like shots, so whoever he would meet would be disappointed, possibly disgusted, and frightened. But maybe it wouldn't matter because when he met them, he would just take them if he wanted them. This isn't just a fat guy who has a thing for young girls, there is something else going on here.

What makes this even more interesting as well as frightening is that police seem to be convinced that more than one person is using the profile, based on the number of devices used to access the accounts and time spent on them.

Kegan never comes out and says someone else is using the profile. He throws his friend Durk under the bus at one point, saying he got drunk, and he might've used my phone when he was passed out.[77] But even then, it's only when he's pressed by police and they say they know someone else has been logging into his accounts that he says something. And that's what makes this even more confusing. Tony Kline looks just as good as Kegan for this crime, or maybe the two of them together.

---

77. Warrant—State of Indiana Vs. Kegan A. Kline. Transcript. https://www.wishtv.com/wp-content/uploads/2022/03/Tx-statement-Kegan-Kline-10-19-2-FINAL-VERSION-Redacted-1.pdf

From both the anthony_shots and EmilyAnn(e) accounts, there was a lot of "my dad" stuff. Questions were asked like, "Would you watch my dad masturbate?" "Would you have sex with my dad?" "Would you have sex with a 40-year-old man now? Would you have done that when you were 9?"[78]

Police said they believe there are two different patterns of writing in the messages, indicating more than one person using the account. They claim to have technical evidence showing two different devices are using these profiles at the same time. They pinged the devices and could tell they both were being used in the house.

In a transcript given to FOX59 by the *Murder Sheet*, Kline spoke to HLN producer Barbara McDonald in a jailhouse interview on December 9, 2021. In the interview, Kline said his father had access to the anthony_shots account. Kline also told McDonald that ISP reportedly told him "they knew it was my dad"[79] who killed Abby and Libby.

> **McDonald**: Do you think you're going to be charged with anything related to Abby and Libby's murder?
>
> **Kline**: No. No, I don't.
>
> **McDonald**: So they haven't, the State Police haven't threatened that?
>
> **Kline**: No. No.
>
> **McDonald**: Do you feel like they're trying to get you to pin this on your dad?
>
> **Kline**: Yes. Yes, I do.

---

78. Warrant—State of Indiana Vs. Kegan A. Kline. Transcript. https://www.wishtv.com/wp-content/uploads/2022/03/Tx-statement-Kegan-Kline-10-19-2-FINAL-VERSION-Redacted-1.pdf

79. FOX59. "A break in the Delphi murders? Transcripts reveal new details." March 24, 2022. https://fox59.com/news/indycrime/a-break-in-the-delphi-murders-transcripts-reveal-new-details/

**McDonald**: And that's probably why he's not speaking to you?

**Kline**: Right. 'Cause when I first got arrested they told me that they knew it was my dad and if th-, if I tell 'em all my charges will be dropped.[80]

In the interview with McDonald, Kline said his father was abusive, once holding guns on him and his mother. He also said his dad had past domestic violence cases filed against him and a history of violence toward women, saying he had "been to jail over beating [his ex-wife] up."[81]

Kline said his father also liked "younger women" and claimed he once slept with a seventeen-year-old when Kline was twenty. If Kegan is telling the truth, his father Tony would have been approximately forty-seven years old at the time.

In the one hundred ninety-four-page transcript of the police's conversation with Kline, he was questioned about using the anthony_shots account to communicate with Libby German the night before her death.

The videotaped statement of Kegan Kline occurred on August 19, 2020.

The interview starts with some innocuous chitchat and niceties. Kline's handcuffs are removed, and he is offered water. During this initial conversation Kline says, "I'm like, the least most violent person."[82]

Detective Vido and Deputy Clinton take over and read Kline his Miranda rights. They explain he is being held

80. FOX59. "A break in the Delphi murders? Transcripts reveal new details." March 24, 2022. https://fox59.com/news/indycrime/a-break-in-the-delphi-murders-transcripts-reveal-new-details/

81. FOX59. "A break in the Delphi murders? Transcripts reveal new details." March 24, 2022. https://fox59.com/news/indycrime/a-break-in-the-delphi-murders-transcripts-reveal-new-details/

82. Warrant—State of Indiana Vs. Kegan A. Kline. Transcript. https://www.wishtv.com/wp-content/uploads/2022/03/Tx-statement-Kegan-Kline-10-19-2-FINAL-VERSION-Redacted-1.pdf

without bond and read his charges, which are so extensive, they take up a page and a half in the transcript. The charges all revolve around child exploitation and child pornography.

The officers begin talking to him about his charges. Kline attempts to deflect, saying he was underage when he was looking for the content they found on his devices. In reality, he was in his early twenties.

Q: The phones, um…

**KLINE**: So, like, I told her that, I can't remember her name, she was like the I don't know, something with the child division umm all those are old video, when I was underage.

*The investigators quickly refute that.*

Q: Well and I want to ma-, and I want to make it clear too that we not only have watched your interviews—

**KLINE**: Right

Q: —but we've personally gone through each device—

**KLINE**: Right, right.

Q: —we've watched the videos—

**KLINE**: Yeah.

Q: We've seen the pictures and I can tell you, you were not underage at that time.

**KLINE**: Of all the underage girls I talked to I was definitely underage, for any of those pictures I got from them.

Q: And, and that's not the data that we have. On-on the metadata of those images, I mean, they're time stamped—[83]

---

83. Warrant—State of Indiana Vs. Kegan A. Kline. Transcript. https://www.wishtv.com/wp-content/uploads/2022/03/Tx-statement-Kegan-Kline-10-19-2-FINAL-VERSION-Redacted-1.pdf

They later discuss his move to Vegas. As expected, there is confusion about the dates he lived there. Kegan is also unable to articulate his address, but he did say he moved out there with his friend, Durk Hayes. He says he has been back from Vegas "for like a year and a half, probably."[84] If true, this would mean he lived in Vegas from June 2017 to late 2018. Later, he amends that to saying he lived there for about a year. He also said he lived in L.A. for a short time, but then later said he would just visit there once a week or so.

The investigators begin to ask him about the name EmilyAnne45 that he used on Kik, which is a messaging app. This turns into questions around conversations between EmilyAnne45 and another account, "Hannah Rostoll." Investigators have evidence of the two chatting about exchanging pornographic material. Both seem to be curious as to what ages the girls are in the photos and videos the other has to share. Both seem to be more interested in girls fifteen and under. They eventually exchange images of what the law enforcement officers refer to as nude thirteen-year-old girls. Each express how "hot" the girls are. Kline admits to investigators he knows "Hannah" is actually a male.

According to law enforcement, at one point the conversation goes like this.

> **EMILYANNE**: so what kind of pics
> **HANNAH:** Whatever you want
> **EMILYANNE**: L.O.L age
> **HANNAH**: 13-16[85]

84. Warrant—State of Indiana Vs. Kegan A. Kline. Transcript. https://www. wishtv.com/wp-content/uploads/2022/03/Tx-statement-Kegan-Kline-10-19-2-FINAL-VERSION-Redacted-1.pdf

85. Warrant—State of Indiana Vs. Kegan A. Kline. Transcript. https://www. wishtv.com/wp-content/uploads/2022/03/Tx-statement-Kegan-Kline-10-19-2-FINAL-VERSION-Redacted-1.pdf

Later they discuss photos of girls as young as three. Kline says he doesn't remember any of this conversation.

Law enforcement pushes Kline, saying this conversation was purely to exchange child pornography including "girls that are like 5 years old."[86] They tell Kline that the device they are most interested in is his iPhone 4. Kline immediately tries to throw his old roomie Durk under the bus, saying maybe he was using his phone and says he gives his password to "a lot of people."[87]

Kline is asked about a polygraph examination that was administered at an earlier date. During this portion of the interview Kline tells the officers that during his polygraph he admitted he would still talk to girls on Kik who were under sixteen even when he was twenty-two. Law enforcement tells Kline they know he was asking for "9 to 13 fuck videos." Kline also admits sharing one photo of a shirtless fourteen-year-old girl with Hannah.

Later in the interview, detectives tell Kegan they are aware of the type of internet searches he is prone to make, such as "little teen ass fucked" and "preteen slut," as well as photos of the bodies of Sandy Hook victims.

The officers go on to mention a Dropbox, to which Kline says, "What do you mean? I never had a Dropbox."

Deputy Clinton responds, "From your Dropbox off your phone, we have started one of the largest child pornography investigations ever undertaken in the state of Indiana."[88]

The officers confront Kline with the fact that while using the screenname EmilyAnne, he told Hannah he likes

86. Warrant—State of Indiana Vs. Kegan A. Kline. Transcript. https://www.wishtv.com/wp-content/uploads/2022/03/Tx-statement-Kegan-Kline-10-19-2-FINAL-VERSION-Redacted-1.pdf

87. Warrant—State of Indiana Vs. Kegan A. Kline. Transcript. https://www.wishtv.com/wp-content/uploads/2022/03/Tx-statement-Kegan-Kline-10-19-2-FINAL-VERSION-Redacted-1.pdf

88. Warrant—State of Indiana Vs. Kegan A. Kline. Transcript. https://www.wishtv.com/wp-content/uploads/2022/03/Tx-statement-Kegan-Kline-10-19-2-FINAL-VERSION-Redacted-1.pdf

girls of any age. They follow that up by confronting Kline about an image sent to him by Hannah. The photo is of a girl (somewhere between the ages of seven and twelve) taking a photo of herself in the mirror, with her pants pulled down, touching her vagina. EmilyAnne responded, "What a little whore."

Law enforcement tells Kline that they believe two people are using his devices. They believe this to be true because the speech, phrasing, and phonetics used are totally different.

The officers try to push harder, telling Kegan he is facing forty-five years in prison and try to get him to flip on his father.

**CLINTON**: We need an answer for this right, It's all you, or [its] you and someone else.

**KLINE**: they told me that last time I was here. About killing two girls. They tried to say that I failed a polygraph and that I did it. Me or my dad. So you understand how I'm like now, these guys are bullshit artists.[89]

The investigators again try to get Kline to turn on his dad, but he throws Durk under the bus once again. Law enforcement reminds Kline the data they have is coming from the home he shared with his dad, not the apartment he supposedly shared with Durk.

Not only that but some of the conversations were focused around having sex with a mature man.

The detectives read Kegan an exchange between EmilyAnne45 and Elenor18, who is ostensibly a thirteen-year-old girl, where Emily asks questions such as, "would

---

89. Warrant—State of Indiana Vs. Kegan A. Kline. Transcript. https://www.wishtv.com/wp-content/uploads/2022/03/Tx-statement-Kegan-Kline-10-19-2-FINAL-VERSION-Redacted-1.pdf

you have sucked a 37-year-old dick when you were 10?" and "would you let a grown man finger you at 8?"[90]

To another girl, EmilyAnne asked, "my dad asked if you think you could deep throat," and "if an older man took you in the bathroom and told you to get on your knees and suck his cock what would you do?"[91] There were numerous other conversations of this nature.

They then pressured Kline about not turning in one of his phones right away, until he deleted all the apps in an attempt to conceal his activity.

Kline admitted to talking to girls as young as thirteen. Law enforcement tells him it's ridiculous to infer someone outside of the house was using the devices, saying, "That would be someone living in the home that was using the device and communicating with these people that were trading child porn, and it, and again, it's not just a random occurrence, were talking years, we're talking months of the same person."[92]

They ask if he and his dad shared devices. Kline said, "No. Not really." He said his father doesn't have his password. He said Tony didn't know anything about the child porn stuff and would never talk to him again if he knew Kegan was involved, and that his dad was "freaking out" about the raid. Law enforcement then said they told Tony about the child porn, so he does know about it. Kegan said his dad never mentioned it.[93]

90. Warrant—State of Indiana Vs. Kegan A. Kline. Transcript. https://www.wishtv.com/wp-content/uploads/2022/03/Tx-statement-Kegan-Kline-10-19-2-FINAL-VERSION-Redacted-1.pdf

91. Warrant—State of Indiana Vs. Kegan A. Kline. Transcript. https://www.wishtv.com/wp-content/uploads/2022/03/Tx-statement-Kegan-Kline-10-19-2-FINAL-VERSION-Redacted-1.pdf

92. Warrant—State of Indiana Vs. Kegan A. Kline. Transcript. https://www.wishtv.com/wp-content/uploads/2022/03/Tx-statement-Kegan-Kline-10-19-2-FINAL-VERSION-Redacted-1.pdf

93. Warrant—State of Indiana Vs. Kegan A. Kline. Transcript. https://www.wishtv.com/wp-content/uploads/2022/03/Tx-statement-Kegan-Kline-10-19-2-FINAL-VERSION-Redacted-1.pdf

Kegan pretended to be a girl because it was easier for him to get girls to talk to him that way.

Finally, they got down to it. Law enforcement said they know he wrote to Libby German and that he admitted to doing so to them before. Kegan replied, "I don't think I ever did though. I think I talked to one of her friends, like I told them."[94]

The investigators pressured Kegan to tell them when he first contacted Libby.

> **KLINE**: I don't know. I literally don't know. It had to be on Instagram or something.
>
> **Q**: Okay. So she added you on Instagram. When was that, would you say?
>
> **KLINE**: I literally have no clue, I don't remember talking to her, really. I didn't even know who she really was until after I saw that on the news and I was like, oh wow, that name. Like, I remembered the name.[95]

The investigators got Kegan to admit he traded messages with Libby while she was at a sleepover, but he said he blocked her because "she was annoying."

It seems Kegan thinks by giving them this they might move on, but they dug in harder. They told him they knew he exchanged photos with Libby using the anthony_shots persona. Kline then admitted to communicating with her via Snapchat and Instagram extensively and also to doing searches about the Delphi investigations while in Vegas.

Then came this exchange where Kline admits he talked to Libby the day she was killed.

---

94. Warrant—State of Indiana Vs. Kegan A. Kline. Transcript. https://www.wishtv.com/wp-content/uploads/2022/03/Tx-statement-Kegan-Kline-10-19-2-FINAL-VERSION-Redacted-1.pdf

95. Warrant—State of Indiana Vs. Kegan A. Kline. Transcript. https://www.wishtv.com/wp-content/uploads/2022/03/Tx-statement-Kegan-Kline-10-19-2-FINAL-VERSION-Redacted-1.pdf

**Q**: and one of the girls that got killed you talked to. Including the day of.

**KLINE**: Okay then I mean a lot of people get—

Q: She—

**KLINE**: killed and then people talked to 'em what do you mean? That doesn't mean I killed them.[96]

Kegan admitted sending a photo to Libby of anthony_ shots in a Ferrari. Then he finally admitted he had been talking to Libby for several days.

The investigators pointed out that on the day of the murder, two devices at Kegan's house were both logged into the anthony_shots device at about the same time. One of the investigators said, "Eight o'clock in the morning at your house, where you and your dad lived, two separate devices see the numbers here how they're the same? Log in, log out. One device. Log in, log out. All within minutes of each other to the same Anthony Shots Snapchat account."[97]

The detective also tells Kline: "Regardless of what you say, there are two different authors of those messages. They're not you. They're both your devices but the phrasing is different. It changes. It's not the same person. So, we know we have multiple logins with Snapchat, we have two different people using Kik messenger, talking to people from your residence."[98]

Later, Kegan is confronted with evidence that he said he was supposed to meet Libby that day.

96. Warrant—State of Indiana Vs. Kegan A. Kline. Transcript. https://www.wishtv.com/wp-content/uploads/2022/03/Tx-statement-Kegan-Kline-10-19-2-FINAL-VERSION-Redacted-1.pdf

97. Warrant—State of Indiana Vs. Kegan A. Kline. Transcript. https://www.wishtv.com/wp-content/uploads/2022/03/Tx-statement-Kegan-Kline-10-19-2-FINAL-VERSION-Redacted-1.pdf

98. Warrant—State of Indiana Vs. Kegan A. Kline. Transcript. https://www.wishtv.com/wp-content/uploads/2022/03/Tx-statement-Kegan-Kline-10-19-2-FINAL-VERSION-Redacted-1.pdf

**Q**: anthony_shots says 'yeah we were supposed to meet but she never showed up.'

**KLINE**: That's a fucking lie. That's a damn lie.[99]

When asked how knew it was a lie, Kegan said, "Because I didn't fucking murder someone, yeah, so I know."[100]

On the day of the ski-mask incident, they told Kegan they know he did internet searches involving the family of the girl who saw Ski-Mask Man. He responds, "Right. Okay."

Kegan also admitted talking to Libby once more.

**Q**: You're the one that talked to her all weekend?

**KLINE**: I guess, yeah.[101]

Later, Deputy Clinton goes further:

**Q**: So now we're worried about grooming. We have-we have a guy that has troves of child pornography on his devices. We have Liberty being groomed and unfortunately she was completely enthralled with anthony_shots. Completely like though, you know, I'm talking to this rich hot guy. I'm you know like as she is completely in love with Anthony_shots.

**KLINE**: Right.[102]

99. Warrant—State of Indiana Vs. Kegan A. Kline. Transcript. https://www.wishtv.com/wp-content/uploads/2022/03/Tx-statement-Kegan-Kline-10-19-2-FINAL-VERSION-Redacted-1.pdf

100. Warrant—State of Indiana Vs. Kegan A. Kline. Transcript. https://www.wishtv.com/wp-content/uploads/2022/03/Tx-statement-Kegan-Kline-10-19-2-FINAL-VERSION-Redacted-1.pdf

101. Warrant—State of Indiana Vs. Kegan A. Kline. Transcript. https://www.wishtv.com/wp-content/uploads/2022/03/Tx-statement-Kegan-Kline-10-19-2-FINAL-VERSION-Redacted-1.pdf

102. Warrant—State of Indiana Vs. Kegan A. Kline. Transcript. https://www.wishtv.com/wp-content/uploads/2022/03/Tx-statement-Kegan-Kline-10-19-2-FINAL-VERSION-Redacted-1.pdf

He was then confronted with the fact he deleted his search history from February 10 through 15. Not only that but his device was searching "non stop" for Delphi information while he is supposed to be in Vegas and one of the investigators said, "You're still sending Snapchats to Libby when you know she's dead."[103]

They pushed Kegan about his alibi, about him and Tony being at Kegan's grandparents by asking him if he often looked at porn at his grandparents' house because "that's what you were doing on your phone."[104]

The investigators told Kegan they believe he knows who killed the girls and remind him once more that Durk would have no ability to have access to his phone when almost all of this was happening. Kegan again said that only he, Kegan, had access to the anthony_shots profile.

Just before the interview ends, the detective reminded Kline that when he was asked if he knew who killed Libby and Abby, "you did say no both times in your polygraph and guess what, that was deception."[105]

The interview concluded with Kegan saying he would do anything he could to help.

This whole interview appears to be incredibly damning. If neither Kegan nor his father were involved in these murders, it will be difficult to wrap one's head around that.

Kline told investigators he didn't exchange photos with Libby but did admit to receiving photos from a friend of hers who was at the same sleepover.

---

103. Warrant—State of Indiana Vs. Kegan A. Kline. Transcript. https://www.wishtv.com/wp-content/uploads/2022/03/Tx-statement-Kegan-Kline-10-19-2-FINAL-VERSION-Redacted-1.pdf

104. Warrant—State of Indiana Vs. Kegan A. Kline. Transcript. https://www.wishtv.com/wp-content/uploads/2022/03/Tx-statement-Kegan-Kline-10-19-2-FINAL-VERSION-Redacted-1.pdf

105. Warrant—State of Indiana Vs. Kegan A. Kline. Transcript. https://www.wishtv.com/wp-content/uploads/2022/03/Tx-statement-Kegan-Kline-10-19-2-FINAL-VERSION-Redacted-1.pdf

Investigators said they knew Libby was speaking to anthony_shots at the sleepover the night before she went to the Delphi trail with Abby. Police believe Libby was being groomed by the account and was "completely enthralled with Anthony Shots."[106]

Kline also said his father was "freaking out" when Kline told him in February 2017 that detectives said Kline was a suspect in the Delphi murders. Kline told McDonald his father weighs two hundred eighty pounds, that he is a deer hunter, and was robust enough to walk through the woods and strong enough to retrieve a deer.

106. Warrant—State of Indiana Vs. Kegan A. Kline. Transcript. https://www.wishtv.com/wp-content/uploads/2022/03/Tx-statement-Kegan-Kline-10-19-2-FINAL-VERSION-Redacted-1.pdf

# It Takes Two

Six of Kegan's devices were seized by detectives during the raid. They consisted of several smartphones, a tablet, and an iPod touch.

According to the affidavit, the iPod touch had last been used in May 2015 and contained explicit images of children. An iPhone, which had also last been used around the same time, contained sexual images of children around the age of fourteen. Additionally, a Samsung Galaxy was found to contain images of children aged between twelve and seventeen. On a second iPhone, investigators reportedly found sexual images of children between twelve and seventeen, adults involved in sexual acts with children between the ages of three and eleven, and images of drugs, and Kline holding a black handgun.

The seized tablet, meanwhile, had conversations on Facebook Messenger, showing the user speaking to young girls and asking them to continue the conversation on Kik or Snapchat.

A second Samsung Galaxy recovered was factory reset on February 23, 2017—nine days after the murders.

During the raid, Tony and Kegan were the only two living there. Police confiscated a whole bunch of devices, but they failed to collect one of his phones. He gave it to them the next day, after an attempt to wipe it clean.

How and why could they not find this phone? Was he hiding it somewhere? Was it stored off the property? Was it just an oversight? What is so different about it?

And why did he bother to turn it in? He isn't so dumb he doesn't know they'll know he has it, so he better look like a good guy and turn it in.

Quickly, they realized he tried to scrub it. While young people are constantly upgrading their devices and this was the one he was using to commit these crimes, it is believed this one device is the only one he used to communicate with Libby. It seems like he is aware that's the phone he wants to try to wipe.

Kegan looks dumb, but he isn't. He admits to things at times and forgets things at times. But it seems like he is protecting someone; whether that is himself or someone else is hard to say. He never throws his dad under the bus, but when he must have an alibi on February 13, he says he and his dad went to his grandparents' house, so now there are multiple alibis. Kegan goes there three or four days a week; it would be easy for them to get confused.

But his dad didn't have to work that day. Tony Kline, who works for Chrysler, doesn't work Mondays.

Not that I ever will need an alibi, as far as you know anyway, but if I do, I will use my folks. That's right, Mom, you remember, I was here that day.

We know anthony_shots talked to Libby right before she was murdered. We know he was also talking to another girl a week later, right before a guy in a ski mask showed up outside her window.

Let's get a bit more into Ski-Mask Man, shall we? According to transcripts, a middle school-age girl named Alexis, in Galveston, Indiana, messaged the anthony_shots account that she wanted to hook up after school. She had been writing back and forth with the account for a while and was infatuated with Anthony.

She said her parents wouldn't be home and shared her address. When she got off the bus a day later, on February 20, 2017, she saw a man in a ski mask peering into her bedroom window and called police.

I mean, come on. To me, it's extremely probable Bridge Guy is Ski-Mask Man. The girls were abducted and killed the Monday before. Not only that, but Ski-Mask Man is also outside of this girl's home about the same time the girls were killed.

I have difficulty thinking that is a coincidence. If it is a coincidence, I would leave Carrol County because you've got two creeps at large out there.

Police asked Kline about Ski-Mask Man specifically and executed a search warrant days after the murders. Data from Kline's computer shows he searched for members of that girl's family on Facebook the day before the peeping incident.

The thing is, this girl wanted to hook up with anthony_ shots. The girl eventually came clean and said she gave her address to a young guy who doesn't look like the guy in the ski mask. Online, he is a young Justin Bieber-type guy; the chances of her giving out her address the day before and then having this dude outside of the house being a coincidence are slim.

This girl knew Liberty German well. Libby stayed at this girl's house weeks before she was killed. Libby and Alexis talked about anthony_shots when she stayed over. Libby said she was infatuated with anthony_shots too. Both wanted to go out with him. To me, it would be a credible hypothesis that she told Kegan via the fake account that she was going to the bridge that day with a friend (at minimum), and (at maximum) had gone there to meet him and brought a friend along for protection, as ironic as that might be.

Why aren't Kline or his father being arrested? The elder Kline has prior convictions for sexual harassment and battery.

Well, the most likely reason is because they don't know which person it could be. Both are reasonable doubt for the other. If you charge Kegan, his defense attorney will say, "He didn't do it, his dad did." If you charge Tony, his defense attorney will say, "He didn't do it, Kegan did."

If they mess up and charge the wrong one, then the case is over. If they had evidence that two people were at the crime scene, I think both these guys would have been charged. The problem is the evidence suggests one person did it.

Years ago, when I said there may be two killers or the killer is getting help possibly through a false alibi, I thought I was going to get laughed out of the room. Here we are, six years later, and at this point in the investigation it is looking like from my perspective that the two best suspects are a father and a son living together and probably participating together in these sick and deviant activities.

They tried everything to get Kegan to break on his dad, but he didn't. Does that mean Kegan didn't do it, so he doesn't feel threatened? Is he scared of his father and won't rat him out?

Or maybe he did do it but he knows if they had anything on him, they would have charged him by now.

I have always been confused about how two guys come up with this type of idea in the first place. Two guys decide to murder, or to abduct and rape women or children—how does that start? Which one of these assholes brought this up first?

"Hey, I've been thinking about raping someone."

"No way! I was thinking about doing that too."

It happens though. On January 27, 2001, two teenagers, James Parker and Robert Tulloch, committed what is known as the Dartmouth murders when they killed Half and Susanne Zantop, both of who were professors at Dartmouth University. Tulloch was the leader of the two, while Parker just followed along. Both wound up pleading guilty: Parker to second-degree murder and Tulloch to first-degree murder.

In another well-known case, a fourteen-year-old boy, Bobby Franks, was murdered by Nathan Leopold and Richard Loeb. Both young men were from wealthy and socially established Jewish families. The two were in a romantic relationship and often committed petty crimes just for the fun of it. They killed Franks simply to commit the perfect crime. And because they could. Both were sentenced to life in prison for murder, with an additional ninety-nine years tacked on for kidnapping.

Sometimes if you're thinking about doing something crazy, or evil, it just helps to have someone else around to make you feel better about yourself.

I was convinced that Tony and Kegan are involved in these murders. I think law enforcement accepts that Tony was using Kegan's phones and catfishing accounts from their home network, and they know which devices and (for the most part) which activity was Tony versus Kegan based on timestamps, writing style, devices, and so on.

The circumstances of the crime strongly suggest that it wasn't random. Therefore, law enforcement has said in press conferences from the beginning that it is possible but not likely that the girls were murdered in a random attack. Common sense and Occam's razor both dictate that these girls were targeted and perhaps even lured to the trails. The location was chosen because the girls would be there, not the other way around.

This is a low-risk environment with low-risk victims. It would be a different calculation if, say, Libby or Abby were alone, riding a bike along a road. Many children have been abducted by a stranger into a car because that's an effective and pretty discreet way to kidnap and kill a child. But taking on two children, one of whom was the size of an adult, in these circumstances? It's unlikely someone looking for a random thrill kill is going to hunt on a trail, on foot, in a remote corner of a very small town, on a Monday, at two in the afternoon, and decide on a pair of victims.

Anecdotal as they may be, it was the interviews with Tony's stepchildren that really convinced me, along with his arrest records/reports which include incidents of domestic violence and harassment.

I know there are a lot of sick people in the world, but pedophilia, sadism, and sociopathy are not exactly a common cocktail. While online pedophiles may be a dime a dozen, the type of person who could or would brutally murder two little girls isn't exactly hiding around every corner.

I believe in coincidences. I think they happen all the time. But this is a big coincidence to accept if you think anthony_shots had nothing to do with this. Even with all the sickos out there, I can't make myself believe these girls interacted with two of the worst types in a twenty-four-hour span. Is it possible? Sure. Is there a more likely alternative? Yes.

According to law enforcement, Kegan (or at least his phone) was on Wi-Fi and actively searching for child porn at his cousin's house on the afternoon of the thirteenth. He and his phone were not with Tony at the grandparents' house as he claims. Not having an alibi certainly isn't proof of guilt, but having your son fabricate one for you that later falls apart doesn't exactly scream innocence either.

Tony could be Bridge Guy. I feel like I can confidently exclude Kegan, I just think he's a bit too big, even in 2017. I know some disagree, but when I look at them side by side, he fails the eye test for me, but Tony doesn't. To me, his features resemble Bridge Guy if Bridge Guy is wearing a hat.

Whatever your criticism of law enforcement may be, the fact remains Tony was in their focus. They simply were not able to eliminate him at the time. They seem to feel as I do: Kegan is a disgusting criminal and a sick person, but he isn't the architect behind a double murder, is not the actual killer, and probably wasn't even present for the crime. I think that he knows his father did this, and that he enabled and helped him in some way, even if it was just by giving him access to Libby. I don't have a very strong opinion on Kegan's level of involvement. I wouldn't be shocked if it was only peripheral nor would I be shocked if it turned out he was instrumental, but regardless, he is secondary to Tony in my opinion.

In this crime, you have what seems to fit more with a targeted attack, and yet from the video, the girls presumably didn't identify the killer on sight. A catfishing scenario fits this perfectly. He knew the girls, but they didn't know him.

The most important thing is we are looking for someone unaccounted for from two to four on that day.

That two-hour window roughly fits into the time the Ski-Mask Man was seen. Do the two things have to be connected? No. But it's hard to shake the idea that they are, considering both this girl and Libby were talking to anthony_shots. Law enforcement says she was eager to meet him.

Tony works for Chrysler; he has worked there for years, making cars. Interesting enough, his work schedule is Tuesday through Friday, and he has had that schedule for years.

Then after the raid, they go to Vegas, which is bizarre. Someone who was ultimately charged with thirty counts of child sexual abuse materials was allowed to leave the state. It seems the police either didn't know they were going, or they didn't consider them suspects.

Kegan lies all the time—about who he is, how much money he has, his lifestyle. That is not terribly uncommon, but someone spending all their time online lying to underage girls is weird. Kegan has presented he was even living and working in Vegas for a period of time, but that can't be substantiated.

If your photo or voice was on TV in a murder investigation, it makes sense to want to leave. But Kegan's half-brother Bart said it was a trip that had been planned for a while and people in the family knew about it. It's so unclear what went on out there and how long they were gone.

Kegan was arrested August 29, 2020, for thirty counts of child sexual abuse material. The charges stem from a search of his Peru, Indiana, home on February 25, 2017, just eleven days after the bodies of Liberty German and Abigail Williams were discovered.

I understand justice can take a long time on occasion but how weird is this? They become aware of his illegal activities in February 2017 yet he isn't charged until three years later. Why the hell did it take so long? This disgusting catfisher was successfully targeting children.

Let's pretend Kegan and Tony have nothing to do with the murders. At the very least, Kegan is a horrible piece of shit just from what he has done. Did he slip through the cracks? What was he up to this whole time?

In an interview with Kegan's half-brother Bart, he tells the story of how he wasn't allowed to use a particular bathroom while growing up because it always had plumbing issues. One day, he used the toilet and to his dismay, clogged it. Tony saw what happened, got pissed, dragged the kid into the bathroom and shoved his head into the toilet, then pulled him out and banged his head into the sink. Bart was hurt and worried he was going to be killed. He escaped and ran out of the house.

When being interviewed, one of the police officers asked Kegan what should happen to a guy who loses it one day and slams his kid's head into the toilet and sink. Kegan said that if someone kills a kid, they should be put to death. Police didn't say he killed a child, so this was a very odd response. I don't think that Kegan had the slightest idea that the officers were directly referring to a story involving his family. If he did, he managed to sell me on another lie.

Then, after the transcripts of Kegan Kline's police interview found its way to the general public, the Indiana State Police made a "cover our ass" statement regarding the lack of haste in taking an obviously dangerous individual off of the streets. The Indiana State Police released that statement regarding Kegan Kline in December 2021:

> The Indiana State Police has received many media inquiries since our December 6th press release concerning "anthony_shots" and eventually the identification of Kegan Kline. Your questions are certainly relevant as they relate to a long, complex, and extremely complicated murder investigation.
>
> During the last nearly five years, we have conducted dozens of secondary investigations based on information we received. One of those investigations included a Possession of Child Pornography case resulting in the arrest of Kegan Kline. The information we had, have, and continue to receive concerning Kline has ebbed and flowed over these last few years. We understand there was a period of time that passed between 2017 and 2020 when Kline was not arrested and incarcerated for Possession of Child Pornography. Once the Indiana State Police presented the criminal case to the Miami County Prosecutor in June of 2020, immediate action was taken by both the Indiana State Police and the Miami County Prosecutor's Office, which ultimately resulted in Kline's arrest.
>
> Like so many other pieces of this investigation, we will always review, learn from, and make any necessary adjustments. We do not believe that any person has done anything intentionally wrong, but we will continue to critically evaluate our efforts.

We know there is enormous interest in the "WHY" of everything we do, but we cannot and will not speculate. One day you will have the opportunity to see and know what we do, and we look forward to that day.[107]

I think they're pretty sure or at least think they are that one of the Klines had to be involved. It's clear though that they lacked the evidence to prove which one. The problem for the prosecution is the other guy. He is your reasonable doubt. If it isn't a slam dunk, you're screwed.

Talk about reasonable doubt. Look at this creepy kid. He did it. Look at this creepy dad. He did it.

There is reasonable doubt even with the child sexual abuse material. It could have been Tony online checking out porn, but Kegan didn't throw Tony under the bus.

They tracked down the model used for the shots profile. The man's name is not being revealed to protect his identity, but he is a model and police officer. "It's frustrating, as a police officer, knowing that my photo was used for so many heinous crimes, and continues to be used as such," he said. "I feel incredibly helpless. I'd love to be there when they find this guy so I can throw the cuffs on him myself."[108]

In August 2022, Indiana State Police confirmed they had a dive team searching a river located just a few miles from the family home of Kline. Investigators would not say what they were looking for in the river nor how it could be connected to the Delphi murders case.

107. WISH-TV. "ISP Releases Statement on Delayed Kegan Kline Arrest, 'Anthony_shots' Profile." December 13, 2021. https://www.wishtv.com/news/crime-watch-8/isp-releases-statement-on-delayed-kegan-kline-arrest-anthony_shots-profile/

108. WTHR. "Man in photos on anthony_shots social media profiles responds to Delphi case." December 9, 2021. https://www.wthr.com/article/news/crime/delphi-girls-murdered/man-anthony-shots-social-media-account-responds-pictures-delphi-murders-abby-german-libby-williams/531-79f59e9f-0b93-4a78-bdf2-34017b2f8c6e

# WHAT DREAMS MAY COME

WWJD is an acronym that I heard for the first time when I was in high school, often used by Christians during times when they are seeking guidance. For those unfamiliar, it stands for WHAT WOULD JESUS DO?

In theory, one is to ask themselves, in a difficult situation, what would Jesus do? And then apply what you believe Jesus would do to your handling of a predicament. When I first heard WWJD and contemplated what that would or should mean for me, I arrived at the conclusion that Jesus would address situations, conflict, and even crisis with a level of peacefulness and understanding I would not be capable of but should strive to achieve. I'm still working on this.

I realize that you are not reading this book to hear me go on a Bible-thumping expedition nor do I plan to do so. But when it comes to a lot of the cases I review for the show, or just to satiate my own curiosities, I often pull out my WWJD card. Except I call it my WHAT WOULD JOHN DO? card. Or to better create my own acronym, maybe I should call it the WWJDD card: WHAT WOULD JOHN DOUGLAS DO?

John Douglas is a living legend. A retired FBI agent, he is sometimes best known as one of the agents who was instrumental in shaping the FBI's Behavioral Science Unit, aka the elite serial crime unit. The man is a literal pioneer of criminal profiling. John Douglas is most often referred to as the Mindhunter, which as many of you are aware was a wonderful series on Netflix based on real-life cases Douglas worked on. But it is also the title of one of Douglas' first books that he wrote with Mark Olshaker, someone who has assisted Douglas in writing many of his books.

Douglas' *Mindhunter* is one I have recommended countless times. In the prologue, titled "I Must Be in Hell," Douglas explains that at one point in his legendary career, he was finishing up the Wayne Williams/Atlanta child murders case in Atlanta, Georgia, when he was called out to San Francisco to work the Trailside Killer case. He was also flying still back and forth between Alaska and Seattle at the same time. In Alaska, Douglas was working on the Robert Hansen case. Hansen was a bakery owner who in his free time would pick up and kill sex workers. In Seattle, Douglas was an advisor for the Green River Task Force. This was one of the largest and longest serial killer investigations in American history. Keep in mind, the FBI headquarters, Douglas' home base, is in Quantico, Virginia. Douglas was regularly flying, working, and living out of hotels in several different time zones, often all in the same week.

This would catch up with him. Douglas eventually needed to be hospitalized due to fatigue, stress, and many other factors. Sadly, the job almost cost him his life. Douglas explains that there simply were not enough hours in a day for him to actively work all these cases at once. So, he employed a strange method where he tried to force himself to dream about the cases he was working and the killers he was trying to catch. For people like Douglas, in his line of work, the longer a case drags on, the longer a killer is out walking free, free to kill and kill again. When it comes to serial killers, if the law enforcement agency doesn't work the case intelligently, thoroughly, and efficiently, then people die and there will be more victims. Directly from Douglas' book, *Mindhunter:* "I'd try to force myself to dream about the case in hopes that that would lead me to some insight about it."[109]

I was elated to read this. First of all, I admired Douglas' dedication to the job and to the work that he was doing. Work that would ultimately help save lives and hopefully, in some small way, deter others from committing similar heinous acts. Secondly, I was surprised by his open-mindedness. Here is an educated individual. A pioneer in his profession. Schooled by the "just the facts, ma'am" buttoned-up agency that was the FBI at the time and he was willing to allow his subconscious dreams to be some small part of a contributing factor in his assistance of these very crucial investigations.

But the real reason I was elated to read this was because it was something I was doing already, completely by accident.

As said throughout this book, my preferred method of absorbing information on these cases is by way of reading. My preferred reading time is in bed with a good true-crime book or the iPad, reading about cases on the internet.

When I read, as most of us do, I become hyper-focused on the subject and the story. I read and digest every paragraph and thought as I slowly work myself into a state where my eyelids become the weight of garage doors, nearly impossible to keep open. Then, I fall asleep. Often into a deep sleep, one in which I hope to experience a vibrant and adventurous dream. But because many a night I am reading true crime right before falling asleep, it is not uncommon for me to dream about a real-life case that I am working on for the show or just reviewing.

Now, let's be clear: I am in the entertainment industry. I am a charitable person and actively work on some victim advocacy programs and cold-case assistance organizations, but the work I do does not hold a candle to the great import of someone like John Douglas.

109. Douglas, John; and Mark Olshaker. *Mindhunter: Inside the FBI's Elite Serial Crime Unit.* (Gallery Books, October 24, 2017).

What would John Douglas do when it comes to the Delphi murders case? We have some idea, due to an impromptu interview he did with *Inside Edition* in May 2019.

Just weeks earlier, the Delphi murders investigation took a sharp right turn when they announced to the public that they were "changing their investigative strategies" with the release of the newer sketch showing the "younger bridge guy." At that same press conference, they released an extended video of how Bridge Guy walks, and audio which they said may hold vital clues. Most specifically, the suspect's use of the word *guys*, which, on the clip is followed by "down the hill."

Of this, Douglas said, "That tactic, if they're going to do it, they should have done it two years ago."[110] Meaning, if they (law enforcement) are going to release information about the case to the public in hopes that the public can help law enforcement by returning information, they should have done that at the beginning. I agree with Douglas. It is not only likely but also easy to understand that this information in the hands of the public is of more value in 2017 than it is today.

On the word *guys*, Douglas says, "'Guys' says to me that maybe he may know these victims. Or it's a person ... someone who interacts with children."[111]

On the background of the suspect, Douglas says that the person who killed the two likely has some kind of criminal history. "You don't wake up one day and commit a double

110. *Inside Edition.* "Who Killed Abby and Libby? 'Mindhunter' John Douglas Offers Insight Into Delphi Murders." May 15, 2019. https://www.insideedition.com/who-killed-abby-and-libby-mindhunter-john-douglas-offers-insight-delphi-murders-52953.

111. *Inside Edition.* "Who Killed Abby and Libby? 'Mindhunter' John Douglas Offers Insight Into Delphi Murders." May 15, 2019. https://www.insideedition.com/who-killed-abby-and-libby-mindhunter-john-douglas-offers-insight-delphi-murders-52953..

homicide like this," he said. "There has to be some kind of trail."[112]

And finally, Douglas says about the suspect's post-offense behavior. "They should also be checking and looking to see people who were here, now they came up with some reason to leave the area."[113]

I was lucky enough to have had the privilege of interviewing John Douglas three times on *True Crime Garage*. Mr. Douglas always has an open invitation to come on the show anytime.

The first time I interviewed him was for a show we released in May 2019 titled "John Douglas—The Mind Hunter." That is episode number 302 on your *True Crime Garage* radio dial. To say that I was both nervous and excited at the opportunity would be an understatement. Douglas was coming on the show, not for my benefit, but as part of the promotional trail for his latest book at the time, *The Killer Across the Table*. I was told originally to limit my questions to the subjects in the book. This was somewhat difficult, given that the book was coming out the same week as our show. I was recording the interview the week before, during which I received an advanced copy from Dey Street, an imprint of HarperCollins.

Here I was, set to interview one of the few heroes I have, but I was scared I was in over my head. I had the task of releasing two episodes that week and the Douglas interview would only be enough for one episode. That meant I was going to have to prepare for the Douglas interview by reading his book, writing out my questions, and then

112. *Inside Edition*. "Who Killed Abby and Libby? 'Mindhunter' John Douglas Offers Insight Into Delphi Murders." May 15, 2019. https://www.insideedition.com/who-killed-abby-and-libby-mindhunter-john-douglas-offers-insight-delphi-murders-52953..

113. *Inside Edition*. "Who Killed Abby and Libby? 'Mindhunter' John Douglas Offers Insight Into Delphi Murders." May 15, 2019. https://www.insideedition.com/who-killed-abby-and-libby-mindhunter-john-douglas-offers-insight-delphi-murders-52953.

conducting the interview all the while putting together another episode about an entirely different case. Some of the requirements for *True Crime Garage* fall into the love/hate category. I both love and hate that we do a new case every week. Sure, sometimes we will spread a case out over the course of four episodes in a two-week timespan, but that week, the way that cookie crumbled—it was going to have to be two episodes each about a different case.

The other case we covered that week was an odd one. The case itself was odd but even more strange, it was a case that a law enforcement agency asked us to cover. This is rare but it happens on occasion. Police know that we can be a good, different, and possibly effective media platform. Sometimes you need someone to put a lot of ears on your case and we have fortunately earned the attention of many ears over the years. So, while I was nervous, overworked, and overwhelmed, I knew that I tend to shine when I find myself "up against it." And I was up against it. I decided to do the only thing that one could. I put my head down and got to work, hoping to have a little fun along the way.

When I called Mr. Douglas at our arranged date and time, the first thing I said was, "Hello, Mr. Douglas. My name is Nic Edwards from the *True Crime Garage* podcast. I'd like to ask you a few questions about Joseph Kondro."

Kondro was just one of several diabolical killers spotlighted in Douglas' new book. He replied, "Sure, Nic. You can ask me about Kondro or anything that you wish to talk about." I was over the moon. Here I was, worried and hoping to impress in a way that would allow me a possible second opportunity to speak with Douglas, and then I get him on the phone and he's a regular guy and as happy to talk about these cases as I am.

The second time I interviewed him, I was told in advance to feel free to ask John about anything I wanted. But knowing that he was coming on the show "not just for his health," he's got a book to promote, after all. I knew

I would revert to another one of my favorite acronyms. KISS—keep it simple, stupid. In that acronym, I'm stupid, by the way. I would limit my topics to cases I knew he was familiar with and his new book at the time, *The Killer's Shadow*. That interview played out in the November 2020 shows, episodes numbers 445 and 446 titled "Mind Hunter: John Douglas."

The last time that I interviewed Mr. Douglas, although hopefully it is not the last time, it turned into a three-episode series called, "When a Killer Calls," which was the name of his latest book. We released these episodes in February 2022. The case was about two murdered girls, Shari Smith and Debra May Helmick. Both poor victims were abducted and killed separately by the hands of the same evil man, Larry Gene Bell. It is unlikely they were his only victims.

Bell displayed what many would call a "signature" in the commission of committing these two murders. A signature is most commonly defined as an act carried out by the perpetrator that is not required in order to commit the crime but rather serves some kind of emotional or psychological need of the offender. The signature comes from within the psyche of the offender and reflects a deep fantasy need that the killer has about his victims. Oddly enough, one of the signatures on display by Bell when he abducted and killed the girls was he insisted on calling Shari Smith's family and speaking to her mother and sister on the phone at length.

This would be the first time that a telephone interview with John Douglas would not be a requirement. We were going to do the interview via the computer, using an audio-only meeting style. This was preferable to me. One, the audio quality is far superior. Two, this meant conducting the interview from the comfort of my home office. The two previous interviews were done in my car. This is because where I live cell service is sometimes spotty and because it was John Douglas that I was interviewing, and I would not dare deal with spotty cell coverage at the risk of annoying

Mr. Douglas. Each time I grabbed my notepad, jumped into my car, and drove twenty-five minutes to Columbus, where I sat in a parking lot where I knew cell phone service was always top notch and conducted the interviews.

On several occasions, I have fallen asleep while looking for clues or reading up on the Delphi case. Sometimes I don't remember dreaming about the case or anything at all. There are at least two times that I can think of where and when I have dreamt of Delphi, both times were after reading about the case extensively immediately before falling asleep.

On one occasion I dreamt that I could read some of the killer's thoughts. I could not "see" the thoughts or understand them. I could only "read" them. I couldn't get any background information on why he was thinking or behaving the way that he was or even his thought process toward his actions. I did not have a full or complete understanding of the who, what, why, or how.

What I could pick up on was that he was determined to kill that day. He was determined to do it near the trails but not on the trails. In the dream, Bridge Guy saw one of the girls and decided to approach. He spotted what he thought was an optimal victim from afar. He had decided well before going to the trails that day that he wanted a female victim and the younger the better. In the dream, this was not due to some sexual preference. No, because there was very little in the way of a sexual component to his motives that day. He wanted a young female victim because he had already decided that a young female victim would stand a much lesser chance of surviving. And the victim surviving was not an option for this man and his plans.

He wanted to catch his victim on or near the bridge. When he arrived that day, he parked near the cemetery. The cemetery was familiar to him. He knew he could walk from the back of the cemetery and get to the trails rather quickly. More importantly, he could park his vehicle in a location that would help to expedite his fleeing the scene. It was much more important that he be able to get out faster than he got in. The other important part of his plans for parking at the cemetery, when it came time for him to leave that day, was he wanted the path of least resistance. His trek from where he intended to make the kill to the security blanket of his vehicle parked at the cemetery would provide him with a shorter walk off the beaten path that would most likely allow him to flee without an eyewitness. When he arrived and made his way to the trails that day, he did not know whom he was going to kill. In fact, he didn't know if he was going to kill at all. He had been there before. Not a lot but a few times. He didn't kill then because he did not find his optimal victim in the location of the bridge.

The Monon High Bridge. To him, the bridge represented almost a trap for his victim. If he were to just see "her" there, he knew she was his. The bridge was his spider's web waiting to catch the unexpecting prey. If he should be there at the trails when his prey was to find itself caught in his spider's web trap, well, then, he would move in for the kill.

Bridge Guy now was on the trail side of the bridge. The same side that Libby and Abby approached the bridge from. He was not concerned about looking for a victim on the trails themselves. No, his concern was minding his trap. The trap was set, so he needed to watch the trap and wait for his optimal prey. He had a predetermined spot off the trails and in the woods. This is an elevated location where he could look down and clearly see the bridge and both sides. He wanted to see someone getting on the bridge and approach from the opposite side that he had come in on. In other words, he wanted to trap someone on the cemetery side of the bridge. He's perched up on a hill somewhere that is both within walking distance of the bridge so he could get to the bridge fast enough that once he made his move, he would be on the bridge before the victim could turn around and start making their way back across, but also deep enough in the woods that he would not be spotted by persons on the trails. He wanted the element of surprise on his side. He also wanted to be able to watch his trap knowing that no one had the ability to watch him while he was doing so. He spotted one of the girls getting on the bridge and, for whatever reason, did not see the other girl. He made his approach. Fast, quick but not running, just walking at a very steady and brisk pace.

Once he got down to the bridge, he saw the girl again. Maybe she looked a little different than she had before when he was on the hill, but he was not homing in on the details because they didn't matter. He simply cared to carry out his plan the way he had carved it out after many nights and a few days of careful and almost meticulous planning. The person he spotted was female, she appeared to be young and appeared to be alone. It was not until he was several steps onto the bridge and had already started to make his way across that he noticed that there were two. But the other person he spotted appeared to be a female as well and she too looked young. By the time he got near the other side of the bridge, he could see no one else ahead of them. They were out there, just the two of them. This was further confirmed to him by the girls' actions and because they stopped and did not continue to walk ahead.

They wanted to turn around and go back. Back to the good and safe side of the bridge. The side where they would like to see someone else, maybe even a familiar face. He turned to see that no one was behind him and if he could corral the girls quickly enough and take them further from the bridge, then he or they would not be seen. Once he caught them at the end of the bridge, he used some form of quiet control. In the dream, it was a gun. He walked them, directing them to where it was that he wanted to go. He needed to maintain control of the girls until they arrived at his predetermined location. This would be off the trail system and onto privately owned land. More specifically Ron Logan's land. In my dream, after Bridge Guy took control of the girls, the only thing he cared about was making sure that they were on Ron Logan's land. He was even double-checking this, so to speak. He wanted to be sure that the girls were on Logan's property because he intended to leave them there. My perception of what I was viewing in the dream was that where they were found was a critical motivating factor for the murders.

When I woke up, I thought, *this is crazy. I am crazy.*

At first, the dream made no sense to me at all. But I couldn't shake it and thought about it several times that morning. I wanted to make sense of it. I thought there could be something there. Some little, tiny nugget of something to delve deeper into. I could not get past the idea that Bridge Guy, in the dream, was consumed with making sure the girls were left on Ron Logan's property. At first, the thought was that this person hated Ron Logan. He was going to kill and so why not leave the victim or victims on the property of a person who lives very nearby and that Bridge Guy also disliked? Seemed easy enough. But then I continued to think on it. He was so purposeful in leaving the victims there. He could have obtained a victim anywhere and very likely somewhere less risky. That would mean that the trails were important to his plans as well and not for the sake of procuring a victim.

So why the trails and why Logan's property? Then the thought occurred to me, what if the intent of leaving the victims on Logan's property was not because Bridge Guy hated Logan? What if it were because he wanted to either frame Logan or cast all the suspicion on him? Not because he hated him but because he wanted to control Logan. Forcing Logan to do something he didn't want to, like move away. Or an all-out frame job that landed Logan in jail and on trial for murder. What if the plan was because of the value of Ron Logan's very desirable property?

I'm not going to get into a whole lesson about Indiana property laws as I don't know them. I did complete a course in State of Ohio real estate law more than a dozen years ago. A theory like this would fall into the old "follow the money" category. In this scenario, Ron Logan's land is the money or the thing of value. According to several online sources, Logan owned forty acres of land. Depending on whom you ask, some may even consider that to be "prime" real estate. At the time of the murders in 2017, from what I could find, he had either owned property or it had been in the Logan family for fifty-three years. Take that for what you will.

I've learned that in some cases, and this is most certainly one of them, you need to be willing to explore but also ready to move on. Getting back to reality, this was a dream with no real hardcore evidence to it at all. Actually, no evidence. It's just a thinking-outside-of-the-box idea. But maybe Douglas was onto something with this dreaming-about-the-case idea. Could he or someone in a position to solve a case use this method to provide themselves with an outside-of-the-box theory or theories?

Yes, and I will tell you why with another dream I had, watching portions of the case events playing out in my sleep.

This dream was much shorter. In this dream, it was simply very brief moments leading up to the actual abduction. This time I could not read anyone's thoughts, but I could witness and understand someone's actions. I could see Libby and I focused in on her face at close range, but I could see and understand some of her actions at the same time. In this dream, something tipped the girls off and told them to be afraid, Libby in particular. This was because the girls had encountered Bridge Guy prior to either of them getting on the bridge.

When they encountered him, we must ask ourselves, was he wearing a face covering at that time? If so, this could have been off-putting to the girls. Or perhaps it was something else. However, they continued on their way to the bridge because he was traveling in the opposite direction, and they assumed he was leaving the trail area and they would not encounter him again.

Why would this make any difference at all? Well, ask yourself this. Let's say it were late at night and you find yourself arriving in a parking lot. You are all set to get out of your vehicle when something catches your eye. It's a man you do not know and for some reason, you get a feeling that this man could be dangerous. What scenario would make you feel a little better? The man was just arriving to the parking lot as you were, or he was heading in the direction of exiting the parking lot?

Now back to the dream. By this point, the girls are on the bridge and Libby spotted the man they had encountered earlier, but now he is approaching the bridge. This totally sets off her spidey-senses. Libby reaches for her phone, gets set to call a parent or even 911, and gets the dreaded NO SERVICE warning or notification. Libby is a fast thinker and so she knows that in situations when and where there is no service, calls cannot be made and many apps are useless, but *some* of the phone's utility apps run off of battery power and the phone's storage. In a desperation play (or a punt, if you will), she films Bridge Guy with her phone, then gets scared and worries Bridge Guy sees her using the phone.

According to ScienceABC.com, "If you happen to be in a place where there is absolutely no network coverage by a service provider, this is bad news. Since there is no network tower nearby that can receive and send your phone's signals, your phone becomes completely ineffective. Given this, it is essential for people who travel to remote places to explore the hinterland and unknown places to have communications security in the form of satellite telephones or radios in emergencies requiring immediate assistance."[114] That, from my understanding, is pertaining to the use of calls and texts.

But how could this be because of Libby's known phone usage that day? According to many sources, at 2:07 p.m., Libby takes a picture of Abby walking on the Monon High Bridge and posts it to her Snapchat story. This picture would be the last communication from Abby or Libby.

She had network coverage and was connecting to a cell tower then, but the Ron Logan warrant indicated, "at approximately 2:13 p.m. which was the time of last contact with LG [Liberty German] and AW [Abigail Williams] by cellular device."[115] Does that mean the cell service was lost at that time?

We don't know but we have all been in the situation when we have network coverage and then minutes or seconds later, boom—we don't. I am certainly not saying that I am right about any of this. In fact, I have never mentioned these dreams at length on *True Crime Garage*.

They are just simply dreams but are interesting angles in which to look at this case.

No one knows for sure why the girls videotaped Bridge Guy. This is a thought that could explain it.

114. ScienceABC.com. "How can Mobile Phones Make Emergency Calls When There's No Network Coverage?" July 8, 2022. https://www.scienceabc.com/innovation/how-can-mobile-phones-make-emergency-calls-when-theres-no-network-coverage.html

115. Logan Warrant. https://interactive.wthr.com/pdfs/logan-warrrant.pdf

# PURGATORY

The previous portions of this book were written before the arrest of Richard Allen on October 28, 2022. So now, I begin to inch my way toward the current day and where the investigation stands. There have been a lot of peaks and valleys experienced by investigators and followers of this case. In between, there has been a lot of waiting and hoping. Hoping that soon these poor girls' families will get some answers, and the community, the State of Indiana, and frankly parents everywhere could rest a little easier at night knowing the threat is gone. Removed. Exterminated like a cockroach. We waited and waited, but it began to feel like we may never get answers or never identify those responsible.

Life moved on after the murders, whether we wanted it to or not. Whether we could handle it or not. Life moved on without Abby and Libby. In all the other cases we have discussed, life moved on without those victims as well, but we held tightly and so dearly to the memories and spirits of those bright lives and beautiful souls everyone loved and missed so much.

The Bible tells us that children go to heaven, and why shouldn't they? Children are the definition of innocent. Abby, Libby, and all the other child victims we have discussed in this book are all uncorrupted by evil, malice, or wrongdoing. They were too young for such sin to enter their hearts and minds. In this case, the only evil that those girls knew was the evil that intercepted them that day on that bridge.

All children go to heaven. Hopefully, there is something peaceful and healing in that notion, especially for those closest to the victims.

I'm not here to thump you with a Bible and if you don't believe in such things, please pardon my mentions of it but don't dismiss it. These cases are, in the greater scheme of things, a battle of good versus evil. We need to know and be reminded that good triumphs over evil. Solving this case by making an arrest would certainly help. The man on the bridge, his image on the television and computer screens walking across that bridge, his voice directing the girls "down the hill." Those are symbols and signs of evil. Pure evil. We need champions of good as well. The champions so clearly are Libby and Abby's families; in some unexplainable way, they were helping us, the public, to cope with and accept this tragedy. Both families showed enormous amounts of courage and grace. Doug Carter and the women and men of the law enforcement agencies working this case and the others discussed in this book are our champions as well.

I've been very lucky. I have not had to experience first-hand tragedy to any degree that is equivalent to the loss discussed in these cases. But regardless of our life experiences, hope and good, and reminders that both exist, are necessary.

Children go to heaven. I thought of the Bible and my own weird version of my own spirituality many times during the late nights poring over this case. It was easy to do. Reach out and grasp tightly that hope. But then hold on for dear life because sometimes these cases can take years or even decades to solve.

We were in purgatory. The wait for something to happen was heavy and seemed endless. I can only begin to imagine what that heavy burden felt like for the investigators. Life and the investigation moved on without Abby and Libby. While that may be a sad thought, it's an important one to remember and can be uplifting when gazed upon from certain angles. They are now in heaven. At peace.

While we sat in purgatory, we could only hope that the killer or killers were experiencing personal and private hell worse than anything we could possibly imagine. On April 22, 2019, during the press conference announcing the new sketch of Bridge Guy, Doug Carter looked and sounded like he was holding back tears. Toward the end of his speech, he said, "To the murderer: I believe you have just a little bit of a conscience left. And I can assure you that how you left them in those woods is not, *is not* what they are experiencing today."[116]

He was right. What the killer remembers of that day and how he left them in those woods is not what Abby and Libby are experiencing today.

Following the lead of Doug Carter, I write this to the murderer of two young girls.

I don't think that you have any conscience left. I agree with Carter one hundred percent, that only a coward would do such a thing. And I too can assure you that how you left them in those woods is not—*is not*—what they are experiencing today. They are in a better place and not because of you, but because of the beautiful lives they created for themselves and the beautiful lives provided to them by the ones that loved them. They were loved in a way that you have not experienced. They gave love that you are incapable of giving.

---

116. WFLITV. April 22, 2019. "Delphi Homicide News Conference: ISP release video, additional audio and a new sketch of the suspect." https://www.youtube.com/watch?v=WfJQINVMWPE

You know this about yourself, and you have known it for a long time. You know that you are different. You know that you are not special. You know that you are damaged goods. Only a coward would do such a thing. When you walked onto the trails and stepped onto that bridge, you were playing out some twisted weird game of power and control. You thought that you would leave there that day feeling different and better. You thought all your deep-rooted personal feelings of inadequacy would be conquered by you then and there that day. You thought the perverted little coward would be elevated to something more than just gross and pathetic. You assumed that you could hurt someone and become more than what you are. You may have even believed that you could be, for the very first time in your life, something special.

But here's the truth of it: You did nothing special. You are not and have never been strong or in control. You were playing this game of power and control, but you were the only one who knew the rules. You were only able to victimize children who were never allowed to know that this game was being played. You stacked the deck against babies. Yes, you may have the images stored in your VCR brain but that is not what they are experiencing today, and they never will again.

What really happened was that you walked out of those woods even more scared and unsure of yourself than ever. You returned to your "life" and your routines more convinced than ever before that you are not special. You are not significant. Your existence is meaningless. You're a fraud and a loser. You are so very scared of everything and everyone but now you experience something you never imagined. Now you fear the ones closest to you. That you may be exposed or exposed by those who surround you. So regardless of what the rest of us are experiencing for you, I hope it's hell.

# Today is the Day!

Any working stiff will tell you that for some mysterious reason, Thursdays just feel different. Perhaps that's because on a Friday, sometimes you have earned the right to piss off if you wish.

On Thursday, October 27, 2022, I was heavily invested in a cold case. It's not uncommon for me to be "working" on several cases. I don't recommend taking on more than three at a time, but I've put myself in a position where I don't get to choose the number of cases I'm involved in.

I refer to what I do as "working" cases. I know it's a strange thing to say. After all, I'm not law enforcement, not even a licensed private investigator, but I am a private investigator for the show. Not always, but a lot of the time, we are doing much more than just covering a story. What we do often involves getting in touch with someone with first-hand knowledge of the victim, the crime, or the investigation. We want to be able to tell you a part of the story that you have never heard before. You can't do that by writing a simple book report. Plus, we are actively asking the public for help on these cases.

I always have next week's case to work on. A full case to try to research, examine, and write down everything along the way. I have cases that I work for a non-profit organization called the Porchlight Project here in Ohio. We assist law enforcement and families in Ohio cold cases. I always have one or two that I am working for them. Not only that, I have the baggage of the last two cases covered on *True Crime Garage* wrapped around me at times like a weighted belt. It's in that two-week window that if we are going to get a lead, that is when it is going to come in.

Then I have the cases I can't let go of. Delphi has been at the top of the list for over six years. But it was not Abby and Libby's case on my mind that night. It was an Ohio cold case. One of the coldest in my recent memory. I had just learned of it three months earlier, but it was a mystery from long ago.

On a November night in 1960, in the tiny town of Paulding, Ohio, someone abducted, raped, and murdered fourteen-year-old Nancy Eagleson. She was walking home with her little sister from an afternoon at the local movie theatre. The Eagleson case was open but of course due to the passage of time, it wasn't what I would call active. There was no physical evidence in Nancy's case. Other than witness statements, there was no evidence at all. No one could agree on a suspect, and I was hooked, almost as deep as Delphi. This thing got its hooks in me and it wasn't going to let go anytime soon.

I was spending that Thursday night tearing through the file I had created. Much of it was the actual police file from the Paulding County Sheriff's Office. Through several channels, I was able to get my hands on my own version of the original police file. There was no physical evidence, but I was hoping that would change. The non-profit I was working for was able to jump through some legal hoops and have the body of Nancy Eagleson exhumed. Hopefully, the exhumation would change the status of our lack of any physical evidence. On Friday morning, I was going to head back up that way toward Paulding to follow up on an item or two. Paulding County shares the state line of Ohio with Indiana. This meant getting up early and driving two and a half hours up to Paulding County. I wanted to get there at a decent time in hopes that I could make it back home by five or six p.m.

I got a good start that morning and made it up there by ten. This was shaping up to be a good day. If everything fell into place, I might be done and home by four.

But then I got a text from a friend in law enforcement in Indiana. The text read, INSIDER BASEBALL... INDIANA STATE POLICE MADE A MASSIVE ARREST TODAY. Then my phone buzzed again. It was a new text from the same sender. That simply read, DELPHI.

I wanted to get home immediately. I was more than two hours away from my home computer. I needed to know more. I finished up what I was doing and rushed through a few more things and by one, I was on the road home. By this point, my phone would not stop. I was getting messages from friends, listeners, other podcasters, and even law enforcement. Everyone was hungry to know more. I was racing toward Delaware County and all I knew was this...

Richard Allen was the man's name. There was going to be a press conference on Monday. Until then, it's Richard Allen from Delphi, he's got a wife and family, he's on Facebook, and there was a big smile on my face.

As I gripped the steering wheel and continued to push the envelope on how fast one can travel without getting pulled over, all I kept thinking was, *Today is the day*.

"Today is the day," I said it to myself. Then I repeated it several times out loud and then yelled it from the top of my lungs, "Today is the day!"

The Delphi double murder investigation was certainly one hell of a roller coaster ride and the cars on the track might as well have been shaped like questions marks. A true case of many highs and so many lows. Many times, there were rumors that seemed credible making the rounds. I often found that with a little digging, I could easily determine that there was no real new news or information coming out regarding the investigation and the rumor was just that, a rumor. Sometimes a cigar is a celebration and other times, a cigar is just a smoke. With Delphi to this point, they all had been just smoke.

*Today is the day.* I don't know who started saying it first, but I knew exactly what it meant. It meant today is the day that we catch the person or persons responsible for murdering two little girls. Becky Patty, Libby's grandmother, posted "Today is the day" almost every day on Twitter.

Just like those crosses that dot the Indiana landscape, "Today is the day" was another symbol of hope. If we start each day off saying that today is the day, well, then, we are sending off well wishes to the families, to law enforcement, and to anyone who may be able to help. It's all about sending out some good vibes into the universe. I love when things return to me, especially when it's a karma thing.

The first thing I was going to do when I got home was check Becky Patty's Twitter feed. I wanted that cigar now more than ever. I wanted to see on Becky's feed, not a hopeful "today is the day" but a definitive "TODAY IS THE DAY!"

After pulling into my driveway, I put the car in park. Before getting out, I checked Becky's Twitter. On her feed was those four words she posted often, but on previous days, the words were always next to some very uplifting image. Most of the time a flower or a sunset, always something inviting and beautiful. On this day, the post was different. "Today is the day!!!" was posted below an image of many of the law enforcement officials who worked the case over the years along with a post from Libby's older sister Kelsi, which confirmed what so many had hoped for and prayed about for over five years.

Someone had been arrested. Details were coming by way of a press conference but that would have to wait until Monday.

October 31, 2022. Halloween. I woke up on this Monday in a cheap hotel room near Cleveland, Ohio. The Captain, my partner in crime, was in England. This would be the first time we were going to be recording an emergency podcast while neither of us were in our garage studio. This presented some technical issues but more than that, it just felt weird.

It was no surprise to me that from Friday afternoon, when the arrest was announced, to that Monday morning, rumors were again swirling like a violent tornado around the ether. How did police identify Richard Allen as Bridge Guy? Were there other persons involved? How did he manage to hide in plain sight for over five years? Was it DNA that provided the break in the case? Everyone wanted to know and of course I did too.

On that Monday, the Captain and I, along with hundreds of thousands of people, tuned into the press conference and hung on every word. What details were they going to tell us? What would we learn about the accused? How did they catch him? Why did it take so long?

Immediately after the press conference, we connected via computer. Rather than talk through what we learned as usual, we hit record. When it is case related, we made a rule long ago: don't talk about the case until we are on microphone. Lightning very rarely strikes twice and if there was going to be some electricity in the conversation, then we want to capture it and get it on the record.

There are two things that I absolutely have become accustomed to with this investigation. If there is going to be "good" information coming out in this case, it will most likely come out on a Monday. There may be news, but the investigators won't really tell you much of anything.

We already knew that the Monday box was going to be checked. At the conclusion of the press conference, the not-much-information box was filled in as well.

We learned nothing of the accused. We learned nothing of the evidence. What we *did* learn was some of the court documents pertaining to the arrest were sealed and the prosecutor wanted to keep it that way. They confirmed what we already knew: Richard Allen, a local man, was formally charged with the murders of Abby and Libby.

We reported as much on our emergency podcast that day. We owed it to our wonderful listeners to discuss the press conference. To offer up our thoughts, insights, and of course even toss in some questions of our own. We did add some information that was not discussed in the press conference. We reported that yes, Richard Allen was local and lived close to the crime scene. In fact, he was one point six miles away. A five-minute drive to where the girls were found. We reported that he is married with one grown child, who was old enough to have a family of their own. We added that he worked at a local CVS and had lived in Delphi since 2007.

One item of particular interest was I found record of Allen filing for and obtaining weapons permit in June 2009. This was a concealed carry firearms permit. This convinced me of two things that were long suspected. First, he lived and worked in close proximity to the trail system and the bridge; there was no doubt in my mind he had been there before and likely regularly. He knew the trails and knew them well. He knew the bridge and had crossed it before that day. He likely even snooped around on the other side of that bridge just to see what was there or, more importantly, was not there. With this kind of first-hand knowledge of the trails and bridge, he would have also known who to expect to see on the trails that day. Meaning, if he was looking for a certain victim type, he went there that day expecting that he just may find what he was looking for.

The second item was this weapons permit. Many of us thought if someone was out there alone and abducted the girls, he would need to process the ability to control them. We know he abducted and at least attempted to control their movements by the recording, but how did he do it? The obvious answer is his concealed firearm. He concealed the gun, of course, from several people there on the trails that day, but when he saw his prey, he swooped in and as he approached, he made this weapon visible to them and intercepted the girls on the bridge.

Then there it was, pulled from my mailbox: the weekly edition of the *Carroll County Comet*. On the front page of the paper was a picture of the accused. Allen looked like an average Joe. Nothing about him was remarkable in appearance or distinguished. He had a goatee with long straggly white and grey hairs that hung below his chin. He was sporting a tight buzz cut and an orange jailhouse jumpsuit. His expression was blank and his eyes were distant. This was the face of evil.

The headline: DELPHI MAN FORMALLY CHARGED WITH TWO COUNTS OF MURDER.

The article read, in part:

> The Indiana State Police (ISP) issued a press release on Monday and conducted a press conference, about the arrest of Richard Matthew Allen, 50, of Delphi for the double homicide of Abigail Williams and Liberty German, which happened Feb. 13, 2017, near the Monon High Bridge near Delphi. Allen was formally charged with two counts of murder on Oct. 28. Allen is being held, without bond, in the White County Jail. ISP indicated the arrest was made Oct. 26 by the "Delphi Double Homicide Task Force" following a long and complex investigation. ...

According to information presented at the Oct. 31 Press Conference, an Omnibus (or preliminary) Hearing is scheduled for Jan. 13 at 9 a.m. and a trial date has been set for March 20 at 9 a.m. [117]

---

117. *Carroll County Comet*. "Delphi man formally charged with two counts of murder." November 2, 2022. https://www.carrollcountycomet.com/articles/delphi-man-formally-charged-with-two-counts-of-murder/

Carroll County Prosecutor Nicholas McLeland said at the press conference the probable cause affidavit and charging information are sealed. This meant we would not be able to learn what exactly led to this man's arrest and what evidence they had to secure the arrest warrant from a judge. The news was good, but the information lacked any details or specifics. Authorities made sure to say that the case remains active and an ongoing investigation, with a reminder of where to direct tips and information from the public by calling 765-564-3535 or email **abbyandlibbytip@ cacoshrf.com**.

At the press conference, a family member of one of the victims told the *Comet* there would be a hearing November 22 to decide what information would be released to the public.

So after a quick cigar and celebration, we returned to purgatory, once again waiting for more, but joining us this time was Richard Allen, who was being held without bond in the White County Jail. For him, I hope it feels like hell.

# THE FACE OF EVIL

Unfortunately, no community is immune from evil entering their lives at any given time. We always hear that old familiar phrase, "That would never happen here." But that, frankly, is just not true.

We would like to think that we can create safe environments for everyone to raise their families. The cynics will say nay, we can and we do. Everyday. We have built and maintained so many wonderful and beautiful neighborhoods and communities in this country. But we can't guard that wall every second of everyday and unfortunately, so often, evil can look just like you and me. We want to believe that if evil were lurking nearby, we would be aware. Art imitates life and in return we can at times believe that the reverse is also true. If life were to imitate art, well, then, we would be able to spot evil. If only that were true. It would be so easy to quickly distinguish the "good guys" from the "bad guys," but that is just not the case.

William Shakespeare said, "Hell is empty and all the devils are here." I refuse to share such a bleak outlook on this beautiful world and the wonderful communities we have created. However, he is not entirely wrong. Evil is real and we have pointed to some prime examples of such throughout these pages.

The case known far and wide and, in many circles, simply as Delphi is one of the most horrific murder cases in Indiana since April Tinsley. In April's case, we waited so very long to see some justice. Thankfully, the good women and men of the Indiana State Police and their counterparts never gave up, they never gave in, and justice came. After the arrest of Richard Allen of Delphi, it was starting to look like justice was on the horizon.

While the arrest unveiled the face of evil and identified the man on the bridge as Richard Allen, once again, strange and cryptic information was trickling out of Carroll County. The arrest was made. The prosecutor requested that the probable cause affidavit leading to the arrest be sealed and the request was granted. What exactly was in that document? Why was it agreed to that this document, which is typically public information, would be sealed?

While we waited for answers, more information was being pushed to the forefront. Carroll County Judge Benjamin Diener issued a strongly worded court order to move the accused into the custody of the Indiana Department of Corrections. Sheriff Leazenby filed the transfer request for, as he put it, "safekeeping." Diener and his court found that the defendant was "in imminent danger of serious bodily injury or death, or represents a substantial threat to the safety of others."[118]

My first thought was, how fun? Bridge Guy is in imminent danger of serious bodily injury or death. Now here is the part when I remind you Richard Allen and everyone else in this great country is, in fact, innocent until proven guilty in a court of law. My timing could not be more appropriate to remind us, as I needed a reminder myself at the exact same time.

Judge Diener wrote about the prisoner transfer and recusing his self from the trial that the decision was "not predicated on any acts or alleged acts of the Defendant"

---

118. WSAZ. "Judge recuses himself from case of slain Indiana girls." November 3, 2022. https://www.wsaz.com/2022/11/03/judge-recuses-himself-case-slain-indiana-girls/

but rather since the arrest was made, there was a "toxic and harmful insistence on public information" about the defendant and the case. Diener said that "YouTube already hosts content regarding family members of this judicial officer including photos." He continued, "The public's blood lust for information, before it exists, is extremely dangerous."[119]

"ALL PUBLIC SERVANTS administering this action do not feel safe and are not protected. All public information will be available the second it exists,'"[120] the judge wrote.

All of this while we wait for the probable cause affidavit and the search of Allen's home and property to be made public.

"When the public peddles misinformation with reckless abandon, we all are not safe,"[121] the judge continued. "The Court notes, for the public, that when Defendant appeared for the initial hearing, he was clad in protective gear. That protection was not to protect Defendant from the Court. That protection was to protect Defendant from the public."[122]

Later, we learned that the Honorable Judge Frances C. Gull was appointed by the Indiana Supreme Court to preside over the court proceedings of the Delphi double homicide case. This appointment of Judge Gull is the right

119. Drusilla Moorhouse. *Buzzfeed.* "Newly Released Details About The Delphi Murders Show How Police Came To Arrest A 50-Year-Old Man. His Lawyers Say He Has 'Nothing To Hide.'" December 6, 2022. https://www.buzzfeednews.com/article/drumoorhouse/delphi-murders-new-details

120. Drusilla Moorhouse. *Buzzfeed.* "Newly Released Details About The Delphi Murders Show How Police Came To Arrest A 50-Year-Old Man. His Lawyers Say He Has 'Nothing To Hide.'" December 6, 2022. https://www.buzzfeednews.com/article/drumoorhouse/delphi-murders-new-details

121. Drusilla Moorhouse. *Buzzfeed.* "Newly Released Details About The Delphi Murders Show How Police Came To Arrest A 50-Year-Old Man. His Lawyers Say He Has 'Nothing To Hide.'" December 6, 2022. https://www.buzzfeednews.com/article/drumoorhouse/delphi-murders-new-details

122. *Carrol County Comet.* "Judge Diener Issues Order – Then Recuses Himself From Double Homicide Case." November 9, 2022. https://www.carrollcountycomet.com/articles/judge-diener-issues-order-then-recuses-himself-from-double-homicide-case/

move, in my opinion. She's very experienced and has a very impressive career.

According to the Allen Superior Court website, Judge Gull has served as a judge in the Allen Superior Court for over twenty-five years and has been re-elected four times. It would take pages to go through her achievements and responsibilities over the years. It's good there is an accomplished judge presiding over this case. We do not want a mistrial. It has gone on far too long. The families and Delphi need to start the healing process and holding the person or persons accountable for this horrific crime is a big step in the direction of healing.

On November 22, there was a scheduled hearing the Carroll County Courthouse to decide what to do about the sealed documents. Should they be released? Why have they not been released? It was also learned that special security measures were to be taken with this hearing. Other scheduled hearings and meetings for that day were cancelled. This measure was taken to try to limit the number of persons in the building on that day. Carroll County officials were expecting so many people in attendance, they were trying to determine the weight limit for the balcony area.

Richard Allen requested court-appointed legal counsel for the proceedings and the request was granted in a very timely manner. Attorneys Bradley Rozzi and Andrew Baldwin were named to be his counsel.

Carroll County Prosecutor Nick McLeland was planning for the trial as well. He requested forty thousand dollars in additional appropriations to his 2022 budget for office supplies, witness fees, and transcripts.

The November 22 hearing to decide if the sealed documents would be unsealed was interesting. I've reviewed hundreds of cases and it is rare that documents are sealed. The prosecution wanted to keep the documents sealed. They cited the safety of witnesses as a strong argument. The defense wanted more transparency from the prosecution and the State's case. Then you have the media, who were pushing for "open records," as they always want more transparency: the Indiana Broadcasters Association, the Associated Press, Circle City Broadcasters, Gannett Satellite Information Network, Indiana Newspapers, and the Hoosier State Press Association filed a brief with the court on November 21, just prior to the hearing.

I didn't have an opinion. Of course, I wanted to see those documents but, in the end, all I really wanted was what was most fair to all parties, but the safety of witnesses trumps all.

Richard Allen's legal counsel had an opinion on the matter. On November 21, they petitioned the Court to conduct a hearing and then release Richard Allen on his own recognizance or set a reasonable bail. The petition stated that Allen's defense has reviewed the probable cause affidavit and because neither the proof of guilt is evident nor the presumption of guilt is strong, he is seeking a hearing to release him on his own recognizance or set a reasonable bail.

Then the Richard Allen probable cause affidavit was released to the public. After the scheduled hearing, the judge unsealed the documents; however, some portions were redacted. This is extremely appropriate considering there are witnesses named in the document.

The probable cause affidavit was eight pages long. The document starts off by describing the scene as it was on February 14, 2017, when the victims were found. It states that, through interviews, electronic records, and surveillance videos, investigators believe that Abby and Libby were dropped off across the road from the Mears' farm at 1:49 p.m. on February 13. The now infamous video from Libby's phone showed the two girls encountered a male subject at 2:23 p.m. on the southeast portion of the Monon High Bridge. The girls are referred to as Victim #1 and Victim #2 in the document.

We can surmise that Victim #2 is likely Libby based on the following statement from the document. "The video recovered from victim 2's phone shows victim 1 walking southeast on the Monon High Bridge while a male subject wearing a dark jacket and jeans walks behind her."[123] We have been told so little by law enforcement about the details known to investigators on the day of the abduction and murders but one item detail that we have been told consistently through the course of the investigation is Libby filmed the suspect with her phone and we have seen the photo of Abby walking on the bridge.

The remainder of this paragraph offers up some previously unreleased detailed information about the abduction. It reads, "As the male subject approaches victim 1 and victim 2, one of the victims mentions, 'gun.' Near the end of the video a male is seen and heard telling the girls, 'Guys, Down the Hill.' The girls then begin to proceed down the hill and the video ends."[124]

There is a lot here that makes this "new" information very hard to swallow. First, we have all wondered about the details of that day. Primarily, the details of how everything went down once contact was first made between the perpetrator and the victims. Here we do in fact learn that yes, the perp was carrying a firearm, and yes, he used this to gain control of the girls and from there he was directing their movements. The part that makes the top of my head want to fly off is, "Near the end of the video a male is seen and heard telling the girls, 'Guys, Down the Hill.'"[125]

123. Probable Cause Affidavit. CAUSEN0. 08C01-22-10-MR-01. https://www.documentcloud.org/documents/23321732-probable-cause-affidavit-filed?responsive=1&title=1?embed=true&responsive=false&sidebar=false

124. Probable Cause Affidavit. CAUSEN0. 08C01-22-10-MR-01. https://www.documentcloud.org/documents/23321732-probable-cause-affidavit-filed?responsive=1&title=1?embed=true&responsive=false&sidebar=false

125. Probable Cause Affidavit. CAUSEN0. 08C01-22-10-MR-01. https://www.documentcloud.org/documents/23321732-probable-cause-affidavit-filed?responsive=1&title=1?embed=true&responsive=false&sidebar=false

We have known for over five years that the man said, "Guys, down the hill." But what is stated here is the male subject *is seen and heard*. Wait a second! Does *seen* mean that they may have had better-quality video images of this guy all along? Was he disguising his face at this time? What the hell does this mean? Are there details in this case which may come out at trial that point more toward the direction of what some of the masses were screaming from the rooftops, "The police don't know what they are doing!" If they had additional video of Bridge Guy captured on Libby's phone, taken at a closer proximity than the man-walking-on-the-bridge video that was released to the public, well, then, I say, shame on you, detectives.

The document goes onto to state that the man shown in the video then ordered the girls to go down the hill and no witnesses saw them after that time. There were no outgoing communications found on the phone after this time as well. The bodies of the two victims were discovered the next day.

The deaths were ruled a homicide. Clothing belonging to both victims was found in Deer Creek, just south of where their bodies were located. The State's key piece of evidence, as far as this document is concerned, is a single .40-caliber unspent round. This was found by investigators at the crime scene. The bullet was located less than two feet away from the of one of the victim's bodies. The unspent round had extraction marks on it.

On October 13, 2022, officers investigating the double homicide executed a search warrant at 1967 N. Whiteman Drive in Delphi. This is the home of Richard Allen. There, officers located jackets, boots, knives, and firearms. One of the guns was a Sig Sauer, Model P226 .40 caliber pistol. After an analysis of the Sig Sauer, a function test, the barrel and overall length measurements, test firing, ammunition compound characterization, and microscopic comparison, the laboratory determined the unspent round found next to one of the victims had been cycled through Richard Allen's Sig Sauer gun.

This further confirms that now that a gun was used in this crime. It does not sound like it was the murder weapon but yes, a gun was used during the crimes committed that day. This document is stating that they know the exact gun that was used that day and the owner of said gun.

They are stating that a bullet was loaded into Richard Allen's Sig Sauer Model P226 .40-caliber gun, then the slide was "racked," which then expelled the bullet before it was fired from the gun. Typically, the bullet will be expelled from the side of the gun's slide. Racking the slide allows the gun to feed the first round from the magazine and load it into the chamber after expelling the round that was already loaded. The gun will expel this round even if it is still a live round.

Per the document, either Allen expelled the still-live bullet out of his Sig Sauer at the murder scene as a threat tactic to scare the girls or attempt to gain control of them, or the bullet was expelled by accident during a struggle. There is one other possibility here that somehow a still-live bullet was racked through his gun and was brought to the crime scene in his pocket or someone else's and ended up found right next to one of the victims.

Per the document, Richard Allen's wife confirmed for police that yes, her husband owned guns and knives and they were stored at their residence. Now, here is where Richard Allen may have created a very large hurdle for his defense team. One that he may not ever be able to clear. He told police that he has never allowed anyone to use or borrow the Sig Sauer firearm and he could offer no explanation about why an unspent bullet that came from his gun was found near the bodies of the victims.

If you had to bet the farm here, what do you think happened?

This statement confirms that scientifically law enforcement can place this specific gun that belongs to Richard Allen at the scene of a double homicide. But can they place the defendant at the crime scene?

Maybe.

The document describes three witness statements and Richard Allen's own admissions placing himself at the trails on the day when the girls were killed. In fact, he told police back in 2017 that he was on the trails that day. He told police that he was on the trail between 1:30 and 3:30 p.m. on the day the victims went missing. He said he arrived at the trails via his personal vehicle. He told police that he parked his car at what he referred to as the old Farm Bureau building and walked to the Freedom Bridge. Once on the Freedom Bridge, he said he saw three females at the bridge. He said that he did not speak with the females. Allen said that he walked from the Freedom Bridge to the Monon High Bridge and did not see anyone along the way. He stated that someone may have seen him and not see them as he was watching a stock ticker on his phone while he walked. He said there were vehicles parked at the trailhead but did not describe them. He told police while on the trails that day, he did not take any photos or videos with his phone or otherwise.

Three juveniles were interviewed by police. They each told police that on February 13, 2017, they witnessed and encountered a man walking from the Freedom Bridge to the Monon High Bridge. They provided a brief description of this man which correlates with the general description of the suspect. Bridge Guy. They added that the man they saw was kind of creepy. Another witness observed a man walking away from the Monon High Bridge. The witness described the man as wearing a blue jacket and blue jeans and he was muddy and bloody; this was just before four p.m.

Some witnesses reported seeing a vehicle parked at the former Child Protective Services building. This is interesting.

Could this be the same vehicle that Doug Carter mentioned at one of the press conferences? He said they were looking for the driver of a vehicle parked at this building or asked if anyone knew who was parked there. The witnesses said the vehicle was noticeable because of the manner in which it was parked. At least one witness stated that the vehicle appeared to be parked in a manner that would purposely conceal the license plate. I find this information interesting, but I believe one could be swayed either way as to if this points to Richard Allen being guilty or innocent. I don't find the descriptions of the vehicle parked "oddly" at the former Child Protective Services building to be an overly convincing match to one of the two vehicles belonging to Richard Allen and his wife.

Allen was again interviewed by investigators on October 13, 2022. What is not clear in the document is if the following was in addition to the statement given by Allen back in 2017. Was this new information? He again admitted he was on the trail but denied knowing the victims and denied any involvement in their murders. He says he went to the Monon High Bridge to watch the fish below. This does not seem very likely to me but it's not out of the realm of possibility.

Investigators reviewed and examined the evidence gathered in the investigation. It's stated in this document that due to the statements and the evidence the State collected that detectives and investigators believe Richard Allen is the man seen on Libby's cell phone video, filmed shortly before the abduction and murders took place, detectives believe he is the man seen in the video approaching them from the Monon High Bridge, and once he got to the other side of the bridge, he then forced the girls down the hill and to the location where they were murdered.

The document was damning but to me, it was not a smoking gun, caught red-handed, open-and-shut case.

I am a gun owner. I've purchased one and been gifted a few. Once in a blue moon, I go and shoot one, but I know very little about guns. So, I talked at length with some of my family and friends whom I would consider to be gun experts. They all agreed that if the analysis of the tests were correct and the statements given by the accused to police were truthful, then the State has a very strong case against Richard Allen. If Indiana can't get a guilty plea from Richard Allen, then they were going to have to rely on expert opinions of the State to get a guilty verdict from the jury.

One question all of us have is, if it really is Richard Allen, then why did it take so long to find him? He lives right near the scene of the crime. He looks like Bridge Guy; he dresses like Bridge Guy; and he even told the police he was there that day. How did he get lost in the shuffle? Did it not ever occur to them that one guy, who already told them he was there that day, makes a pretty darn good suspect? Some sources have said the original statement to the police was overlooked due to a clerical error and it was only when law enforcement circled back to look over all the evidence again that Allen's statement was found.

At the hearing, the prosecution gave a statement that I found to be strange. Equally odd was the reaction from the defense team. The prosecution stated that they did not know how many players were involved in the homicides. This, of course, left the door open to there being an accomplice or other parties being involved. I had long suspected that two people were involved but this document does not have evidence listed that suggests anyone but Richard Allen had anything to do with the crime. The defense said the same in their reaction to the statement from the prosecution. This made me wonder: one, just how strong the State believes their case against Richard Allen to be and two, why wouldn't the defense leave that possibility open as well? This would seem like there was some wiggle room for reasonable doubt, or at the least a plea deal bargaining chip for Allen, should he be able to provide proof that someone else was in fact involved.

The other item in the PCA that stood out was the witness statements around the vehicle. The document does not definitively say so but implies the vehicle parked at the former Child Protective Services building was Richard Allen's. This was troubling because the descriptions provided by the witnesses don't match up with the general descriptions of the two vehicles belonging to Richard Allen and his wife.

Richard Allen says he parked at the Farm Bureau building and walked to the Freedom Bridge. If he is the perpetrator, we certainly would not expect him to give us a completely truthful statement to police. But is he trying to cover for himself here or does he simply not know the name of the building?

From the document:

[redacted] advised when she was leaving she noted a vehicle was parked in an odd manner at the old child protective services building. She said it was not odd for vehicles to be parked there but she noticed it was odd because of the manner it was parked, backed in near the building. Investigators received a tip from [redacted] in which he stated he was on his way to Delphi on State Road 25 around 2:10pm and February 13th, 2017. He observed a purple PT Cruiser or a small SUV type vehicle parked on the south side of the old "CPS" building. He stated it appeared as though it was backed in as to conceal the license plate of the vehicle. [redacted] advised he remembered seeing a smaller dark colored car parked at the old CPS building. He described it as possibly a "smart" car.[126]

On page five of the eight-page document we learn that "[i]nvestigators discovered Richard Allen owned two vehicles in 2017 —a 2016 black Ford Focus and a 2006 gray Ford 500."[127] From the vehicle descriptions provided I don't believe that they are describing either a Ford Focus or Ford 500. A Ford 500 is a mid-sized sedan. None of the descriptions even come close to how one would describe a 2006 Ford 500. Allen's 2016 black Ford Focus, however, is a different story entirely. The one witness described a smaller, dark-colored car, possibly a "smart" car. I would agree that Allen's Focus fits this description. Investigators observed a vehicle that resembled Allen's 2016 Ford Focus on the Hoosier Harvestore surveillance video at 1:27 p.m. traveling westbound on CR 300 North in front of the Hoosier Harvestore, which coincided with Allen's statement that he arrived at the trails around 1:30 p.m. So we cannot confirm nor refute that the vehicle described by this witness is in fact Richard Allen's vehicle. But what we can say is that we know, unless someone let Richard Allen borrow a vehicle that day, he was not driving a PT Cruiser or small SUV on February 13, 2017.

Another interesting angle to this bit of information is how the vehicle was parked. If, in fact, this vehicle belonged to the perpetrator, this gives us some potential insights into the mind of the killer and his planning for carrying out the crimes and getting away undetected. First, this vehicle was noted and remembered by more than one witness, based on

---

126. Probable Cause Affidavit. CAUSEN0. 08C01-22-10-MR-01. https://www. documentcloud.org/documents/23321732-probable-cause-affidavit-filed?respo nsive=1&title=1?embed=true&responsive=false&sidebar=false

127. Probable Cause Affidavit. CAUSEN0. 08C01-22-10-MR-01. https://www. documentcloud.org/documents/23321732-probable-cause-affidavit-filed?respo nsive=1&title=1?embed=true&responsive=false&sidebar=false

the odd way it was parked. It's even suggested it was parked this way to conceal the license plate of the vehicle.

This would indicate a plan. An effort by the perpetrator to conceal his identity before even stepping foot onto the trails that day. He planned to commit crimes there that day. Or had this person planned to commit crimes at the trails before and therefore took precautions every time he was on the trails, searching for a victim? The former CPS building is not particularly close to the Monon High Bridge. Not for the purposes of these types of crimes anyway. It's not incredibly far from the bridge to where the vehicle was parked, however.

I have long suspected that the killer planned to abduct a victim or victims and then transport them to another location via a vehicle. If the vehicle described by these witnesses belongs to the killer, then that was not his plan at all. Choosing to park there would indicate one of two possibilities. Either he did not intend to kill anyone that day, which seems unlikely based on the suspicious manner in which the vehicle was parked, but the urge overtook him and he killed anyway, or he was looking for a victim that day and had no intention of that victim leaving the woods alive.

After the judge ordered the probable cause affidavit to be released in redacted form to the public, prosecutor Nicholas McLeland filed a motion asking Judge Gull to prohibit the parties, counsel, law enforcement officials, court personnel, coroner, and family members from disseminating information or releasing any extra-judicial statements by means of public communication.

McLeland contends, in the order, the case has received extensive treatment in the news media. He said it is reasonable to believe that the media will continue to cover this cause of action extensively and that the publicity will prejudice a fair trial. McLeland asked the Court to put an order in place which would ensure that the parties abide by Indiana rules of professional conduct.

Then the attorneys for Richard Allen had a press release of their own. In a statement provided to the media, in which they referred to their client as Rick, they stated why they believe that their client is innocent of the charges of murder.

The statement reads:

> We have received multiple requests from local and national media for interviews and comment since the unsealing of the probable cause affidavit. It would be virtually impossible to comply with these requests and continue to focus on the merits of Rick's defense. Therefore, we offer up these thoughts: We do not want to try this case in the media and we intend to adhere to the Indiana Rules of Professional Conduct that provide guidance on pretrial publicity. However, the police and prosecutor's office have conducted many press conferences over the five-plus years of this investigation and following our client's arrest. On the other hand, Rick's ability to assert his innocence has been reduced to only one short, post-hearing press conference. Accordingly, we feel it appropriate, necessary, and within the bounds of our rules of professional conduct to make a few comments concerning the probable cause affidavit and Rick's innocence. Rick is a 50-year-old man who has never been arrested nor accused of any crime in his entire life. He is innocent and completely confused as to why he has been charged with these crimes. The police did not contact Rick after Libby German and Abby Williams went missing, rather Rick contacted the police and voluntarily discussed being on the trail that day. Like many people in Delphi, Rick wanted to help any way he could. Rick contacted the police to let them know that he had walked on the trail that

day, as he often did. Without Rick coming forward, the police probably would not have had any way of knowing that he was on the trail that day. Rick volunteered to meet with a Conservation Officer outside of the local grocery store to offer up details of his trip to the trail on the day in question. Rick tried to assist with the investigation and told the police that he did recall seeing three younger girls on the trail that day. His contact with the girls was brief and of little significance. Rick does not recall if this interaction with the Conservation Officer was tape-recorded but believes that the Conservation Officer scribbled notes on a notepad as Rick spoke to him.

After Rick shared his information with law enforcement officials, he went back to his job at the local CVS and didn't hear from the police for more than 5 years. The next time Rick heard from the police was in October, 2022. This was approximately two weeks before a contested Sheriff's election and within days of a federal lawsuit filed against the Carroll County Sheriff's Office by its former second in command, Michael Thomas. In the lawsuit, Thomas claims that he (Thomas) "had made suggestions and offered assistance in the investigation of a high-profile child homicide investigation" but those suggestions and offers were rejected by the Sheriff. Thomas further claimed that the Sheriff and others in the department feared the disagreements with Thomas would become publicized as a result of the political campaign for Sheriff. Thomas claims in the suit that he was ultimately demoted and replaced by Tony Liggett, who later that year won the 2022 election for Sheriff. Furthermore, Thomas claims he was also removed from high profile cases. Rick was ultimately arrested on or about October 28, 2022. In the 5+ years since Rick volunteered to provide information to the police, Rick did not get rid of his vehicle or his guns and did not throw out his clothing. He did not alter his appearance; he did not relocate himself to another community. He did what any innocent man would do and continued with his normal routine. The probable cause affidavit seems to suggest that a single magic bullet is proof of Rick's guilt. It is a bit premature to engage in any detailed discussions regarding the veracity of this evidence until more discovery is received, but it is safe to say that the discipline of tool-mark identification (ballistics) is anything but a science. The entire discipline has been under attack in courtrooms across this country as being unreliable and lacking any scientific validity. We anticipate a vigorous legal and factual challenge to any claims by the prosecution as to the reliability of its conclusions concerning the single magic bullet. On Rick's behalf, we argued to have the PCA unsealed. Rick has nothing to hide. As importantly, we were hoping that we would receive tips that would assist us in proving up his innocence. Not surprisingly, we have been inundated with tips from a variety of sources, all of which will be vetted by our team. Although it is the burden of the prosecutor to prove Rick's guilt beyond a reasonable doubt, the defense team looks forward to conducting its own investigation concerning Rick's innocence. We appreciate those that have reached out to support his cause. The prosecutor mentioned, at the last hearing, his belief that others may have been involved in the killing, yet there was no mention in the PCA about a second suspect involved in the killing. The defense is confused by such discrepancies in the investigation and will be in a better position to respond as more discovery is received. Rick Allen owned a Ford Focus in February of 2017. His Ford Focus is not, in any way, similar to the distinctive look of the PT Cruiser or Smart Car that was described by the witnesses. It seems that the CCSD is trying to bend facts to fit their narrative. At this point in time, we have received very limited information about this case and look forward to having something more to view than that which was offered up in the sparse PCA. Moving forward, it is our intent to scrutinize the discovery, as it is received, and give the necessary attention to the volumes of tips that we are receiving. To the extent we continue to discover information that points to Rick's innocence, we will offer up this information to the public, so long as we are not prohibited from doing so as a result of the recent request by the Prosecutor for a gag order or by the Indiana Rules of Professional Conduct.[128]

Before the end of November 2022, attorneys for Richard Allen requested a change of venue for the upcoming trial. This is standard procedure, especially in a high-profile case. There are obvious reasons to believe the jury pool could be tainted with people who may have already made up their minds that he is guilty. Carroll County is not the most populous county. There were only a little over an estimated twenty thousand residents in 2018. Delphi is the county seat of Carroll. In 2020, the estimated population of Delphi was under three thousand residents. The reports were that over three hundred people were at the trails on February 13, 2017, searching for the girls before they were later found. That is over ten percent of the town's population who were there that day. Those people are much too close to this case to be an impartial member of the jury.

---

128. Press Release. https://interactive.wthr.com/pdfs/press-release-for-richard-allen.pdf; WISH-TV. "Delphi murders suspect's attorneys: Richard Allen is innocent, confused by charges." December 1, 2022. https://www.wishtv.com/news/crime-watch-8/delphi-murders-suspects-attorneys-richard-allen-is-innocent-confused-by-charges/

Richard Allen's defense team did their homework and concluded the following: fifty percent of Carroll County residents conducted online searches of Richard Allen in the last few days of October 2022, following Allen's arrest. The attorneys compared this to the city of Fort Wayne, Indiana, located in Allen County. I know this is not really an apples-to-apples comparison, comparing a county to a city; however, Fort Wayne has a much larger population that it would be absurd to compare it to Delphi. Fort Wayne has an estimated population of over two hundred sixty thousand residents making it well over ten times larger than Carroll County. In Fort Wayne, the defense team stated, less than four percent of the population searched the internet for Richard Allen; a much smaller percentage from Carroll County.

I'm not pro-defense here with Richard Allen. But this case has gone unsolved and unresolved for far too long. We just need to get everything right. No mistakes. Do everything by the book so we make sure we've got the right guy and he goes away forever.

Richard Allen's defense requested a venue no less than one hundred fifty miles from Carroll County. Fort Wayne is less than one hundred miles from Carroll County, and I think that would suffice. However, while moving the trial may appear to be most fair for both sides, it does create one rather large logistical issue for the trial. It is not uncommon for the jury to tour the crime scene. This has certainly taken place in many infamous murder trials. Heck, many may recall that during the Nicole Brown Simpson and Ronald Goldman murder trial, the jury toured the Simpson home. Given the unique nature of the Delphi crime scene, I would expect a tour of the area to be helpful to the prosecution.

Another reason given to move the trial may be bias swayed the other direction. Richard Allen worked at CVS, a popular store in Delphi for many years, both before and after the murders. Many of the residents of Carroll County have likely had interactions with Allen at some point during daily routines or while out running errands.

In the end, I believe the good judge made the right decision. She decided that the trial will take place in Carroll County and the jury will be made up of residents from Allen County.

Both sides are doing their jobs well. This is going to be an interesting trial for sure.

Richard Allen is due to have his day in court to either be proven guilty of two counts of premeditated homicide or to prove his innocence in the matter. He—like all charged with crimes in this country—is innocent until proven guilty.

# NOTE

While we were all following along to the court proceedings regarding Allen, the Indiana State Police, and the *Carroll County Comet* issued a reminder to the public on the sixth anniversary of the deaths of Keyana Davis, eleven; Keyara Phillips, nine; Kerrielle McDonald, seven; and Kionnie Welch, five, who were tragically killed in a house fire in Flora, Indiana, on November 21, 2016. The Indiana State Police continues to use all resources in an effort to solve the crime. The investigation is ongoing, and detectives continue to investigate all tips and leads that are received.

The Indiana State Fire Marshal has offered a reward of up to five thousand dollars for information leading to the arrest and conviction of the person(s) responsible for the fire. ISP urges anyone with information to contact the tip line at 1-800-382-4628. For more information, visit the case page at the Indiana State Police website at **www.in.gov/isp/crimereporting/flora-arson/**.

As of this writing, the murders of cousins Lyric Cook-Morrissey and Elizabeth Collins are still unsolved. If you have any information about the circumstances surrounding the disappearance and deaths of Lyric Cook-Morrissey and

Elizabeth Collins, please call the Evansdale Police tip line at 232-6682 or Cedar Valley Crime Stoppers at 855-300-8477. A $150,000 reward, raised privately and by the FBI, is available for information leading to an arrest and conviction in the case.

Additionally, Cedar Valley Crime Stoppers has offered a $50,000 reward[129] for anyone coming forward with information that simply leads to an arrest.

This remains true for the murder investigation of Tim Watkins as well. If you have information concerning the death of Tim Watkins, you are urged to call the El Paso County, Colorado Sheriff's Office tip line at 719-520-7777.

129. Cedar Valley Crime Stoppers. https://www.facebook.com/CVCrimestoppers/photos/a.280856372015917/1940580429376828/

# ACKNOWLEDGMENTS

Writing a book has always been a dream of mine. Ever since I was a kid, I was inspired to put pen to paper and create, to piece together an intriguing tale by pulling together the mysteries and adventures folded away and hidden in the darkest recesses of my mind.

That is easily said in a couple of sentences but, of course, not so easily done.

Not everyone is lucky enough to have an audience. Trust me, that is something that is not lost on me. I am incredibly honored and lucky to have a loyal listenership that my partner in crime, The Captain, and I built together over the course of the last several years. I am very proud of the hard work and the accomplishments that we set out to achieve and then did so together. There is still more to come.

Many of you know that often we create our own good luck. This is done by making smart decisions, hard work, and sacrifices. I believe this to be one of the most valuable lessons we can pass along to our children, students, and heck, it's not too late to teach that to some of our friends either. It's through that hard work that we earned our audience and it's through hard work that we hope to maintain that audience. Before I forget, thanks for listening.

When we first started *True Crime Garage,* the Captain and I were both working regular nine-to-five-type jobs. Many people believe that the beer drinking that takes place on the show really is just some sort of confirmation of us being slackers. In reality, it is just the opposite.

When we started *True Crime Garage*, we each conducted every bit of the work it took to put together the show in what was to be our free time. Hell, I was working a rather demanding job. My typical day was a forty-minute commute each morning into downtown Columbus to arrive at 7:50 and then sneaking out of there sometime between 5 and 5:30 if I was lucky. Lunch was a five-minute session of scarfing down a tuna fish sandwich, standing over the sink, that I had packed up the night before.

Research and writing for our little garage show came in the late, lonely hours of the night. I spent my nights pounding away on an old laptop at a corner desk in my basement, hoping I don't forget to hit SAVE before shutting down for the night. This meant twice-a-week regular trips to the library on evenings or weekends and hoping there would not be too many people there to get in my way. Recording the show in those days meant driving directly from work for forty minutes to a makeshift garage studio. Sometimes it was seven p.m. before we would hit the record button and I had left my house twelve hours prior. The beer drinking in the studio kept me sane and motivated to keep plugging away during another late night. After the show, I'd drive about forty minutes or so home, hang it up around midnight, and then get back up at 6:15 the next day for another drive to downtown Columbus.

I fail as a slacker. The beers were simply the midnight oil and I was happy to burn it.

I got that work ethic from my parents. My father Skip is a retired police detective who was "on call" every two weeks for about as many years as I can remember. I watched him get called away in the middle of the night after working his regular shift night after night. I hope that it is rare for a child to feel bad for their parent. I know there were a lot of months that I felt bad for him. The force and the streets damn near worked him to death some weeks. That didn't stop him from taking me to work with him on career day each year. I also very much appreciated seeing the Notre Dame football calendar hanging up in his office. My father was not a fan. I mistakenly bought him the calendar for Christmas one year, having no idea that he didn't like the Golden Domers. He hung it up anyway and probably endured a good ribbing on more than one occasion, seeing how we lived in Buckeye nation.

My mother Barb is incredibly hard-working as well. She was the principal for several schools in the Columbus City school and other districts. Later in her career, she did a stint that involved working at some tough and underfunded schools. Basically, this meant that when the school board needed someone to come in and clean up a real shit hole, they called her. And she would always rise to the challenge. She can be quite the motivator and tough woman when she needs to be. When I was little, I often tagged along with her to her work in the summer months. This is what lead me to an early love of books. She was there to work, not to babysit me. So, she would walk me into the school library and tell me, "Okay, I'll be back in a couple of hours." The time alone for me would fly by. I wanted to leaf through everything I could get my hands on. No telling how many books and magazines I left incorrectly stored out of place on the shelves of those schools.

My wife Tonya has been more than an inspiration, she has been something much more needed and much more important—my best friend. I'm not easily understood. Sometimes I need help understanding myself and she just gets it.

My stepmother Marsha taught me love, acceptance, and understanding, and how to better show that to those around me.

My brother Andrew reminds me that it is important to do things your own way and to stick to your guns no matter what. Watching and listening to my sister McKenzie and my stepdaughter Dallas has allowed me to have a real understanding of the magic and miracle that it is to be a parent and, more importantly, a mother.

To my brother Patrick, who at many times throughout my life has been one of my very best and closest friends; you made this dream come true for me. Thank you.

*For More News About Nic Edwards and Brian Whitney, Signup For Our Newsletter:*

**http://wbp.bz/newsletter**


*Word-of-mouth is critical to an author's long-term success. If you appreciated this book please leave a review on the Amazon sales page:*

**http://wbp.bz/delphi**

# Index

**DEATH BY TALONS**
http://wbp.bz/deathbytalons

# LOU AND JONBENÉT

## A Legendary Lawman's Quest To Solve
## A Child Beauty Queen's Murder

# John Wesley Anderson

**LOU & JONBENET**
http://wbp.bz/louandjonbenet

**LOVE ME TO DEATH**
http://wbp.bz/loveme

**PRECIOUS FEW CLUES**

http://wbp.bz/precious

Printed in Great Britain
by Amazon